THE LIGHTHOUSES
OF NEW ENGLAND
1716-1973

Edward Rowe Snow

Illustrated

⚓

DODD, MEAD & COMPANY, NEW YORK

ISBN: 0-396-06827-8
Library of Congress Catalog Card Number: 73-6031

Printed in the United States of America
by The Cornwall Press, Inc., Cornwall, N. Y.

To the children of
my nephew Edward Donald and his wife Judith,
Sophia Ellen and Hesper Elizabeth Snow

Preface

The first edition of *The Lighthouses of New England,* published in 1944 under the title *Famous Lighthouses of New England,* enjoyed considerable success in its time, but, unfortunately, has long been out of print. Twenty-nine years have passed since the book was first published, and it seemed a good idea to bring it up to date. Since 1944 many alterations have taken place, both in the lighthouse service and in individual lighthouses. The history of these great lighthouses and their keepers is all here, available for the next generation.

In the preparation of the first edition of the book I was helped by the late Rear Admiral W. N. Derby and his staff of the Boston Coast Guard District. Aiding me in the present book were Captain Robert A. Lee of Portland, Maine, and Commanding Officer Kenneth Black, now at Rockland, Maine.

Those whose personal services for this book were outstanding include my daughter, Dorothy Snow Bicknell, Frederick G. S. Clow, Arthur Cunningham, James Douglass, Walter Spahr Ehrenfeld, Marie Hansen, Melina Herron, Barbara Heywood, Joseph Kolb, Robert E. Moody, Richard Nakashian, Joel O'Brien, William Pyne, Elva Ruiz, Helen Salkowski, Alfred K. Schroeder, Donald Snow, Winthrop James Snow, and Susan Williams.

The internationally known South Shore journalist, John R. Herbert, made many important suggestions for this volume.

My wife, Anna-Myrle Snow, as always, worked long and faithfully day and night so that the book would be ready in time.

If I have neglected to mention any particular organization or person, I do hope that I shall be forgiven.

EDWARD ROWE SNOW

Contents

List of Illustrations

Following page 142

Introduction

Lighthouses, from ancient times, have fascinated and intrigued members of the human race. There is something about a lighted beacon that suggests hope and trust and appeals to the better instincts of all mankind.

In early times the only systems of illumination were huge bonfires built on a high hill, or kettles of tar burning from the top of a pole. But some time in the more recent past the idea of lighthouse illumination in fact the first real lighthouse—was devised by a combination of events. The following story, which comes from Liverpool, England, explains how modern lighthouses began.

A Liverpool gentleman, as the story goes, told a friend that he could read the small print of a newspaper at a distance of thirty feet by the light of a farthing candle. He was immediately challenged on this seemingly absurd statement and made a bet that he could prove his assertion. The following evening a small group of scientifically inclined men met for the demonstration. The gentleman from Liverpool then lit a farthing candle at one end of the stage he was standing on, fastened a concave mirror at the proper distance behind it to obtain a focus of approximately thirty feet, sat down in his chair at the distance agreed upon, and read aloud clearly and carefully the small print of the local paper published that same day.

In the audience was a clock master, who after returning home that evening reasoned with himself as to why that same mirror could not be used as the basis for experiments that might give light to mariners at sea. After several months of work, the first practical lighthouse system was devised, and used with great success until Fresnel's improved methods of illumination superseded the earlier invention. At least that is the way they tell the story in Liverpool.

In 1822 a French scientist named Augustin Fresnel perfected a light that had refracting lenses with prisms at top and bottom, as the illustration in this volume indicates. The refraction bent the light into a thin area of concentration. At the center of the lens room was a powerful magnifying glass. Fresnel built seven sizes of lenses, which he called orders.

The definition of a first-order or second-order lighthouse station is rarely understood. A first-order station means that the distance inside the lantern tower from the actual center of the lantern where the flame or light is located to the lens that surrounds the flame is 36 2/10 inches. A second-order station has a similar measurement of 27 6/10 inches, and because of its shorter distance from flame or light to lens, has correspondingly less power in the rays of light it gives. Third- and fourth-order stations, respectively 19 7/10 and 9 8/10 inches, have a similar diminution of power. There actually is a higher classification than the first order known as the hyperradial, which has a measurement of 52 3/10 inches.

American lighthouses were slow to be established in this country. First was Boston Light, then Brant Point at Nantucket, Beavertail at Rhode Island, and New London in Connecticut.

The career of Winslow Lewis coincides with the more active years of development of the New England lighthouse system. One of the most important lighthouse men of the last century, Lewis was born at Wellfleet, Massachusetts, in 1770. Completing an active career at sea by 1810, in the War of 1812 he commanded the Boston Sea-Fencibles, a group composed of mariners who were organized to defend Boston's islands and waterfront. Captured by the British while on his way to visit a lighthouse, he was later freed.

In 1810 he had obtained a patent for a reflecting, magnifying lantern to illuminate lighthouse towers, which was a great improvement on other lights. The next year he installed his invention at Boston Light, where it proved to be satisfactory, using only half the amount of oil formerly consumed. Because of his success, Lewis was commissioned by Secretary of the Treasury Albert Gallatin to place his lamps and reflectors in all forty nine lighthouses then in the United States. Lewis was given $20,000 for his invention, and a proportional share in the oil saving that his patent made possible. He was allowed the value of half the oil saved at all the lighthouses, figured on the basis of the consumption of an average year before his oil-saving invention was put in. Seven years later he signed a second contract with the government, whereby he was allowed the value of one-third of the oil saved because of his invention.

In 1815 he signed a contract to supply all lighthouses for seven years with the best sperm oil, and to visit each lighthouse annually and report conditions there.

Many of Lewis's other inventions were outstanding. He introduced a reflector made of copper, plated with silver on its concave surface, which was modeled into the shape of a paraboloid. It was Lewis who first fitted American lighthouses with the Argand lamp, invented by Aimé Argand early in the eighteenth century. This improved lamp used a new type of tube-shaped wick set between two cylinders.

When the Fresnel lens was invented, Lewis at first did not

approve, but later he came to admit that it was superior to the paraboloid and Argand lamp.

By 1820 Lewis was an extremely busy man, as the lighthouses of this country had grown to seventy in number. Before his death, he constructed one hundred lighthouses.

During his lifetime Winslow Lewis was embarrassed by his own nephew, Isaiah William Penn Lewis, better known as I. W. P. Lewis, who as an inspector of American lighthouses in 1843, continually found fault with his uncle's work and with lighthouses and keepers in general. Actually, Winslow Lewis did much to make American lighthouses more effective and more economical.

In 1843 when young I. W. P. Lewis arrived back in Washington from his inspection trip, he misrepresented the Light House establishment to members of Congress and the Secretary of the Treasury, according to Stephen Pleasonton, his object being to take the management out of the hands of the Treasury Department officials and place it under the Topographical Corps. Perhaps as a result of his activities, the Topographical Corps was actually given the task of building the Minot's Ledge Light in 1847, the tower that fell into the sea in 1851.

The government allowed open bidding for the oil contract in 1832, and Winslow Lewis was underbid by a group of "wealthy oil dealers from New Bedford." Stephen Pleasonton, the famous Fifth Auditor of the Treasury, in charge of American lighthouses, thereupon entered into contract with Charles W. Morgan, Samuel Rodman, Jr., William R. Rodman, and Edward Merrill, all of New Bedford, Massachusetts, for the above-mentioned men to supply the Government with a "sufficient quantity of best spermaceti strained oil," at the rate of $31.98 annually for each lamp "that shall be lit." There were then 1,932 lamps in American lighthouses. Five years later there were 2,147 lamps in the country, and the New Bedford contractors received $35.87 per lamp for another five-year period.

The reader can well understand that the lighthouse department was suffering from growing pains in the period from 1790 to 1850. However, for what they had to work with, men like Alexander Hamilton and Albert Gallatin conducted lighthouse affairs to produce results that were amazingly satisfactory.

The vicissitudes of the Lighthouse Service have been many. The Treasury Department has taken turns with the Department of Commerce in managing the lighthouse service from earliest times until 1939. In that year the entire lighthouse system was placed under the Coast Guard. At the dramatic time of Pearl Harbor, the Navy took over the Coast Guard, and at the end of World War II the Navy gave up control. The men of the Coast Guard have quickly taken the places of the old-time lighthouse keepers, who, one by one, have retired from the service. Continuing the traditions of the Lighthouse Department, the Coast Guard is achieving splendid results at all the American lighthouses today.

But the long period of activity enjoyed by the men of the old Lighthouse Department up and down the Atlantic, on the Mississippi, in the Pacific, and on the Great Lakes should not be forgotten. The heroic lighthouse keepers of yesterday and their brave women-folk cannot be allowed to step into the past with their saga unsung—a story of romance, adventure, loneliness and danger.

PART I

LIGHTHOUSES OF MAINE

1

Matinicus Rock Light

Matinicus Rock is a lonely, isolated ledge of approximately thirty odd acres, located off the entrance to Penobscot Bay in Maine, twenty-two miles out into the ocean. Matinicus Island, with its thriving settlement six miles away, is the nearest island of importance.

In 1826 the distant Rock was deeded to Massachusetts, and a lighthouse was begun and completed the next year. Constructed of wood, the new building consisted of two lighthouse towers, one built into each end of the keeper's residence.

Competition was keen for the position of light keeper at Matinicus Rock. The following letter, written to President John Quincy Adams by Fifth Auditor Pleasonton from Washington, is of interest in this respect:

June 8, 1827

"Sir,

"I have the honor to enclose the recommendations in favor of the following persons to be Keeper of the Light house on Mantinicus Rock in the State of Maine, viz: John

A. Shaw, Isaac Tolman, Samuel Holmes, John Wales, William Dyer, William Young and Esaias Preble.

"The appointment of John A. Shaw is respectfully submitted, and that his salary be fixed at four hundred and fifty dollars per annum.

I am, S. PLEASONTON, *Fifth Auditor*."

President Adams approved the appointment of Keeper Shaw on June 26, 1827, and Isaac Ilsley was notified at once. He was Maine's district superintendent, and had several lighthouses under his management. John Alder Shaw, informed of his appointment by Ilsley, soon reached Matinicus Rock. Within a few weeks he experienced a gale, which convinced him the building would not last too long. He was right. After a few great northeast storms had swept across the island, smashing and shattering the wooden lighthouses, the government decided to erect more substantial buildings to face the mighty power of the wintry North Atlantic gales.

I quote portions of the old logbook that was kept at Matinicus Rock from 1829 until 1839:

"3 Sept 1829 a heavy gail of wind to N W
31 Oct 1829—a saver [severe] gail Broak over rock
 9 Nov. 1829—a bad storm
24 Nov.—a man of war pased hear to Day.
25 Jan, 1830—A vilant Snow Storm
30 Jan. 1830—A Sataday night Very cold
 9 Feb.—trim and set up All night
21 Feb.—1 chooner passed hear today."

Whenever Keeper Shaw left the island or was ill his wife ran the lights. One such incident is mentioned:

"23 May 1830—The keeper very sick
June 1830—The keeper is Beter and he aught to be"

The log book stops abruptly on Sunday, March 20, 1831, when Keeper Shaw was removed from the island in a very sick condition. Taken to a Portland hospital, he died there on April 29, 1831, at the age of sixty-nine. The new temporary keeper appears to have been Abner Knowles, who arrived at the Rock to take charge on May 7, and "found all things in good order."

He was followed by Phineas Spear, who was also taken sick and carried to the mainland, where he died in April 1834.

The month of November 1836 was a terrible one, with a rapid succession of storms and gales. Knowles wrote:

"Nov. 3, 1836—Rainstorm N.E. waves washed into well and salted the water"

Other storms occurred on the 12th, 15th, 17th, and 18th, while a heavy gale hit on the 21st from the east southeast. The 27th was "very cold and blustering," and a "fresh breeze" swept the island on the 29th.

In 1846 a new substantial granite dwelling with two strong towers at each end was constructed. The old dwelling was left standing to be utilized as a storehouse, but the two wooden towers were torn down. At the time, Samuel S. Abbott was keeper, having been appointed in 1839.

It was in the spring of 1853 that Abbie Burgess received her first view of Matinicus Rock, the island that was to be her only home for many years, when her father moved out to the island as keeper of the light. Accompanying Keeper Burgess were his invalid wife, four girls and a boy. The boy soon became a fisherman and spent most of his time in the Bay Chaleur, north of New Brunswick, leaving Abbie, at fourteen, the only one old enough to help out with the chores on the island.

The Rock, Abbie found, was a desolate spot where no trees or even grass would grow. It was so low in the water that every year spray dashed completely over the island. She did not feel any more cheerful when she examined the old logbook of the former keepers and found that no less than seven times in ten years the giant waves of the Atlantic, pushed into billows thirty and even forty feet high, had surged across the island.

Abbie read with consternation the records of one particular year, 1839. On Sunday, January 27, a terrible storm swept right across the rock with waves mountain high. The keeper and his family were forced to flee for their lives from the lighthouse when seven successive waves battered the weakened structure, completely demolishing it. It was a terrible experience for the keeper that year, but the extreme simplicity of lighthouse journalists prevailed when the time for the entry came on the evening of the disaster. The brief record for January 27, 1839, was

"Lighthouse tore down by the sea"

For two days after the storm, Abbie read, no welcome gleam shone out from Matinicus Rock, but finally, she noticed in the entry for January 29, the keeper was able to hang a temporary beacon from a jury-rigged mast, so that ships at sea could be guided away from the dangers of the cruel ledges in the vicinity.

The tower was eventually repaired, and the stone residence where Abbie was then reading the log had been completed a few years later.

Night after night when she had put the younger children to bed, Abbie would assist her father in the twin towers at the island, lighting all the twenty-eight lamps with such feminine efficiency that her father soon called her his assistant keeper. He would often journey to the mainland to sell lobsters, and on his return, Burgess would find that Abbie had conducted the light with just as much skill as he had ever used. By the time she was seventeen, Abbie was really the guiding spirit of the rock, and the sailors passing by would speak of the girl who ran the lighthouse. The extra income earned by lobster fishing proved a welcome addition to Burgess' salary of $450 a year, especially when expensive medicine had to be provided for his invalid wife.

Abbie also kept hens on the island, five in number, and they became her special pets. Unless one has lived for months cut off from the rest of the world, it is hard to realize the importance of having a pet of some sort for a companion.

The old log book with its items about storms and dangers from the sea proved absorbing reading for the young lighthouse heroine. Many winter nights when the thin summer oil would burn poorly in the below-zero temperature, Abbie would have to sit up all night nursing the wicks along, and she would study the log book by the hour. Abbie began to wonder whether any storms such as those mentioned in the book could possibly sweep the ledge while she was there, for she knew that her invalid mother was steadily growing weaker and could not be moved during a gale if the lighthouse was destroyed as that of 1839 had been.

She studied the situation carefully and changed her mother's room from the old building to what she believed was the strongest part of the new structure, a chamber just in back of the higher of the two lighthouse towers. A month after the change had been made, in December 1855, a great storm hit the rock and swept against the old dwelling, but only spray hit the windows of her mother's new bedroom. Abbie felt that her decision had been a wise one.

The following month, January 1856, Keeper Burgess was forced to go to Rockland to purchase supplies and food. He said farewell in the usual fashion to his wife, but he took Abbie aside and told her that only extreme necessity prompted his trip; the lighthouse cutter had not made its regular September call and it was dangerous to let the winter trap them at the island without sufficient provisions. "I can depend on you, Abbie," were his last words as he slid the dory down over the slippery rocks and jumped in for his long sail to Rockland, twenty-five miles away.

Abbie and the children watched their father's sail from the top of the lighthouse until it vanished in the distance. Almost before they sat down to lunch, however, the wind veered to northeast, and the first signs of a bad storm began.

Her younger brother had left the rock months before and was then aboard a fishing vessel in the Bay Chaleur, so Abbie was alone at the light with her helpless mother and the younger girls of the family. For three days the storm increased in intensity, and in the early morning hours of the fourth day Abbie was startled by several great billows that roared right across the island and battered against the heavy granite building itself.

With the coming of dawn that terrible morning of January 19, 1856, Abbie looked over at the old dwelling house where her mother had been living before Abbie decided to move her to the new building. The old home had been totally destroyed, and not a stone of the foundation was still in place. Abbie shivered when she thought what would have happened to her mother in the other building, the timbers of which were even then being scattered all around Penobscot Bay. Abbie continues the story herself:

"The new dwelling was flooded and the windows had to be secured to prevent the violence of the spray from breaking them in. As the tide came, the sea rose higher and higher, till the only endurable places were the light-towers. If they stood we were saved, otherwise our fate was only too certain. But for some reason, I know not why, I had no misgivings, and went on with my work as usual. For four weeks, owing to rough weather, no landing could be effected on the Rock. During this time we were without the assistance of any male member of our family. Though at times greatly exhausted with my labors, not once did the lights fail. Under God I was able to perform all my accustomed duties as well as my father's.

"You know the hens were our only companions. Becoming convinced, as the gale increased, that unless they were brought into the house they would be lost, I said to mother: 'I must try to save them.' She advised me not to attempt it. The thought, however, of parting with them without an effort was not to be endured, so seizing a basket, I ran out a few yards after the rollers had passed and the sea fell off a little, with the water knee deep, to the coop, and rescued all but one. It was the work of a moment, and I was back in the house with the door fastened, but I was none too quick, for at that instant my little sister, standing at the window, exclaimed: 'Oh, look! look there! the worst sea is coming!'

"That wave destroyed the old dwelling and swept the Rock. . . . The sea is never still, and when agitated, its roar shuts out every other sound, even drowning our voices."

Her father returned several days later and the lighthouse keeper thankfully greeted his wife and children. Abbie was praised again and again for her heroism.

In 1857 Abbie was left with her brother on the rock during a storm, again when the father was on the mainland securing provisions. During a lull in the gale, her brother started away for food in a small skiff. Neither he nor his father came back for the next twenty-one days, during which time the family was reduced to a daily diet of one cup of corn meal mush and an egg. Finally father and son returned with plenty of food, but they found Abbie exhausted from worry about them, for she feared that both had drowned.

The election of Abraham Lincoln as President caused Keeper Burgess to lose his job, for the keepers were politically appointed at this time. One day after the election he met a friend, Captain John Grant, on the streets of Rockland.

"Hell, John, why don't you apply for my job?"

"I wouldn't do that to you, Sammy," was the reply.

"Well, there is no one else I would rather let have it, and as I am not going to be able to keep it, why don't you ask for it?"

So in this strange fashion Keeper Burgess resigned from the lighthouse service and Captain Grant took his place, in the year 1861.

Abbie Burgess, who had fallen in love with the rocky ledge, remained at the house of the Grant family to acquaint them with the lighthouse station. Grant's son, who had been appointed assistant keeper, became interested in the twenty-two-year-old girl. Before the year ended Abbie Burgess and young Isaac H. Grant were married. Not long afterward Abbie Grant was officially appointed an assistant keeper at the lonely towers. Four children were born to the happy couple before they left Matinicus Rock.

A Confederate raider, the *Tallahassee,* was active in the waters of Penobscot Bay during the Civil War, and Keeper John Grant, anxious for the safety of his people ashore, saw the raider appear just off the rock and make for the fishing fleet then close by. One by one the crews of the fishermen were taken off and placed on one small craft; then all the other fishing vessels were burned. The following day the burned hull of one of them, the *Magnolia,* washed ashore at

Criehaven, while a coaster was beached at the Rock. The war was to strike much closer home, however. Keeper Grant's son Jarvis was the first from around Matinicus to enlist, joining the army at Rockland. He was killed in the Battle of Bull Run.

During the year 1875 a chance arose for Abbie's husband to be keeper at White Head Light, a short distance from Spruce head, about twenty miles inland from Matinicus. So Abbie and her family left the rock. The Grant family lived at White Head for fifteen years, enduring many great storms that swept across the ledges around the tower during the long Maine winters.

Captain Grant stayed on at the rock until 1890, retiring that year in favor of his son, William G. Grant, who was promoted from assistant keeper.

James E. Hall, a descendant of Ebenezer Hall, who was killed by the Indians at Matinicus in 1757, was an assistant keeper under William Grant. When Grant ended his career at Matinicus Rock in 1900, James Hall was made head keeper. While Hall was keeper, the brig *Atlanta* slid over the dangerous Zepher Ledges and had to be beached at Seal Island, a few miles northeast of the rock. The brig was a total loss, but her great cargo of lathes proved a welcome gift to the fishermen of Criehaven and Matinicus.

Keeper Hall left Matinicus Rock in 1908 and was succeeded by Merton E. Tolman. Eight years later Hall was killed in a rock-blasting accident while serving as keeper at Grindle Point Light, Islesboro, Maine. Tolman, who was one of the Matinicus Island Tolmans, remained at the rock until 1911, when Charles G. Dyer became the head keeper. Frank O. Hilt, a sturdy giant from St. George, was made third assistant in 1913. Three years later Keeper Dyer resigned, to be succeeded by Arthur B. Mitchell, who served during World War I. Frank Hilt took over in 1919, remaining at the rock until 1928, when he was transferred to the historic Portland Head Light.

In 1933 Keeper R. W. Powers experienced a storm at the light that was fully as disastrous as the one young Abigail Burgess encountered back in 1857. The waves swept right through his kitchen, leaving the debris piled waist deep.

But no one else is as closely associated with the rock as Abbie Burgess Grant. Often through her active and happy lifetime, Abbie looked back to the days when she was in complete charge of the important Matinicus Rock Station. Many times she wished that she were back there again. About the year 1891 she wrote from White Head Light as follows:

"Sometimes I think the time is not far distant when I shall climb these lighthouse stairs no more. It has almost seemed to me that the light was part of myself. When we had care of the old lard-oil lamps on Matinicus Rock, they were more difficult to tend than these lamps are. . . . Many nights I have watched the lights my part of the night, and then could not sleep the rest of the night, thinking nervously what might happen should the lights fail.

"In all these years I always put the lamps in order in the morning and I lit them at sunset. These old lamps . . . on Matinicus Rock . . . I often dream of them. When I dream of them it always seems to me that I have been away a long while, and I am hurrying toward the Rock to light the lamps there before sunset. . . . I feel a great deal more worried in my dreams than when I am awake.

"I wonder if the care of the lighthouse will follow my soul after it has left this worn out body! If I ever have a gravestone, I would like it in the form of a lighthouse or beacon."

This wish was carried out many years later in the presence of the former governor of Connecticut, Wilbert Snow, and a group from Massachusetts.

2

Mount Desert Rock

Far out from any other island, rock, or ledge, separated for weeks and even months at a time from all physical connections with the American mainland, Mount Desert Rock and its important lighthouse seem a part of another world. I have made several flights over this far-distant isle of the deep, and can never overcome a feeling of uneasiness while circling above the rocky ledge in a small land plane. The rock is twenty-two miles from the nearest harbor on Mount Desert Island, and twenty-six miles from the mainland.

Sieur Samuel de Champlain is responsible for the naming of Mount Desert Rock. He first came to the island of Mount Desert in September 1604. The great French adventurer sailed within sight of the rock on many occasions during the next few years, but never returned to settle at Mount Desert Island as he had planned. Incidentally, the pronunciation of Mount Desert is the same as dessert, the last part of a meal.

It was in the year 1830 that the first beacon was lighted at Mount Desert Rock, the loneliest of all New England lighthouse stations. Yes, Matinicus Rock, Boon Island, and Minot's Light also are isolated, but a glance at the chart will show that Mount Desert is all by itself, whereas Boon Island is only nine miles from shore, Matinicus Rock has neighboring islands, and Minot's Light is not too far from Cohasset. The first tower on the rock was of peculiar design. The lantern rested on timbers placed across the roof of the keeper's dwelling, and was exactly fifty-six and a half feet above the ocean.

The play of the giant waves across Mount Desert Rock cannot be realized by the average reader. In 1842 a stone eighteen feet long, fourteen feet wide and six feet thick, weighing fifty-seven tons, was thrown out of its place by the sea, according to the lighthouse records in Washington. At another time a seventy-five-ton boulder was moved sixty feet during one storm!

Keepers in innumerable cases have not stayed long at Mount Desert Rock. Many have been the reasons. Some have resigned because of loneliness, while negligence of the keeper, politics, and personal ambitions of others have been sufficient cause for dismissal. Jacob S. Richardson was keeper at Mount Desert Rock in 1849 and heard complaints had been made against him. His letter to the Secretary of the Treasury follows:

Mt. Desert, (Maine)
April 1849

"To the Secretary of the Treasury
"Sir:

"The undersigned, Keeper of Mt. Desert Rock Light, in the state of Maine, deems it his duty to send you this communication—from having heard that charges having been made against him, by some who are applicants for the place he now holds—to the effect that he has been guilty of neglect of duty, etc.

"The undersigned is so conscious of a strick fulfilment of his duty, in ever respect, since he took charge of the Light, that he unhesitatingly courts and solicits the most rigid scrutiny. He can only find any reason for this course of his opponents, from the fact that they are very desirous to have him removed. This, however, cannot form, in any correct and upright mind, any excuse for so unfair a course of procedure—and the undersigned has no fear that it will work to his injury in the case before you.

"Any investigations or inquiries, from your office, if deemed necessary under the circumstances, will be met with alacrity.

"Enclosed are some papers, which will show the opinion and knowledge on this subject, of individuals well acquainted with the facts in the case.

Very respectfully yours,
JACOB S. RICHARDSON"

In spite of the above letter, Keeper Richardson was removed from Mount Desert Rock in favor of David King on November 14, 1850.

In 1857 a Fresnel lens was installed in a new lantern at Mount Desert Rock, seventy-five feet above the play of the sea. The tower itself is fifty-eight feet high, with a sturdy, broad base, gradually sloping inward in a graceful curve. Its two-second flash four times a minute is well known to mariners off the Maine coast. Before 1898 Mount Desert Rock had a fixed white beam.

The fog horn at Mount Desert is technically listed as a "diaphragm, air group of 2 blasts every 30 seconds, blast 2 seconds, silent 1 second, blast 1 second, silent 26 seconds, with a bell sounding if horn is temporarily disabled." The radio beacon transmits on 288 kilocycles in groups of one dash and three dots. The antenna lead is at the light tower. Mount Desert Rock can be used as a distance-finding station, and the computation is done by comparing the radio and sounding devices as to the relative extra time taken by the sound device.

A shipwreck occurred off lonely Mount Desert Rock back in the 1880's. The *Helen and Mary,* hailing from Halifax with a great deckload of deals and a cargo of granite below, was sailing near Mount Desert Rock. Threatening weather made First Mate Nelson White suggest to Captain Jared Parker, who was also the owner, that it would be wise to run for either Eastport or Jonesport. Captain Parker's wife, who was Mate White's sister, was aboard with her baby, but the captain decided that White was unduly alarmed, and stubbornly continued on his course.

The sky grew darker and the waves mounted higher and higher, until sections of the deckload began to wash overboard. By this time the captain agreed with the mate, but it was too late. Just as the order was given to shorten sail, over the vessel went, and all aboard piled into two boats. White waited to get aboard the second boat along with the captain, after seeing the crew and the captain's wife off in the first craft. As the captain and mate were launching their boat, the schooner settled slowly into the water and sank out of sight. Both men were carried under water, but the mate soon came to the surface and struck out for some floating wreckage. Within a short time he sighted a large section of the deck load, upon which he clambered.

Looking around him, he saw the first boat bottom up, but no other living person was visible. Shortly afterward the mate noticed a little bundle floating in the water, heading straight for the deck load. Stretching out to grab it as it passed, the mate soon had the bundle in his arms. It was the baby daughter of his sister. The effort almost washed the mate off the floating wood, but he twisted his wrist into the lashings and clung on.

The baby had been wrapped in a heavy oilskin belonging to her father, the captain, and the air inside had kept the whole mass afloat so that the baby was scarcely wet in spite of her remarkable adventure. White then tied the baby to his breast, secured himself to the deck load, and lay down to rest. Hours passed. Nothing happened the rest of the day, and darkness found the two survivors still clinging to their slender hold on life, drifting somewhere off Mount Desert Rock. Perhaps they floated close to the rock itself, but the sailor was too tired to notice. By noon of the next day the floating mass had reached a point perhaps ten miles off the Maine coast.

Shortly afterward White was sighted by the crew of the lighthouse tender *Iris* and taken aboard with the baby, who was still well and active. According to Mary Crowninshield, authority for the story, both of the shipwrecked survivors entirely recovered from their trying ordeal and were later put ashore at Prospect Harbor. Nothing was ever heard from any of the others aboard the ill-fated *Helen and Mary*, so undoubtedly they were drowned when the vessel capsized and sank somewhere off Mount Desert Rock.

A strange accident took place in the early 1890's near Mount Desert Rock. A Maine fisherman was hauling his trawls off the island, and the next day the keeper at Mount Desert noticed that the fisherman's trawl was still in the same position he had seen it the day before. Believing something was wrong, he rowed out to the vessel and found it deserted, with a line over the side. When he pulled up the line, the keeper made the ghastly discovery of the fisherman's body, his hand caught in one of the trawling hooks. Getting the body aboard, he pulled up the rest of the line and found a halibut, weighing well over a hundred pounds. Evidently the halibut had pulled the fisherman overboard when his hand caught in the hook.

On December 9, 1902, during a bitterly cold spell, the tug

Astral with a crew of eighteen was towing a barge in the vicinity of the rock. Because of heavy vapor, the tug crashed against the ledge at Mount Desert Rock at the northeast point. Keeper Fred M. Robbins finally succeeded in getting a line aboard and those in the crew who could move came ashore one by one. One of the crew, however, had already frozen to death. Another, the second engineer, was in such a terribly weakened condition that he had to be assisted.

Almost every one of the seventeen survivors had been frozen either in the legs or hands, and they had to be treated at once. Mrs. Robbins did excellent nursing for the next few days, so that eventually every man who reached shore safely recovered.

All this time the barge was off the island, and the vapor prevented the barge crew from realizing that the tug had been wrecked. Finally they learned the truth, and decided to hoist sail and make for the mainland, where they could send help to the crew of the tug. The barge was picked up off the Rockland Breakwater and towed into the harbor there.

A wrecking crew was sent out from Boston, and what happened then is a matter of opinion. Captain John T. Sterling, in his fine volume *Lighthouses of the Maine Coast,* quotes the keeper as saying that the weather never was finer and a landing should have been made without too much trouble. However, the story in the Boston papers indicated a different state of affairs, and the members of the crew of the rescue vessel were rewarded for their landing at lonely Mount Desert Rock during the middle of winter to take off seventeen survivors of the ill-fated tug *Astral.*

On rare occasions each year the crew at Mount Desert Rock and their families are visited by the lighthouse tender. Almost every article or commodity imaginable is part of the cargo which the tender unloads at this distant ledge. Medical supplies, anchors, mantles, oil, toilet accessories, rope, stationery, dories, and canned goods are some of the items that are "taken aboard" the light station.

One of the most unusual struggles for beauty in the world takes place every spring at Mount Desert Rock. Year after year earth is brought out from the mainland, to be tucked into scores of crevices and split rocks in the vicinity of the lighthouse. Seeds of all types are planted in the earth, and the flowers seem to grow with an unexpected vigor and hardiness at this distant rock. Myriads of colored patches are seen by the occasional visitor as the summer progresses, and early autumn is the most glorious season of all. The desolate rock by this time has been changed to a garden of paradise, with scores of different flowers giving a strangely attractive background to Mount Desert Rock Light.

Then, when the first storms of winter start sweeping across the rocky ledge, they take every last vestige of earth out to sea with them, and long before spring the island is barren and desolate.

The winters at Mount Desert are not as lonely as they were a century ago, of course, with the telephone, radio and TV making the long hours more bearable. Nevertheless, few persons would willingly choose Mount Desert Rock for their permanent abode.

3

West Quoddy, Moose Peak, and Libby Islands Lights

Three of the easternmost major lighthouses in the United States are located at Passamaquoddy Head, Mistake Island, and the Libby Islands. They are West Quoddy Light, Moose Peak Light, and the Libby Islands Light.

In 1806 it became apparent that there was need for a lighthouse near the port of Passamaquoddy. Lewis F. Delesdernier invited five leading citizens to assist him in choosing a suitable site for the erection of the lighthouse. Joseph Sturdivant, Samuel Blanchard, Isaac Sturdivant, Ozias Blanchard, and Thomas Dexter reached the decision quoted in part below:

"We . . . take the liberty to suggest that the site on the mainland the bank being forty feet above the high water—is the most projecting & the nearest to acceptability that we are of opinion that this is the most elligable [sic] and judicious that can be pitched upon for the purpose and that in our judgment the elevation should not be less than 75 feet above the surface of the ground exclusive of the lantern."

Two summers went by before the lighthouse was completed and the oil ready for the light. On August 23, 1808, Delesdernier wrote to Secretary of the Treasury Albert Gallatin that all was in readiness for the lighthouse to begin its illumination, although many things were still needed before the station would be properly outfitted, such as a ladder to descend to the beach below, and suitable provisions for the keeper, who was forced to reside a long distance from home. Thomas Dexter was appointed keeper, with a salary of $250 a year.

Dexter could not exist on such a low salary, however, because the soil near the light would not support a garden, and he was obliged to bring all his provisions the entire distance from town. Finally in July 1810 Keeper Dexter's salary was raised to $300.

Robert Mills tells us in his *American Light-House Guide* of 1850 that West Quoddy Light was a "harbor light, and *stationary*, elevated 90 feet above the level of the sea, and may be seen at a distance of 7 leagues in clear weather. It is situated on West Quoddy head in latitude 44° 49′ 18″ N., longitude 66° 57′ 19″ W. Attached to this lighthouse is a bell (of alarm) weighing 1000 pounds, which in foggy weather will strike ten times in a minute, and may be heard at the distance of five miles in calm weather. If bound into West Quoddy passage, give the Sail Rocks, which lie directly off the light, a birth of half a cable's length, then haul directly round the head, when you may anchor in 7 or 8 fathoms, hard bottom. A stranger should not attempt to go through this passage without a pilot."

The fog signals at West Quoddy have been the subject of much comment and even controversy. Captain Joseph Smith, aboard the Revenue Cutter *Morris*, made a survey of the lights of Maine in 1837, and was especially concerned about the fog bell then at West Quoddy Head. The first bell placed on the location in 1820 was one of the earliest anywhere along the Maine coast. Seven years later the keeper was given sixty dollars a year extra for ringing the fog bell in bad weather to keep sailing vessels away from Sail Rocks. But Captain Smith was dissatisfied with the 1837 bell, which he found was the fourth in the seventeen years that fog bell service had been provided at the station. The first bell weighed 500 pounds, the second 241 pounds, the third 1,565 pounds, and the fourth was actually a cast steel bar, triangular in form, fourteen feet six inches long. Captain Smith expressed himself as follows:

"I believe that a sharp-toned bell of 4,000 pounds weight, struck by machinery properly constructed and proportioned to the bell, would answer all the purposes of a work of this description."

On many occasions we visited Howard Gray, an outstanding, meticulous keeper. His painting of the red and white stripes that identified the tower was masterful.

The present tower was erected in 1858, and has stood with only minor changes since that time. West Quoddy Light has a flash of two seconds, followed by a two-second eclipse. Then comes another flash of two seconds, and a nine-second eclipse. This occurs four times every minute with a flash of 45,000 candlepower.

Moose Peak Light and the Libby Islands Light are located nine miles apart. Libby Islands Light is the easternmost primary light in the United States, and for many years was known as the Machias Light. Built in 1822, it is four years older than Moose Peak, which was erected in 1826 on Mistake Island. Moose Peak Light is seventy-two feet above the sea, with a beam of 1,100,000 candles, while Libby Islands Light has 25,000 candlepower from a height of ninety-one feet.

Libby Islands Light is now equipped with a diaphone, having a two-second air blast and a thirteen-second silent period. There is a bell that rings if the diaphone for any reason should become disabled. Moose Peak Light has a diaphragm horn, giving a group of two air blasts every thirty seconds consisting of a second-and-a-half blast, a two-second silent period, a blast of one-and-a-half seconds, and then a silent period lasting twenty-five seconds.

Keeper Henry M. Cuskley was appointed to Libby Islands in 1903. He told me that the most outstanding incident in his experience at Libby Islands was around 1906, when the three-masted schooner *Ella G. Ells* was wrecked. His statement follows:

"The three-masted schooner Ella G. Ells, bound light from N. Y. to St. John, N. B., ran ashore during a heavy fog, July 4 about 1906, on the outside of the larger Libby Islands and all hands but the Captain were lost. The captain floated ashore on the roof of the ship's cabin."

There have been other serious wrecks in the vicinity of the two lights, among them the *Fame,* the *Princeport,* the *Lockhart,* the *John H. Myers,* and the *Caledonia.* The loss of the *Caledonia* was one of the worst disasters in the history of the Libby Islands. In December 1878 the schooner *Caledonia* hit the cruel, unyielding ledges of Big Libby Island with such terrific force that Captain Davidson, helpless to maneuver his vessel in the gigantic seas, was thrown overboard. Two passengers were still aboard when Keeper Charles Drisko saw the wreck the next morning, but the captain and his men had all drowned. A volunteer life saving crew rescued the survivors later in the day, and a short time afterward the bodies of the captain and the other sailors washed ashore.

The wreck of the packet *Sarah* in 1835 became a legend up and down the Maine coast. There are many variations of the story of the shipwreck, which has been preserved in poem and song, including an ancient ballad known as the *Loss of Sarah*.

4

Petit Manan Light

On a tiny island out in the sea, between Narraguagus Bay and Frenchman's Bay, the government in 1817 erected a lighthouse. The island, known as Petit Manan, is located about fourteen miles westward of Bar Harbor and is connected by a dangerous reef to Petit Manan Point on the mainland. On this reef the sea breaks with unusual violence during storms or high winds.

There is very little information about the early history of the light station. We do know that by 1831 conditions at the island had become so bad in every sense that an investigation was ordered. Stephen Pleasonton, Fifth Auditor of the Treasury, wrote to John Chandler, Superintendent of all Maine lights, in September of that year. Part of his letter follows:

"Petit Manan (called Titmanan) . . . is stated to be 'Very bad indeed—built of worse materials than Desert Light—the lantern in good order, as regards the Lamps and Reflectors, but otherwise positively dirty—dwelling house much out of repair and leaking badly—the man has gone off, being tired of his state of independence—His wife had charge of the whole concern.' This Light house I discover was built in 1817, by Frederick and William Pope, under Mr. Dearborn's superintendence. You will cause the necessary repairs to be made here, before the season be too far advanced; and if the Keeper has actually left the establishment to his wife, you will report the fact, and another appointment will be recommended."

The lighthouse was repaired and the keeper, whose name was Leighton, eventually returned to the island. Taken ill the following year, Leighton died a short time later. His long-suffering wife then asked the government for the position of lighthouse keeper, as she had actually run the light for many years. The government ruled against her, however, and appointed Patrick Campbell the new keeper of Petit Manan Light.

In 1851 the Lighthouse Department at Washington was under investigation, and all of the lighthouses were visited. Petit Manan, at the time, was found to have twelve fifteen-inch reflectors in the tower. These reflectors were so placed as to cover a complete arc of 360 degrees around the island. The light was a weak one of the fourth order, unfortunately, and was rarely seen more than eight or nine miles away from the island. Later the same year a fog signal bell was installed on the island. In 1855 the buildings were torn down and reconstructed. A second-order lens was installed in the tower.

It is the height of this stately tower at Petit Manan which impresses the visitor. One hundred and nineteen feet into the heavens the slender, graceful shaft reaches, until it seems to challenge the clouds themselves. The cast-iron steps were subjected to an unusual accident in 1869, when the heavy weights of the clock fell from the top of the tower, snapping off eighteen of the steps before crashing to the floor of the lighthouse. Fortunately, no one was climbing the stairs at the time.

That same year of 1869 a steam fog signal was installed, but the bell was retained for emergency use and is still on the station. The water supply for the steam fog signal created quite a problem, however, for a nearby swamp was found to contain too much vegetable matter. Finally the old keeper's dwelling was roofed over and fitted with gutters, which carried rain water into two wooden tanks in the cellar. Pipes ran from the cellar to the fog signal station, and the water problem was solved.

Loosened as the result of a great storm in 1856, and then further weakened by a series of unusual gales which swept Petit Manan in 1886, the top of the tall tower began in 1887 to break away from the rest of the granite structure, two courses below the watch room. That winter it was a dangerous assignment to be up at the top of the tower in a gale, for the entire upper section would rock back and forth in an alarming fashion. During the following summer extensive repairs were made. The watch room and lantern were secured to the lower part of the tower by six iron tie rods that passed through an iron strut in the granite and then went down to a bolt thirty feet below the deck. Had repairs been neglected, it is believed probable that the great December gale of 1887 would have caused the top of Petit Manan Light to topple off its base to the ground far below.

On August 4, 1929, Keeper Pierre A. Fagonde noticed the wreck of a schooner on the bar. Calling his assistant Earle B. Ashby, Fagonde went with him down to the scene, but there was no one aboard the wreck. Actually the four officers and crew of the vessel, which was later identified as the Canadian schooner *Valdare,* had rowed several miles over to Narraguagas Light, where the keeper even then was giving them aid and shelter.

In spite of strenuous efforts to save some of the cargo, Keeper Fagonde and his assistant were unable to salvage much of importance because of the heavy seas that constantly swept across the *Valdare* as she was battered to pieces.

Every two minutes Petit Manan has a two-second flash of 1,900,000 candles. The two-second flash fades to a steady light of 60,000 candlepower, which can be seen for 118 seconds of the two-minute period.

5

Saddleback Light

Saddleback Ledge is a rocky area that juts out from the ocean at the entrance to Isle au Haut Bay, part of the larger East Penobscot Bay. The ledge is actually included in the area known as Vinalhaven, although situated nearer to Isle au Haut than the larger island of Vinalhaven.

Three years after the tragic fire aboard the *Royal Tar,* which occurred in 1836, the Saddleback Ledge Light was first established. The *Royal Tar,* carrying circus performers and animals, burned and went down within sight of the ledge.

The first keeper at lonely Saddleback Ledge arrived on the rocky shores in 1839. Whether he had any previous lighthouse experience is not known, but we can be sure that he came to dread the wintry months out on the ice-covered rock, with great storms sweeping in out of the Atlantic, their giant breakers shooting entirely over the rocky ledge, the light, and the keeper's home.

Early correspondence in regard to a lighthouse in the vicinity had centered on Great Spoon Island, located eastward of Isle au Haut. Captain Joseph Smith of the United States

Navy had already mentioned that Saddleback Ledge was much better suited for a lighthouse, and wrote to Commodore Isaac Chauncey on June 5, 1837. In his letter Smith stated that a light at Spoon Island would be of no benefit to coastwise traffic except for vessels approaching Blue Hill and Ellsworth, but he believed even those local schooners and ships would have trouble keeping off the many ledges and sunken rocks in the immediate vicinity. Summing up the situation, Smith said that "a light upon the aforesaid *ledge* would be of great and general advantage, while one on Spoon Island would be beneficial to but few." Half a year later Commodore Chauncey agreed to place a light at Saddleback Ledge, and Smith won his fight. The lighthouse was put up by an expert mason, and his work made a good impression even on fault-finding I. W. P. Lewis.

A Fresnel lens was installed at Saddleback Ledge in 1855, while in 1885 a very acceptable landing derrick was erected at the edge of the rock for an easier method of getting on and off the island.

Keeper W. W. Wells was overturned in the winter of 1925 while attempting a landing at Saddleback Ledge, and was about to give up hope of being rescued when he saw lobsterman George Wells approaching. The fisherman pulled Keeper Wells from the water just as the keeper decided he could stay up no longer. At the time the spindrift was several feet deep and the surf was hitting high on the ledge.

When landing at Saddleback, the keepers feared a snowstorm more than anything else, for usually a heavy sea accompanies the storm. Added to the risks from the high seas there was the danger of the derrick boom of the lighthouse suddenly appearing out of the storm.

In his delightful volume entitled *Ranging the Maine Coast*, Alfred E. Loomis tells us of his doubt about birds flying to their death against lighthouse towers, but Keeper

Wells out at Saddleback Ledge in the winter of 1927 was witness to a wholesale event of this nature. With the coming of a storm from the southeast, birds began to hit the tower in great number just as Wells was clearing away the supper dishes. Bird after bird crashed into the lantern, evidently confused by the light, and some of them weighed ten pounds. Before morning more than 120 birds had either killed themselves or become unconscious because of their collision with the lantern. One bird had attained such velocity that it pierced the outer lantern glass to hit against the costly glass prisms.

The lighthouse has been discontinued.

6

Owl's Head Light

At the entrance to the attractive seaport of Rockland, Maine, is a high, wave-swept promontory, visible to all who sail up or down Penobscot Bay. Pine trees and grassy terraces vie with each other for possession of this rocky headland, while at the very peak of the cliff, partly surrounded by spruce trees, is a lighthouse. Anyone who sails in the vicinity recognizes the location at once as Owl's Head.

The headland has been the scene of many battles, shipwrecks, and other dramatic episodes since the advent of the white man. When the Indians ruled the coast, they called it Medadacut. Many claim Owl's Head is the English translation. The owl's head which gives the promontory its name is easily identified in the rocky cliff by the two cavelike hollows which form the eyes and a ridge which makes the bridge of the owl's nose. Rocks that jut out on either side of the bridge form two eyeballs. The spruce trees are said to be so old that they outrival almost any others along the Maine coast, with hanging moss creating a picturesque effect.

One of the first white men who landed at Owl's Head was the great Indian fighter Colonel Benjamin Church, who at the time of his pursuit of the red men in 1696 anchored off Monhegan to deceive the Indian warriors. Then, in the dead of night, Church ordered his entire party into whale boats in which they rowed all the distance to Owl's Head, arriving there at dawn. In spite of his carefully laid plans, Colonel Church found that the Indians had already fled the vicinity.

In the year 1745 young Thomas Sanders, on board a vessel captained by his father, was decoyed ashore by an Indian at Owl's Head. Once away from the ship, Sanders was surrounded by several red men and captured. His father later sent a ransom of fifty pounds, but young Sanders insisted on getting safe conduct back to the coast before paying the money. While walking through the dense woods, he borrowed his guard's gun to shoot ducks, fled into the underbrush, and thus escaped. Burying the ransom in the woods, he finally reached the coast, where he was soon aboard a Gloucester vessel bound back home. Fifteen years later he was sailing in the vicinity of Owl's Head and was becalmed. Remembering the cache of money, Captain Sanders went ashore and retrieved it from its hiding place.

On June 7, 1757, thirty war canoes landed at Owl's Head and in the battle that followed with the white men, two Penobscot Indians were killed and promptly scalped by Captain Joseph Cox, leader of the American forces.

After the Revolution, Thomaston and the entire surrounding vicinity was rapidly building up a substantial lime and shipping business. In 1822 lime sold from 84 cents to $1.08 a barrel, while schooners from Owl's Head made voyages to Europe, returning with cargoes of salt. Sail after sail passed the attractive Maine promontory, but many of them were wrecked in fog and storm before they made port. Agitation started for the erection of a lighthouse, and when in 1823 the steamer *Maine* made regular stops at Owl's Head, plans

were developed to build a light high on the nearby headland.

The penetrating finger of political ramifications reached
even to beautiful Owl's Head. The following three letters are
included without further comment:

July 27, 1825

"Sir,

"I have the honor to enclose the recommendations in
favor of sundry persons to be keeper of the Light House at
Owl's Head, in the State of Maine. The appointment of
Captain Joseph P. Chandler is respectfully submitted and
that his salary be fixed at three hundred and fifty dollars per
annum,

I am, S. PLEASONTON."

August 22, 1825

"Sir,

"I have now to inform you that the President has appointed Isaac Stearns to be Keeper of the Light House on
Owl's Head. You will be pleased to give him notice of his
appointment, and that his salary is fixed at three hundred
and fifty dollars per annum.

I am, S. PLEASONTON."

Treasury Office, Fifth Auditor's Office
November 3, 1825

"Sir,

"Captain Joseph P. Chandler, of the town of Monmouth,
was some short time ago very respectably recommended for
the office of Keeper of the Owl's Head Light House, but at
that time PARTICULAR CIRCUMSTANCES induced the President
to confer the appointment on another person. The Keeper
of Plumb Island Light House having resigned, another va-

cancy is created in your district, which the President is disposed to fill by the appointment of Captain Chandler if that measure should be agreeable to him. . . .

S. PLEASONTON,

Fifth Auditor & Actg. Com. of the REV. ISAAC ILSLEY, *Esq."*

In September 1825, Keeper Isaac Stearns illuminated Owl's Head Light for the first time. The granite tower had been built at the highest peak of the promontory, eighty-two feet above the sea, with the focal point of the light one hundred feet above the water. For the next thirteen years Keeper Stearns was active at the lighthouse. He retired in the year 1838, at which time he was succeeded by William Masters.

Perley Haines was appointed keeper of Owl's Head Light in 1841, and the next year was an exciting one for him. In September 1842, the steam frigate *Missouri* passed his lighthouse on its voyage to what is now Rockland, Maine, and immense crowds gathered on the headlands as she sailed in by Owl's Head. Throngs visited the *Missouri* the next week at her pier.

A great southeast storm which lashed the Maine coast the last day of November 1842 threw two vessels ashore at Owl's Head, and Keeper Haines did what he could to alleviate the sufferings of the mariners, all of whom were saved.

On many occasions the region around Owl's Head has been closed by ice. At such times adventuresome Rockland hikers have made unusual trips far out from the inner harbor. My father, Edward Sumpter Snow, told me of some long trips made over the frozen surfaces in the years between 1870 and 1886. Alton Hall Blackington, New England lecturer and photographer, also told numerous adventures that befell him while walking in the outer bay over the ice.

One of the strange tales of the sea occurred in 1844. On November 9 the brig *Maine* sailed out by Owl's Head bound for New Orleans on her first voyage. Captain Thorndike had a cargo of lime with a ship's company of nine men. From the time she disappeared off Owl's Head Light nothing was heard of her for three years. Then, aboard a Saint George's vessel a strange discovery was made. A ship's atlas, a fine mahogany chest, and a navigation book were left on the vessel by a group of Portuguese sailors who had deserted the ship after receiving advance pay at Vera Cruz. When the ship arrived back in Maine, relatives of the *Maine's* officers recognized the articles as having belonged to the three officers, Captain Thorndike, and his two mates, Abiezer Coombs and George Cooper. Nothing more was ever heard from the brig, her officers, or her crew. How the Portuguese sailors obtained the articles has been conjectured many times by the relatives and friends of the missing men, but without ever solving the problem. For many years, the loss of the brig *Maine* was discussed as Rockland's greatest marine mystery.

William Masters again became keeper of Owl's Head Light in 1845. In the equinoctial gale of March 21, 1847, the schooner *Hero* smashed against the rocky shore at Owl's Head, while another unfortunate craft, the sloop *Louisa,* hit at Crockett's Point.

In August 1849, Masters resigned in favor of Henry Achorn. The next year a terrific storm sent vessels ashore all along the coast. On January 24, 1850, the schooner *Dove* went ashore at Ash Point. The vessel, owned by Captain William H. Crockett of Rockland, was a total loss.

One of the strangest events in the entire history of Maine took place between Owl's Head and Spruce Head in the year 1850. During the terrible December 22 gale of that year five vessels were thrown ashore between the beach at Owl's Head and Spruce Head, about eight miles away. The weather was far below zero that night, and spray froze on each of the five wrecked ships until they were encased in ice several inches thick.

A coasting schooner, owned by Henry Butters of Haverhill, had been anchored off Jameson's Point when the storm broke. Aboard the schooner were three persons, the mate, his bride-to-be, and a deck hand. The captain had left the ship at Rockland for some mysterious reason. Some said at the time that he had been discharged, others believed that he had merely fled from the vessel because of a strange premonition.

The schooner's cables snapped sometime before midnight, and the vessel was pushed across the harbor by the terrific winds and waves, finally being thrown with great force against the cruel ledges just off Spruce Head. Although she filled at once, the schooner did not sink, as the rocky cradle where she hit held her, her decks just above water.

Down below, the girl had already retired for the evening, but when the schooner crashed, the young woman grabbed a large blanket and hurried up on deck. The three frightened people huddled in the shelter of the taffrail. Every monstrous wave that roared in at them out of the storm left its covering of spray, which soon froze into solid ice. Something had to be done at once, or they would all perish.

The mate then thought of a plan. Making the girl lie down next to the taffrail, he lay down beside her and then covered her with the blanket. The deck hand crawled in beside the mate, and the blanket was pulled over so that all three were under its protection. The bitter night wore on. The tide rose higher and higher, until every single wave broke directly across the schooner. Each successive wave left its thin covering of ice which soon built up to a depth of several inches over the blanket, under which the three helpless people lay. Heavier and heavier grew the weight of the ice, and finally the two lovers, shut off from the air, lost consciousness.

Then the tide started to turn and go out, and as morning came, the deckhand, who had kept hacking with his sheath knife to keep a small air hole open through the thick ice, took heart. Striking and slashing at the heavy icy covering that had entombed him with his two companions, at times using his bleeding hands as clubs, he chopped and punched his way out from under the ice cap that had built itself up over the three shipwrecked victims. Without question, the heavy woolen blanket had saved his life. It was then six o'clock in the morning.

After resting a few moments from the strenuous exertions of escaping from the ice cap, the sailor crawled to the rail nearest shore, clambered over the side, and dropped to the icy rocks below. Working his way on hands and knees, he finally reached the high-tide mark, and then collapsed from exhaustion. It was still below zero, so he forced himself to get up and continue his efforts. Foot by foot, yard by yard, the bruised and bleeding man fought his way through the heavy drifts of snow that lined the shore. Now falling, now upright, the sailor made steady progress inland, until finally he reached a road. In the distance he saw a pung driven by Keeper Masters of Owl's Head Light coming slowly his way. Knowing that he was to be saved, he fell across the highway in a dead faint.

Brought to the keeper's home, the sailor was quickly revived and asked to tell his story. When the keeper and his family realized that the boy and girl were still aboard ship under the heavy blanket and several inches of ice, they made plans to reach the schooner. Retracing the sailor's steps in the snow, the members of the rescue party were soon able to see the masts of the schooner showing above the snowdrifts.

A short time later several of the rescue party boarded the schooner. Guided by the directions given them, they arrived at the taffrail where the two lovers were encased in the ice.

Chopping and cutting around their forms, the men soon were able to lift the frozen pair up from the deck, although it was agreed that they had probably frozen to death. The boy and girl were carried over the side and handed down to others waiting below. The rescuers decided that an effort should be made to revive them. Within a half hour they were taken to a home where they were treated with application of cold water. At first the water's temperature was almost freezing, and then it was gradually raised until it reached approximately fifty-five degrees. Next the hands and feet of the two frozen people were slowly raised and lowered, and their bodies ceaselessly massaged.

The girl was the first to awaken from her deathlike sleep, stirring slightly after two hours' attention. Her lover took almost a full hour more to respond to the steady treatment, but he finally showed signs of life, and a few moments later actually opened his eyes.

Both were covered with warm blankets and made to rest. Several weeks elapsed before they were able to get up and walk, but when spring came they had almost completely recovered. The following June their marriage took place. The story of their strange experience was told up and down the Maine coast for many generations. It is not known whether any of their descendants are still living.

The deckhand fared worse, however. Whether it was from his more exposed position, or because of his efforts in reaching help, he never fully recovered from his terrifying experiences on that bitter December night in 1850. He did not go to sea again, but became a well-known figure on the local waterfront.

Francis W. Underwood, first editor of the esteemed *Atlantic Monthly,* participated in what might be called an escapade of unusual nature. A member of the crew of Robert Carter's sloop *Helen,* he went ashore with Carter and Henry

Ware, Harvard University, 1843, in search of liquid refreshments at Owl's Head. Underwood's costume was wholly acceptable to the best social circles of the day, while Ware and Carter were outfitted in ancient red shirts and pantaloons, their heads covered by disreputable old felt hats.

Unsuccessful in their quest to obtain spiritual solace the three mariners made their way over the road to nearby Rockland, finally reaching there just as a band concert was breaking up. "To our surprise, it proved to be a handsome, city-like place, with well-built brick blocks and granite sidewalks," were Carter's comments on his first sight of Rockland. In Rockland, Underwood was able to purchase some Wolfe's Aromatic Schiedam Schnapps, after which the long hike back to Owl's Head was commenced. By this time a chill wind had brought raw, damp air from the ocean, and a drizzle of rain was beginning.

After a tiring hike back to Owl's Head, the three adventurers reached the beach opposite the *Helen* and shouted for the *Helen's* skiff. Their efforts awakened the occupants of almost every other craft except their own, with the result that they were beseiged with emphatic requests voiced in appropriate language to be quiet. After everyone in the neighborhood, including the keeper of Owl's Head Lighthouse, had protested against this midnight disturbance, the three decided to beat a hasty retreat.

A short distance away they found what appeared to be a one-story schoolhouse building. As one of the windows was open, the men agreed to force an entrance and spend the night in the Owl's Head schoolhouse. The editor of the *Atlantic Monthly* asked the others for a hand up, and he was lifted to the level of the window. Raising it higher, he stepped one foot inside and was about to follow with the other when a terrific shriek pierced the silence. It was the shrill cry of a frightened woman:

"Thieves! Murder! Help!"

It was an extremely embarrassing situation in which the editor of the *Atlantic Monthly* found himself, for he had mistaken a dwelling house for a school building, and they had broken into a lady's bedroom. In his haste to leave the scene he knocked off his new hat and heard it rolling around the floor of the bedroom, but he did not wait to recover it. All three men ran for their lives away from the building, just in time to hear a few choice Owl's Head oaths sent in their direction by an angry man. They ran all the faster, expecting to hear bullets whistling over their heads, but none came. A few minutes later they were hiking along the Owl's Head waterfront, looking for a skiff. Finding a small dory, they rowed out to the *Helen,* aroused the snoring captain, sent him back with the dory, and went to bed. Just as they were turning in they realized that the object of their journey, the schnapps, had been left behind near the house. They did not go back for it.

At four o'clock the sloop was started on its journey up the coast, away from the dangers of Owl's Head and Rockland. Not a single member of the crew, according to Carter, dared "to make our appearance in Rockland in the character of burglars caught in the act of breaking into a dwelling-house at Owl's Head."

Keeper Joseph G. Maddocks came to Owl's Head Light in 1873. Ten years before, at the Battle of Gettysburg, he had been wounded in the arm. Previous to the war he was a shipbuilder, but because of his wounds he was unable to continue in shipping circles and so became a lighthouse keeper. He married Clara Emery, of Owl's Head, and they had five children.

The fuel consumed in the lantern in 1873 was lard oil. Keeper Maddocks had to keep a constant fire in the wintertime to prevent the lard oil from freezing. Afterward kerosene took the place of lard oil, while electricity from the Maine Central line now supplies the current to illuminate the bay. When Keeper Maddocks first came, the fog bell was on the shed, an ordinary bell, rung by hand—then came the tidewater bell on the rocks below the lighthouse.

In heavy storms spray went completely over the house itself, located on the cliff. Just before one of the storms Keeper Maddocks saw a small fishing boat out in the bay. Darkness was falling. In the morning he found a cod line washed up on the rocks in front of the house. As he pulled at the line he found it led into deep water, and seemed to be fastened to something cumbersome. Obtaining his skiff, he rowed over by the rocks and discovered a man's body entangled in the line. It was the fisherman who had been out in the storm the night before.

At eleven o'clock one night, when everyone else was in bed, Mrs. Maddocks was rocking the baby. Suddenly she heard footsteps come up on the porch and saw four men peering in at her through the window. Their boat had been smashed on the rocks and they were wet and hungry. Awakening her husband, Mrs. Maddocks prepared a meal for the unfortunate seamen, while the keeper dried them off and arranged to get someone to take them back to Rockland. The men had been on a fishing cruise, but their schooner was smashed to pieces and everything aboard was lost.

I spoke with Mrs. Maddocks when she was 102 years old. She recalled the many years she had spent at Owl's Head. One winter the whole bay froze over for miles around. Keeper Maddocks and his wife watched a horse and sleigh cross the expanse of ice between Rockland and Vinalhaven, while scores of people walked out over the ice drawing their sleds after them.

Mrs. Maddocks told of the sixteen acres of land belonging

to the lighthouse reservation at Owl's Head. Incidentally, there were more than eleven shipwrecks around Owl's Head before Keeper Maddocks left in 1896.

The last regular keeper of the old Lighthouse Service at Owl's Head was Augustus B. Hamor. Entering the service in 1913, he was sent to Egg Rock near Bar Harbor. He remained there seventeen years and was then transferred to Owl's Head Light in June 1930.

One day, as I was sitting in the dining room of the Owl's Head home of Keeper Hamor's daughter, Pauline, she told me the story of her springer spaniel Spot, who loved the signal bell and the boats of the bay. His whole interest in life seemed centered on the lighthouse, the fog bell, and the shipping that passed the promontory. He was always watching for boats to pass the light, and as soon as they would get near enough to the cliff, Spot would run over to the bell rope and give it a few quick tugs with his teeth, pulling with all his strength until the peal of the bell would echo out over Penobscot Bay. Then, as the craft answered with either whistles or bell, the happy dog would dash down to the water's edge and bark at the passing vessel. It was a joyous life.

One of the best-loved of all the craft that sailed by the light was the Matinicus mail boat, captained by Stuart Ames of Rockland. Quite often Mrs. Ames would call up the light station to ask whether they had seen the mail boat coming from Matinicus, and in this way Mrs. Ames had a little advance notice about the time to put dinner on for her husband.

One terribly stormy night, when the snow-laden wind was cutting in across the island, the telephone rang. It was the wife of Captain Ames, who was terribly worried about her husband, then several hours overdue.

"My husband speaks so often of your dog, Spot. Do you

think that he might be able to hear the mail boat's whistle?" asked the frantic wife. Keeper Hamor replied that they would let the dog out and see what might happen. But after a half hour outside in the gale, Spot returned to the house and scratched at the door to be let in. He had a dejected air, which told the others that he had not heard the mail boat. Lying down in his dry corner, Spot was about to go to sleep, when suddenly he raised up on his haunches, his ears alerted and every muscle in his body tense with expectation. Spot had heard the whistle of the mail boat.

Springing up from his corner, he scampered across the hallway and barked to be let out. The others watched him scramble through the great drifts on his way to the lighthouse bell, but he was unable to reach the signal, for the snow had piled up several feet high in the vicinity. Prevented from reaching the bell, the dog made his way along the edge of the cliff, where the wind was sweeping the snow clear, and reached the point nearest to the boat, barking furiously all the time. Keeper Hamor went out into the storm and followed the dog.

Soon he, too, could hear the whistle of the mail boat, and realized that if the dog's bark could be heard by Captain Ames, he in turn would know where he was and be able to get his bearings in spite of the storm. After a period of violent barking, there came an answer out of the storm—three distant blasts of the mail boat's whistle—a signal indicating he had heard the barking dog. The Matinicus boat was even then charting a safe course for Rockland.

Two hours later a grateful wife called up the Hamor residence and expressed her thanks to the spaniel Spot, who had saved the Matinicus mail boat from disaster. Spot was then sleeping soundly in his corner, proudly dreaming of his feat of rescue. The spaniel is now buried near the fog horn he loved so well.

The present keeper at the light is David Bennett, who with his wife, Jane, and son, Chriss, has served here two years. The beacon is scheduled for automation, according to Rockland Coast Guard Base Commander Kenneth Black.

7

Whitehead Light

The gray, granite lighthouse at Whitehead Island, erected in 1852, can be seen from all ships passing through Muscle Ridge Channel off Rockland, Maine. Although the official light list volume of the Coast Guard claims the first tower at Whitehead was not built until 1807, the following episode makes it seem reasonable to assume that the light was in operation there as early as 1805.

In 1807 the Whitehead oil scandal became public knowledge in Thomaston and what is now Rockland. Evidence showed that beginning in 1805 the keeper of Whitehead Light, Ellis Dolph, sold oil to various prominent citizens of Thomaston. Those who bought the oil did so in good faith, as they were told it was from a surplus supply which he had accumulated at the island. For the next two years Keeper Dolph sold gallon after gallon of what later was found to be United States property. Finally, because of the extra demands which Dolph made on the lighthouse schooner, an inspector was dispatched from Boston to inquire into the need for so much oil.

The inspector arrived in Thomaston and made a few judicious inquiries. He talked with Elisha Snow, Jr., the writer's great-great-grandfather, who told the investigator that he had purchased a barrel of oil from Dolph in 1805. Deacon Snow wrote out the following statement:

> Thomaston, Febr. 17 1807
> "I hereby certify that in the fall of 1805 . . .
> "I purchased a barrel of Spermiciti oil of Ellis Dolph keeper of the light on White Head, which I afterwards was confident was states property
> ELISHA SNOW JR."

Over at St. George, Hezekiah Prince made a similar statement, adding that in Thomaston he had seen Dolph sell more than two hundred gallons of the oil within the last two years. He signed the following:

> St. George Feb 17 1807
> "I hereby certify that I have this day seen a barrel of Spermaciti Oil at Mrs. Joseph Coombs store in Thomaston which sᵈ Coombs bought of Ellis Dowlt . . .
> HEZᴴ PRINCE"

Prince also revealed that the Reverend E. M. Hall had purchased two and a half gallons of the government oil.

Coombs signed a statement to the effect that he had purchased the barrel of oil in his store the previous October. Keeper Dolph was dishonorably dismissed from the service, but whether or not he had to make amends for his wrongdoing is not recorded at Washington.

Winslow Lewis, who built many lighthouse lanterns and supplied oil for their lamps, visited Whitehead Light in 1813. On finding that the keeper, Ebenezer Otis, was not conducting his duties in accordance with the best principles of the service, Lewis recommended that Otis be dismissed. Otis asked for another chance, stating that he had been seriously ill.

Otis was retained at Whitehead, but his health did not improve and he died in July 1816.

Five years later Samuel Davis was appointed keeper. In 1830 Luther Whitman put up a fog bell and machinery at Whitehead. The same year a new lighthouse and dwelling house were built at Whitehead by Jeremiah Berry.

At the request of Colonel Loammi Baldwin, noted engineer, an appropriation was made by Congress around 1837 for the erection of a fog bell "at the entrance to Penobscot Bay on Whitehead, to be rung by power from the tide" on a plan arranged by Andrew Morse, Jr. This bell was erected and worked successfully for several years. In 1840 the matter of its economical suitability was discussed. A description of the machinery follows, taken from a letter written by John Ruggles and Sullivan Dwight:

"The power which rings the bell is obtained by the rise and fall of the tide and the swells, which at that place are constant and unceasing. One end of a large stick of timber, near thirty feet long, projects out upon the water the other end being confined by braces and chains to the middle of another stout timber, some 20 feet long, which lies along the shore, hinged at each end of a projecting rock, both together forming a T. From their point of junction a small timber rises vertically to the height of 18 or 20 feet, being well braced to its position; to the upper part of this mast is attached a chain, which, with a continuous rod of iron, extends up to the bellhouse, a distance of about 140 feet. This chain receives from the vibrations of the outer end of the long timber, and a "take-up-weight" in the bell-house, a constant reciprocating motion, which, acting upon the machinery in the bell-house, winds up the heavy weight of about 2,000 pounds, that drives both the regulating and striking part of the apparatus. As ordinarily there is too much power, when the weight is wound up there is a gear which throws the connecting wheel out, leaving the float to act without effect until needed. Bell is struck four times a minute by 15 pound hammers. Object sought has been fully and successfully accomplished by it, and that for such purpose it is a valuable invention.

JOHN RUGGLES
SULLIVAN DWIGHT"

On December 3, 1840, the Commander of the Steamer *North America,* Thomas Howes, praised the bell in the statement quoted below:

"To Andrew Morse, Jr.

"Sir: Having been repeatedly guided in my course by the sound of your 'Perpetual Fog-Bell,' now in successful operation at White Head on the coast of Maine, and being fully satisfied that your invention is invaluable to the commercial interest generally, I can cheerfully give my testimony in favor of it. . . . As your invention has stood the test of the sea unharmed while in its most violent state of agitation, with the float, by which the power to ring the bell is obtained, boldly exposed to its full force, I cannot but feel the fullest assurance of its success to resist the force which you shall think it practicable to apply it."

S. H. Howes, commander of the famous Steamer *Bangor,* on December 4 wrote as follows:

"I consider this bell as the only completely successful attempt which has ever been made to navigate our waters in dense fogs. I am master of the steamboat Bangor, which plies between Boston and Bangor, by way of Portland. For the last two seasons I have been able to run my boat into and out of Penobscot Bay in the thick fogs which frequently occur, by the aid of one of Mr. Morse's fog-bells, situate on White Head, a promontory in the mouth of the bay. Without the assistance of this bell, I should have been compelled very frequently to have stopped on my passage. . . . I sincerely hope that these bells will be placed all along this dangerous coast."

The Keeper of Whitehead Light, William Perry, Jr., writing from St. George, added his commendation:

Dec 12 1840

"To the Public, About the 1st of June last, I received an appointment to take charge as keeper of the light-house and fog-bell at White Head, in place of Marshall's Point light-house. . . . I have since that time had charge of the bell machinery established by Mr. Morse. This arrangement has been perfectly successful."

The Morse fog signal was used for several years afterward, but finally gave way to improved methods. However, the fog bell utilizing the rise and fall of the waves off Whitehead Island actually worked successfully and was one of the earliest American attempts to harness the ocean.

The William Perry mentioned above soon lost his position at Whitehead because of political manipulations, but came back again, as will be seen by the following letter:

Thomaston April 2 1849

"To the Hon. Secy of the Treasury, United States

"I take pleasure in saying that I have been personally

acquainted with Mr. William Perry, Sr. for some years—that he is a person of good moral habits and strict integrity—that he has been the keeper of the Lighthouse at White Head, St. George, Maine since 1845—and was also keeper of same in 1840 and removed in 1841 for political opinions (as reported to me)—I have no doubt Mr. Perry is in every respect well qualified to discharge the duties of that station to the satisfaction of those interested therein—and I have never heard of any complaint against him,—and have no doubt he has given general satisfaction and I have no desire to see him removed—although I 'differ with him in politicks'

Respectfully yours, GEO. ABBOTT"

When I visited the light in April 1945, Coastguardsman Ernest Kretschmer, stationed at Whitehead, told me the graves of two sailors were on the island. They were wrecked on the shores of Whitehead sometime before 1805 and froze to death on the island. They were found by residents of the mainland the following spring and were buried in the same grave on the island. Kretschmer also told me that Whitehead has snow and ice in the crevices around the ledges on the island as late as June 1 in many years.

8

Monhegan Island Light

"We descried the land, which bare from vs. North-North-East; but because it blew a great gale of winde, the sea very high and neere night, not to fit to come upon an unknownen coast, we stood off till two a clocke in the morning, being Saturday. . . . It appeared a meane high land, as we after found it, being but an Iland of some six miles in compasse, but I hope the most fortunate euer yet discoured. . . . This Iland is woody, grouen with Firre, Birch, Oke, and Beech, as farre as we saw along the shore; and so likely to be within."

Thus did Captain Waymouth's narrator James Rosier describe his first view of Monhegan Island in May 1605. Champlain also sighted this well-known New England landfall two months later in the same year, and christened the location *La Nef,* for he believed it resembled a ship from a distance. Of course, the island was well known to the Indians long before this time. Monhegan, translated from their tongue, stands for *The Island*. It meant just one thing to them, the island where the white men came year after year.

John Smith named the island *Barties*. Although his memory is perpetuated by a monument there, Smith's attempt to name this island was no more successful than in the case of the Isles of Shoals or Cape Ann. Few except historians have ever heard of *Barties*.

The pirate Dixey Bull was active in the vicinity of Monhegan Island before his capture and execution in England, but the red men caused the most exciting events in Monhegan's history. During King Philip's War the Indians began their depredations against the white people of Maine. Coastal settlements like Casco and Georgetown were attacked, alarming the countryside. Hubbard, the Indian historian, tells us that a hundred or so of the inhabitants of the mainland fled from their homes to Monhegan Island,

"resolving there to tarry till they had heard from Boston, from whence Mr. Colicot & Mr. Wiswell promised to do their utmost Endeavor to send help. There they settled three Gaurds, and appointed five & twenty to Watch every Night, not knowing but that the Indians might come every Hour. . . . No boats could be sent to Sea for fear of weakning the Island."

After vainly appealing to Boston for aid the refugees obtained several vessels which landed them at three different locations along the coast: Piscataqua, Salem, and Boston. But for the native fishermen of Monhegan, that month of August 1676 remained long in memory, with the thoughts of the hundred homeless people who visited them so suddenly and then went away.

Deacon Shem Drowne, known in Boston town for his grasshopper, which still stands atop old Faneuil Hall, bought Monhegan Island in 1749, owning it for the next six years.

During the War of 1812 the famous sea battle between the *Boxer* and the *Enterprise* was fought between Monhegan

Island and Port Clyde on September 5, 1814. The people of Monhegan were gathered on the highest bluff to watch the thrilling encounter. My own great grandmother, Lucy W. Snow, stood on the roof of her home on nearby Metinic Island. The encounter ended in an American victory, with both captains slain in the battle.

As the waters of Maine became more and more important for coastwise traffic it was seen that Monhegan Island, which was the first point sighted in most trans-Atlantic voyages, was the logical place for a lighthouse. The tower was built there in 1824. On July 2 of that year Keeper Thomas B. Seavey illuminated Monhegan Light for the first time. His career at this station lasted ten years, when he was succeeded by George B. Wormell, who remained until 1841.

Joseph F. Humphrey became keeper on March 29, 1861. The Civil War broke out two weeks later, and his two sons, Albert and Edward, enlisted. Humphrey died the following December, but his capable wife, Betty Morrow Humphrey, became the official keeper in his place. During all the bitter months of the Civil War, even when rebel raiders were sinking vessels near Monhegan Island, she remained at her post, the bright beams of Monhegan Light sending out their warnings every night. Her younger son, Albert, who had enlisted at seventeen, was killed in 1864. Edward was disabled and returned home to help at the lighthouse. With his help, Betty Humphrey kept the lights of Monhegan Island burning until 1880, a total of eighteen years in all. Hired at $820 a year, she was forced to accept a cut to $700 on April 11, 1876.

During the time of Betty Humphrey's service at Monhegan Island, a satisfactory plan for a fog signal was worked out. The fog signal established around 1854, had not given sufficient warning to ships off the island, so in 1870 a Daboll trumpet was set up at neighboring Manana Island, half a mile west of the lighthouse. Proving little if any advancement, the trumpet was discontinued and a steam whistle was erected back at the lighthouse. In 1874, with objections still being made about the weakness of the fog signals heard from Monhegan Island, the government admitted that it was impossible to "secure a better site."

Arrangements were then made that allowed the fog signal to be relocated at Manana Island. The report of 1876 again expresses disappointment with the existing signal, and in 1877 a new first-class Daboll trumpet was set up at Manana Island. A telegraph wire connecting the two islands was also installed, so that Mrs. Humphrey, high in her tower on Monhegan Island could press a button if a fog bank began to roll in. The button operated a large electric gong situated on the bedroom wall of Fog Signal Keeper Frank Adams. Thus, whenever she saw a fog approaching at night, Mrs. Humphrey would ring the gong in Keeper Adams' bedroom at Manana Island. Adams would spring from his bed and start the fog signal going.

Sidney Studley was keeper at Monhegan from 1880 until 1883, when William Stanley took his place, retaining the position for nineteen years. The next keeper was Daniel Stevens. Others who have been stationed at Monhegan include Keepers Pierce, Wallace, Orne, Handley, Dyer, Woodward, Hutchins, Robinson, Foss and Wilson B. Carter.

The lighthouse sends out its flashes from a height of 178 feet above the ocean with a candlepower of 170,000. Over at the Manana Fog Station, the diaphragm horn gives a group of two terrific blasts every minute. The old fog bell with its cracked lip still stands ready to perform emergency duty, if needed.

Monhegan appears much longer but is actually less than a mile and a half in length, and its highest promontory is 160 feet above the waves. Broocher's Cave is one of the interesting locations here that all visitors should see. Dead Man's Cove,

Washerwoman Ledge, and Pulpit Rock are some of the titles bestowed upon other locations at Monhegan Island, which is nine miles from the nearest point of New England's mainland.

9

Pemaquid Point

The early history of Pemaquid, Maine, is both exciting and mysterious. The ancient cellar holes, the old pavement of disputed origin, the stories of Dixie Bull the pirate, Governor Phips, and Pasco Chubb, all give the entire area an unusual interest to the casual visitor. A learned gentleman in 1710 found a gravestone of 1695 in the burial ground with the simple initials H M and the date. It was the last resting place of Hugh March, killed by the Indians, who were very active in this part of Maine.

Commander Pasco Chubb was attacked at his Pemaquid fort in August 1696 by D'Iberville, the French commander. After a few shells had landed inside the fortification, with the subsequent repercussions causing terror and confusion, Chubb, visibly unnerved, surrendered. One hundred men inside the fort were thus forced to give up without firing a gun. A tortured Indian prisoner was freed by D'Iberville. Later some Indians caught Chubb near his home in Andover, Massachusetts, and killed him. Some say Chubb was killed because of his mistreatment of the Indian prisoner.

Erected in 1827 at the edge of a rocky promontory on the

mainland, Pemaquid Point Light is one of the prettiest lights on the entire coast. Isaac Dunham of Bath, Maine, first received the position of keeper.

As the years passed, it became the custom of the keeper to have a farm along with his running of the light, and Keeper Dunham, who later became the first keeper at Minot's Ledge Light, built several barns and other houses that he believed were worth $1,100. When he was transferred in 1837 he asked the new keeper, Nathaniel Gamage, for an adjustment of the property he had developed. Gamage paid Dunham $1,100.

In 1841, after Gamage had been working the farm and the lighthouse together, newly elected President Benjamin Harrison removed Gamage in favor of J. P. Means. Means was not particularly interested in paying out money for the farm, but agreed to give Gamage a moderate amount for rent. This did not satisfy Gamage, who appealed for help to President John Tyler, who had succeeded to the Presidency at the death of Harrison.

President Tyler asked Secretary of the Treasury John Spencer to investigate the affair, and Spencer found out from Keeper Means that he would be willing to arbitrate the matter and pay Gamage outright. If the two did not agree on what a fair price was Means was willing to leave the appraisal of the buildings and property to some disinterested person. When Gamage heard this, he replied by saying that all he had received in two years was $30, and of this amount, $4 was for shoemaking. He said that he had been obliged to take what the keeper would pay, which was less than $15 a year for his property. On July 1843 Gamage said that the only way justice could be done was to give him back his position, but he did not get the appointment again.

In the year 1903 the keeper of Pemaquid Point Light was

Captain Clarence Marr, a life saver of long experience and the hero of many spectacular rescues.

On the afternoon of September 16 a dense fog lifted suddenly to disclose a stormy, dangerous sky, and the wind began to breeze up from the south-southwest. Several miles out to sea was the fishing schooner *George F. Edmunds,* with her captain, Willard Poole, beginning to worry about the gathering storm, and wondering if he should run through the Western Gut for the tiny harbor of South Bristol, Maine, or perhaps continue down the coast and try for Portland. According to William P. Sawyer of Pemaquid Point, who interviewed the two survivors on September 17, Captain Poole decided to make for South Bristol Harbor. He shaped his course for Pemaquid Point Light, a beacon he was destined never to pass. The captain of the sixteen men on the *Edmunds* was the only one who knew anything about Pemaquid Point or the adjacent waters. In William Sawyer's own words,

"Poole shaped his course for John's Bay, presumably steering for the Pemaquid Point Ledge buoy which could be located more easily by steering for a while toward the lighthouse on Pemaquid Point. The buoy lies about a mile off the lighthouse in a southerly direction. But before starting for Bristol the skipper of another mackerel seiner was told by Poole to follow the *Edmunds* and he could find himself in a snug little haven. This skipper did so for a while but when he heard the distant roar of surf, didn't like the looks of things as he was unacquainted with the waters in that vicinity. So he changed his course to Portland where he arrived next day . . . .

"Meantime the gale increased in fury and when Poole and his schooner had reached a point estimated by one of the surviving members of his crew to have been a mile or two off Pemaquid Point, an unusually heavy gust struck the schooner. The boat was then luffed into the wind and the mainsail reefed, after which the course was resumed for John's Bay. Poole knew, as every mariner brought up in South Bristol did, that the extremity of Pemaquid Point is indented by a small cove called sometimes Lighthouse Cove and that this indentation forms two points. On the east the lighthouse is situated while on the westerly point bounded by John's Bay there is no beacon. Running into John's Bay from the southard a course cannot be laid by steering directly for the lighthouse but must be shaped to the westward to clear the other point. Poole must have realized this fact and calculated the drift of the schooner while the mainsail was being reefed, but his calculations were wrong by only 800 to 1000 feet, for instead of quite clearing the westerly point and entering the Bay, the vessel crashed upon the rocky shores and was soon dashed into fragments."

It was a terrible disaster. Captain Poole and thirteen of his crew perished. Only two fishermen were saved. In the same storm the *Sadie and Lillie* hit close by. Weston Curtis saw the disaster and got a line aboard the wreck. Two men reached shore, but when Captain William S. Harding started to leave the schooner, the lines snarked and jammed, with the unfortunate man drowning in the heavy surf before help could reach him. It was a storm which Pemaquid Point residents remembered for many years.

The body of William P. Sawyer, who wrote the description of the Pemaquid Point shipwreck, was found near the lighthouse on September 17, 1945.

The light is now unattended.

10

Hendrick's Head Light

On the east side of the mouth of the Sheepscot River, Maine, in Latitude North 43° 49′ and Longitude West 69° 41′, is Hendrick's Head, where for many years the cheerful beam of Hendrick's Head Light guided the sailor at sea. The lighthouse no longer sends out its cheerful rays to warn mariners of the shoals nearby, but there are many stories and incidents connected with this location which will be told for years to come.

It was in the year 1829 that the first lighthouse was erected on this rocky promontory six miles from Boothbay. In 1875 the last tower was erected, a square building greatly resembling the Wood End Light at Cape Cod but having a covered way which led to the keeper's dwelling.

In Mills' *American Light-House Guide* for 1845, Hendrick's Head Light is described as a fixed, white light, elevated 39 feet above the level of the sea. Sailing directions suggested that "if bound up the Sheepscot River, passing Seguin Light to the southward, steer N. E. until you bring Hendrick's Head Light to bear N. a little westerly, then run for it, keeping a larboard shore close aboard."

During a wild gale that occurred in March, a century or more ago, the keeper of Hendrick's Head Light noticed a vessel ashore on a ledge about half a mile off the point. A dense snowstorm had prevented the captain of the vessel from seeing the lighthouse until it was too late, and "she fetched up all standing." Those on board took to the rigging at once, and the keeper could see the great seas mercilessly pounding the unfortunate craft, each wave covering the human figures in the shrouds with tons of icy water that soon froze them hard to the ratlines.

Debating for several minutes on whether he could launch a dory into the breakers ten and fifteen feet high then hitting the shore, the keeper went down along the rocky ledges to see if there was any possible way to help the doomed people aboard the shipwreck. But the seas hit with such overwhelming force, and the wind carried the biting spray with such tremendous power that the keeper finally decided there was nothing anyone could do for the sailors aboard the ill-fated craft.

As darkness came on that terrible day the keeper and his wife lit a huge bonfire to let the people aboard the vessel know that they had been seen. Barely an hour later a remarkable incident took place. The keeper had gone down to the shore again to see if any wreckage was coming up on the beach. He suddenly noticed a large bundle "tossing light and coming ashore." He ran over to the cove where his boathouse was located and grabbed a boathook and a line. The bundle gradually worked in toward the ledge where the keeper was standing, and in a few minutes it started to drift toward a small beach near the point. The keeper, fastening the line about his waist, told his wife to hold tight to the other end while he waded into the raging surf. Just as a towering breaker loomed over him, he thrust the boathook into the fastening on the bundle, and then he and the bundle were hurled up on the sand by the terrific force of the oncoming wave. Letting go the boathook, he grabbed at the bundle and crawled above the reach of the next wave.

After resting for a moment from the effects of his pummeling from the surf, the keeper found that he had rescued two feather beds from the deep! But as the feather beds were tied together in a manner to indicate something was inside, he took out his sheath knife and soon cut the fastenings. There, in the middle of the strange bundle, was a box, and in the box was a baby girl, alive and crying as though her heart would break!

Without stopping to untie the line around his waist, he ran with the infant toward the house, his wife shouting advice and running as fast as she could behind him. Reaching the house, he hurried into the kitchen, where the fire made the room warm and comfortable. Then his wife caught up with him and took charge. Within a few minutes the baby was warm and cozy.

The keeper, believing that he could perhaps signal to the luckless mariners aboard the wreck that the baby had been saved, dashed out again into the gale to the huge bonfire, where he planned to wave out to the vessel and indicate the baby was safe. But when he reached the fire and looked out over the raging seas, a violent snow squall prevented his sighting the craft. A few moments later the squall let up, revealing that the ship was gone. Pieces of wreckage soon began to come ashore, including a stove-in lifeboat, a wooden shoe, and many broken spars.

Returning to the box that had contained the baby, the keeper found two blankets, a locket, and a message from the mother in which she commended her child to God. The keeper and his wife, who had recently buried their own child, adopted the baby girl shortly afterward.

Another tale concerns Keeper Charles L. Knight, who was

active at Hendrick's Head in the period between world wars I and II. One night he left the lighthouse residence to mail an official report, and passed a dignified woman walking in the opposite direction. Puzzled as to why she, a stranger, was in that lonely section of Southport after dark, Keeper Knight was about to speak to her, but thought better of it and continued to the Post Office, where he found that the postmaster had also seen the woman. After discussing who the stranger was for a few minutes, Knight hurried back along the road to overtake the woman, but failed to find her. The next day when the tide went out, her drowned body, weighted down with a flatiron, was found on the shore.

Later her remains were taken to the local cemetery in Southport and given a decent burial, although no one ever learned her name. Many in the vicinity say she has returned to haunt the lonely beach where she committed suicide, and there are those who have walked the deserted stretch of highway during the winter months who claim to have seen her furtive form flitting from headland to headland.

Hendrick's Head Light was later given up by the government, and although the tower was allowed to remain as a daytime marker, the mariner must depend on the Marrs Ledge Beacon, lighted during the summer months by the Southport Yacht Club, or the Cuckolds, that fascinating and unusual lighthouse a thousand yards to the "southard" of Cape Newagen.

11

Seguin Light

High on a rocky island, two miles southward of the mouth of the beautiful Kennebec River, stands the rugged granite tower of Seguin Lighthouse. There is no loftier beacon in all the State of Maine, for its light flashes out into the darkness from a height of 180 feet above the sea. Seguin, situated in North Latitude 43° 42', and in Longitude West 69° 45', is one of the major lights along the New England coast. There is a flash of 80,000 candlepower.

In William Strachey's 1612 account of George Popham's voyage, the island is called "Sutquin," possibly a corruption of *satquin,* the unpleasant Indian name meaning to make an oral emission. In John Smith's writings we find that he refers to the Sagadahock River and then mentions the isle of Satguin. When Champlain sailed down the coast in what yachtsman-author Alfred E. Loomis believes was a two-masted pinnace, the Frenchman decided that Seguin Island looked more like a turtle or tortoise than anything else. Many times while flying over Seguin, I have been struck by the resemblance the island bears to that well-known member of the reptile family.

It was in 1795 that the importance of Seguin's location was

realized and a lighthouse built there. The first keeper was a colorful character, Major John Polersky, who fought in the American Revolution. When the major moved out to Seguin he found it was a steep, rocky island about half a mile long, with a green stretch of grass running down to the rocks on the easterly side.

The career of Major Polersky at Seguin Island was not a happy one. Because his salary was always inadequate, he appealed for aid many times. Writing in May 12, 1796, to General Benjamin Lincoln, the former major openly discussed his troubles:

"You know my dear General all the difficulties and expenses a light at Seguin is attended to and I dont want to have extravagent wagers, but should like to save myself. The first three years will cost me money out of my pocket which I can make you sensible of. There is no feed on the island, I must carry two cows for my family and keep them on hay, summer and winter, which I must purchase and carry on the island, with the greatest difficulty. I must keep also a horse on hay to haul or carry my oil, provisions, firewood, etc. etc. I must purchase a good boat, which cost me at list 100 dolar. I must purchase every individual necessity for my family till I can raise it. I must built some sort of a small barn for my cattle and hay. I must hire one man in case of sickness . . . . Now my dear General I hope you will take it into consideration I must request the favour of you to assist an old soldier . . . I expect to go on the island next week in order to make some preparations, toward the time I shall be called upon if the time of my tending the light could be ascertained for five or six years I should take it as a favor. In expectation of a favourable answer I remain

with the highest esteem your humble servant

JOHN POLERSKY"

Anxious to help his former fellow officer, General Lincoln communicated at once with his superior, the Commissioner of the Revenue, who was not impressed. The Commissioner wrote as follows:

"In the case of Major Polersky, there are the advantages of plenty of fuel, without expense, upon the public land, the opportunity to fish for his family use, or even for sale, a boat to fish in will be furnished for passing to the main, there is land for tillage and grass, and for a plentiful garden . . . . The salaries of keepers appear to have been subjected to some miscalculation on their part from the unnecessary degree of former standing, which some of the candidates have had. It is plain at first view, that the above duties are not in their nature adapted to the standing of a field officer, or of a Major of Brigade."

By 1800 the house at Seguin was rotting away because of the action of the fog and salt air, and the bridge used to cross over the gully on the way up from the landing beach was about to collapse. District Superintendent Lincoln visited Major Polersky at his island home the same year, but did not dare trust the weight of his portly frame to the collapsing timbers. "The access is difficult for me," reported the honest general. Repairs of a minor nature were then authorized.

Although General Lincoln did what he could to ease the burden of this faithful Revolutionary hero, matters became worse. Seguin Island in its exposed location was a poor place to try to make a success of a combination farming and fishing life. Storm after storm swept in from the northeast and southeast, smashing boats and vessels with heartless regularity. A twenty-five-dollar boat, an eight-dollar canoe, and a large boat worth three hundred dollars all were smashed within a year of the major's arrival on the island. And so all means of provision were removed, for with his fishing and sailing vessels sunk, Major Polersky and his helper, a good fisherman, were marooned on the island for months. The sufferings that Polersky went through were severe. Death finally came to relieve him of his earthly troubles and thus ended the career of a man who deserved a better fate.

Winslow Lewis installed a new lantern at Seguin in 1817, but the wooden tower had gone to pieces to such an extent that Lewis feared that the lighthouse could not "much longer sustain the Lanthorn." Congress appropriated the necessary funds, and the wooden lighthouse at Seguin Island was replaced in 1819 by a fine stone tower at a cost of $2,500. The constant gales that swept in from the Atlantic eventually conquered the manmade tower. By the middle of the century another edifice was necessary. Congress finally passed a bill authorizing a new tower that was built in 1857 to a height of fifty-three feet, at a cost of $35,000. With minor changes, the lighthouse still stands today, the top of the edifice 185 feet above the sea.

Various attempts have been made through the years to provide a school for the children of the lighthouse keepers at Seguin Island; these efforts were not successful for a very long period of time. Whenever the school was not operating, the resourceful wives of the keepers who could afford to do so left the island to have their children educated at nearby Bath. E. V. Mitchell in his book *Anchor to Windward* tells us that when the school building was closed for the last time, it was utilized for the island cow.

Frank E. Bracey became keeper of the Seguin Lighthouse in the year 1926. One of the faithful veterans of the old lighthouse service, Captain Bracey had an interesting career which began aboard the Portland Lightship in 1920. After five years of rolling and pitching off Cape Elizabeth, Bracey transferred to Seguin Island Light, where he remained another five years.

He was proud of the fact that the Boston to Maine boat had made out the gleam of Seguin Light from a distance of forty-two miles. In 1931 Bracey transferred to Eagle Island Light in Penobscot Bay, but he always remembered his five years on Seguin Island off Cape Small.

"The fog horn was among the most powerful along the coast," Keeper Bracey told me. "Its concussion has put out an oil lantern set on the ground eight feet below the horn itself. I have seen seagulls which were flying by actually knocked down by the force of the concussion. Once during a northeast snowstorm the horn was heard at far away Bath, fourteen miles north of Seguin Island. It is said that the snow acted as a sound carrier."

Keeper Bracey remembered the winding iron stairway that leads up to the turret just below the light. Countless times he carried the kerosene up those steps to feed the cylinder near the air compressor. In this cylinder the fuel for a night's lighting was stored. The compressed air forced the fuel oil to the landing above, where the Welsbach mantle sat on its mechanical throne in the center of the lantern roof. A tube leading up through the floor below fed the oil by means of an inverted U-fashioned vaporizer to the all-important Welsbach mantle which formed the lighting unit for the Seguin beacon.

In 1931 Keeper Bracey was interviewed about his activities at sundown.

"When we light the light we swing the Welsbach mantle to one side. Then we put this little alcohol lamp in its place and light that. By keeping the alcohol lamp burning for eighteen minutes beneath the vaporizer, the oil vapor in the tube reaches the boiling point and ignites. Then we take out the lamp and swing the mantle into its place. The hot vapor passes through a screen and into the mantle. From then on, the light keeps burning until we put it out by shutting off the vapor supply.

"Seguin is what we call a fixed light. Some lights are flashing lights. They seem to revolve and flash brighter at certain intervals. Well, in those lights, glass prisms revolve around the light by clockwork. A certain highly magnifying section of the prism, known as the "bull's-eye," sends out an intense beam of light. We burn about two gallons of oil in the summer and two and a half in the winter. On a clear night we can see eleven lights from here."

Seguin's foghorn is housed at another part of the plateau at the top of the island several hundred feet away. Two twenty-eight-horsepower semi-Diesel engines operating on fuel oil drive compressed air into the diaphone. Whenever fog, vapor, or snow obscure the view, the foghorn is put into operation, its powerful double blasts sounding three times every minute.

It is well that the fog signal at Seguin is a powerful one, for Seguin Island has more fog, year after year, than any location in the United States. The fog signal is on about one-seventh of the whole year; in fact during one single year the diaphone registered 2,734 hours, or more than 30 percent of the time.

When we visited Seguin two summers ago with Coast Guard Captain Robert A. Lee, we were royally entertained. We were pulled up in the dory by the donkey engine in the boat shed, and then began the long hike on the wooden walkway to the lighthouse.

After eating, we went through the covered way into the lighthouse itself, where we found that the Welsbach gas mantle described by Keeper Bracey had been replaced by electrically operated light bulbs.

12

Halfway Rock Light

About ten miles eastward of Portland Head Light, deep in Casco Bay, is a pinnacled, jagged ledge on which stands Halfway Rock Light. In storms and rough seas the waves sweep entirely over the ledges, which extend for several hundred yards to the north and south of the light.

Agitation for a lighthouse at Halfway Rock began more than a century ago when First Lieutenant Green Walden wrote a letter to Captain Joseph Smith, who was inspecting lighthouses and possible sites in the district. Walden said that a light proposed for Mark Island in Casco Bay would be worse than useless, as it would confuse navigators. "I would beg leave to suggest the propriety of erecting a monument on Halfway Rock," were the concluding remarks of Walden.

Captain Smith concurred in Walden's belief, but thirty years passed and no lighthouse was erected at Halfway Rock. In 1869 fifty thousand dollars was appropriated and construction began at once. The tower was almost finished in 1870 when work stopped for lack of funds. The following year an additional appropriation allowed the light to be completed, and it was illuminated for the first time on August

15, 1871. The light is shown seventy-six feet above the sea.

The first keeper of Halfway Rock was Captain John T. Sterling, a relative of Robert Thayer Sterling, the writer-light keeper. He was justly proud of his attractive station in Casco Bay, and had many visitors during the summer months.

Halfway Rock Light has an unusual system of flashing. According to the *Light List* volume, it is: "Fixed white, alternating with fixed red light, with five sec. red flash in red period, every 90 sec."

The normal white light is 18,000 candlepower, the red flash is of 800,000 strength, and the red light has a beam of 190,000.

In her delightful book *All Among the Lighthouses,* Mary B. Crowninshield mentions a visit ashore at Halfway Rock in 1885. The lighthouse inspector invites the children of his sister and another young friend to make the regular lighthouse tour with him on the lighthouse Tender *Iris.* We read of their visit to Halfway Rock Light:

"The bow oarsman tossed and cleverly boated his oar; then, seizing the painter, dexterously jumped ashore, and, with the assistance of the keepers, who had come down to meet the inspector, hauled the boat well up on the ways, and held her steady until the party were out of her; and then they all walked up to the lighthouse together, the keepers looking fine in their uniforms. 'Such an improvement,' Violet had told the boys, 'over the old way, when they wore anything they happened to have on hand,'—the blue cloth suit with gilt ornaments and buttons giving them a fine and dignified appearance.

" 'That's a queer thing,' said the observing John, as they neared the tower, 'looks like an Esquimau's hut.'

" 'Yes,' answered Uncle Tom. 'That was built for a boathouse,—a sort of concrete affair; but you see how little room there is here, and as we had to have another set of boat-ways, it had to be sacrificed.'

"The boys followed Uncle Tom into a circular room at the base of the tower, which seemed to them a sort of store-room. . . . Uncle Tom's sea-boots were vanishing at the top of the narrow circular iron stairway, and John and Cortland quickly followed. The first room entered was the kitchen of the establishment. There, every thing looked in the best possible order, with its neat pantry, finely polished cooking-stove, and shining utensils. The next flight of stairs brought them to another room, the bedroom of the principal keeper; and above this was a second room, with two beds for the assistant keepers. A fourth flight of stairs brought them out in the watch-room, where the keeper remains on duty all night, to see that the light does not go out, and to keep guard generally. . . .

"The keeper opened a door in the lens. . . . The inspector assured himself that the lamp was well cared for, and in good working order,—indeed he asked the opinion on this point of a young man who had come ashore. . . . This young man seemed to speak as one having authority, and the boys found that Uncle Tom spoke of him to the keeper as 'the lampist,' and to him as Mr. Shafer; and that the lampist, though he spoke English but indifferently, seemed to be at home in all matters pertaining to the lamp.

" 'Wind that clock, Hank,' called down the keeper to his assistant in the watch-room below. 'Click, click, click, click,' went the clock. And now a queer frame-work, made of bronze, and set at intervals with perpendicular prisms, outside of which were red panes of glass, began to revolve slowly around the lens proper, and even Cortland could understand, that when it so revolved, the light from the lens could only show forth during the interval, or when there was no red glass to color the light; but, that whenever the colored pane of glass passed any given point, from that point a red beam must shine out across the water."

On September 13, 1966, my wife, Anna-Myrle, and I, together with our daughter Dorothy and my brother Win, went ashore at Halfway Rock from the motor boat *Subojoy*. Head Keeper Horace A. Leverett and assistants Robert Shillace and Edward Hannula greeted us. We toured the lighthouse, and Keeper Leverett explained how the fog horn worked.

Severe damage was suffered in the terrible gale of February 18, 1972, when the fuel tank for the generator was washed off the island so that there was no electricity for heat or power for the light for some time. The wood walkway and part of the boat ramp were destroyed. The crew was taken off by helicopter.

13

Portland Head Light

Portland Head and its light seem to symbolize the State of Maine—rocky coast, breaking waves, sparkling water and clear, pure sea air. Built on the headland after which the city was named, for the promontory was known as Portland Head as early as 1750, this tower stands against the sky, with its identifying ridge built out from the flush sides of the stone edifice two-thirds of the distance to the top.

It was in 1787 that the construction of Portland Head Light began, under the supervision of the Commonwealth of Massachusetts, of which Maine was then a part. Taken over by the federal government, the lighthouse was finished under the direction of John Nichols and Jonathan Bryant. By 1790 the edifice had reached a height of fifty-eight feet and was considered finished. When the officials climbed to the top of the tower, however, they found that a neighboring headland unfortunately shut out the view of the Portland Head Light entirely, and decided that additional height would have to be given the tower. Authority to raise the tower to its desired height finally came from Alexander Hamilton, Secretary of the Treasury.

The original lantern as planned was fairly large, but because of the sloping sides and extra height of the tower, the reduced area at the top was found too small for the lantern the authorities had chosen to install. Finally, a smaller lantern was obtained, and the lighthouse was finished without further delay.

Many of the nautically inclined citizens of Portland were eager to be appointed as keeper of the new lighthouse, but the choice finally narrowed down to two individuals, Captain Joseph Greenleaf and Barzillai Delano. Greenleaf was recommended by Portland's Collector Nathaniel F. Fosdick on November 2, 1790, while Delano was the choice of two of the committeemen who arranged for the construction of the tower.

Captain Joseph Greenleaf won the appointment, receiving official notice from President George Washington himself in a letter written January 7, 1791. Although Greenleaf was the first keeper, when his career ended after a few years at Portland Head, there was Barzillai Delano waiting for the position, and it was given to him.

A few years after the tower had been built it was found damp and uninhabitable. General Benjamin Lincoln, Massachusetts Lighthouse Superintendent, suggested as a remedy that pine planks could be used to enclose the walls of the lighthouse, after which three or four iron hoops could secure the planks to the stone walls of the tower itself. A good coat of shingles, "well painted," according to Lincoln, would complete the unusual plan, which, as far as is known, was never carried out.

General Henry Dearborn visited Portland Head Light in the fall of 1810, and interviewed Keeper Delano about repairing the sagging structure. As the flooring was rotting away, it was decided that new timbers were necessary. When the carpenter arrived to make the repairs, he found that

Delano had stored practically the entire year's supply of oil in the room where the alterations were to be made and it reached almost to the ceiling. The lighthouse keeper was afraid the whole building might collapse if radical changes were made with the heavy weight of oil shifted. Therefore, nothing was attempted that year, and the carpenter was forced to return the following summer to make his repairs.

Because of a complaint about Portland Head Light received by Tench Coxe, Commissioner of the Revenue at the Capital in Philadelphia, Benjamin Lincoln made a thorough investigation. A sea captain complained that he had been unable to see the light while approaching the harbor. Lincoln's investigation revealed that there was no method of ventilation in the tower to carry off the smoke, so that quite often the tubes of glass were heavily coated over. Lincoln then explained to Coxe how the diameter at the top of the tower had been reduced to a little less than six feet because of the extra height needed to clear the nearby headland, but in spite of this, "there is room enough to burn almost any quantity of oil and yet if the lamps are properly arranged space enough to clean the glass." Lincoln was doubtful that the lamps were as weak as claimed, stating he was "a little surprised if the Lights are badly kept that no Master of Vessel should have hinted it to me. They are every week at this Office and often two or three in a week." He also expressed the hope that politics were not entering into the matter.

An outdoor oil shed was built two years later, and also a cistern protected from the spray by a rock fence. The expense of these tasks was considered high, $179.07, but, according to Lincoln, the people of Portland "would not perform it for less."

In 1820, when the State of Maine was set off from its mother, Massachusetts, the new state received local jurisdiction over its lighthouses, with supervision from Washington, of course. Portland Head Light thus received a new supervisor, Isaac Ilsley of Portland.

In the same year the long career of Keeper Delano at Portland Head Light came to an end, when he died in service at the lighthouse. The new keeper was Joshua Freeman.

In September 1850 thirteen twenty-one-inch reflectors were put in place, and the next year another lantern was installed. The new apparatus was a substantial improvement, but a few years later, after the Fresnel lenses were installed at other New England stations, the coastal pilots were quick to voice their disapproval of the weaker rays of Portland Head Light.

When representatives of the newly commissioned Lighthouse Board visited Portland Head on July 5, 1852, Keeper John F. Watts had a strange story to tell them. At the time he took the position no one could tell him how to operate the light, and he was forced to hire a man for two days to teach him how to do it. He pointed out that the reflectors, less than two years old, were badly scratched. The members of the board were surprised to find that the keeper's fog horn was only blown in accordance with private arrangement with certain steamers. Keeper Watts lived in a dwelling house that was in very poor condition, and the lighthouse itself was being undermined by rats.

As a result of the Lighthouse Board's report, as well as considerable criticism from the Portland shipmasters, a Fresnel lens was installed in 1855, the private foghorn was replaced by a regular fog bell operated in bad weather for all shipping, and necessary repairs were made at the base of the tower.

During the Civil War, raids on shipping in and out of Portland Harbor became almost commonplace. Because of the necessity for ships at sea to sight Portland Head Light as soon as possible, it was agreed that the edifice should be raised even higher. When the war ended, the tower was increased in height by eight feet, and a new set of lenses was installed.

The September gale of 1869, which left its mark at so many other lighthouses and lifesaving stations along the coast, did not spare Portland Head. The storm ripped the great fog signal bell from its fastening and hurled it into a nearby gully. A new fog bell tower was built in 1870 with a Stevens striker, and was in turn replaced by a Daboll trumpet that had seen service at Monhegan Island. In 1872 a second class trumpet replaced the Monhegan signal, and in 1887 Boston Light's old twenty-four-inch caloric engine was installed at Portland Head.

Four years earlier Portland Head Light had been lowered twenty feet, only to be raised twenty feet the following year. No one yet seems to be able to explain these changes. Finally, in 1885, Portland Head Light was made a second order station by enlarging the tower at the top and putting a more powerful lens in place. The new light was first illuminated on January 15, 1885.

Portland Head Light in peacetime is an occulting white light. The light flashes, then it occults, or goes through a period of darkness, before the next flash. Every two seconds of the night the beam of light is seen from its tower 101 feet in the air.

Two famous shipwrecks will always be associated with Portland Head Light, the steamer *Bohemian* and the ship *Anne C. Maguire*. The *Bohemian* sailed from Liverpool on February 4, 1864, but stormy weather delayed her several days, so that it was late on the afternoon of February 22 when she made Portland Head Light. A peculiar hazy condition then prevailing misled Captain Borland into thinking he was some distance off shore. Suddenly the *Bohemian* crashed on Alden's Rock, slid off, and began to leak badly.

The Captain ordered all hands to the lifeboats, but in the

confusion the Number 2 lifeboat, heavily loaded, dropped into the sea and many were drowned. The other lifeboats were successfully launched, and all aboard landed safely. Among the survivors was a little boy, John E. Fitzgerald, who later became the best-known and best-loved Irish leader of Boston's 1890's.

The other disaster was that of the *Anne C. Maguire*. Thousands who journey down to the light look out where the *Maguire* hit to read the inscription painted on the rock: "In memory of the ship Annie C. Maguire, wrecked here, Dec. 24, 1886." It was an unusual shipwreck, as the vessel was in legal trouble, and Keeper Joshua Strout had been notified by the sheriff to be on the lookout for her. He never expected the *Maguire* to come ashore in his front yard, however.

A thick snowstorm that was almost a blizzard filled the air at the time Captain O'Neil of the *Maguire* lost his bearings, causing the vessel to smash right up on the ledge. Every member of the ship's company got ashore safely. The sheriff then served his papers. The captain, who was worrying about the fact that all his worldly wealth was aboard the vessel, later found that his wife had placed the money in a hat box, which she had carried to safety upon leaving the ship.

Keeper Strout was a member of a family that served at Portland Head Light Station for almost sixty years. In 1867 Joshua F. Strout as head keeper received $620 a year, while his wife, May, received $480 as assistant keeper. When Strout retired, his son Joseph W. Strout took his place. Joseph Strout remained at Portland Head for more than half a century, and was dearly loved by all who knew him.

Frank O. Hilt then became keeper at Portland Head. He built behind Portland Head Light an interesting innovation, a giant checkerboard.

Sailing out beyond Portland Head, you can barely make out the white rock where Henry Wadsworth Longfellow sat so often in the days when he was composing his poetry. Possibly the first thoughts of the following lines came to him at Portland Head:

> And as the evening darkens, lo! how bright
> Through the deep purple of the twilight air,
> Beams forth the sudden radiance of its light
> With strange unearthly splendour in its glare!
>
> And the great ships sail outward and return
> Bending and blowing o'er the billowy swells;
> And ever joyful, as they see it burn,
> They wave their silent welcomes and farewells.

14

Cape Elizabeth Light

One of the most interesting locations in the area around Portland Maine, is the Cape Elizabeth Lighthouse Station, located several miles southeast of the Pine Tree State's largest city. Built back in the year 1828, the light has had many unusual events connected with its history.

In 1811 General Dearborn wrote to Secretary of the Treasury Gallatin that he had arranged to erect a monument or marker for the identification of Cape Elizabeth by ships at sea, and on June 3 of that year final plans were agreed upon whereby the monument would be forty feet high with a twenty-foot base. But the daytime marker, of course, was not a guide to ships at night, and agitation gradually crystalized into the approval by Congress to build a lighthouse at Cape Elizabeth.

Fifteen months later the contract was awarded to the lowest bidder, Jeremiah Berry, who constructed the two rubble-stone towers for $4,250. Twelve acres of Cape Elizabeth land were purchased at the same time, at a price "of $50. beyond the authority heretofore given."

During the construction of the towers, the local representative, Isaac Ilsley, visited the scene to superintend the workmen, and later included his own expenses in the accounts sent to Washington. Stephen Pleasonton took exception to the expense, saying that a commission of 2½ per cent was sufficient, and ended with the sentence, "You will therefore strike out of the account for Cape Elizabeth light houses the charge for superintendence of the workmen."

President John Quincy Adams appointed Elisha Jordan as the first keeper at Cape Elizabeth Lights in October 1828. Jordan had been chosen from a list of eighteen candidates, including Josiah Waistcoat, Isaiah Snow, Amos Wormwell, and Alexander Goldthwait. Jordan's salary was placed at $450 a year, and he was instructed to reside at the station and make it a habit to be at home.

Mrs. Amelia D. Chamberlain, at the age of nineteen, became the assistant keeper at Cape Elizabeth. Mrs. Chamberlain was a witness to the thrilling wreck of the steamer *Bohemian* in the year 1864. The next spring she assisted in draping the lighthouse towers with black bunting in mourning for the death of President Abraham Lincoln.

A Fresnel lens had been installed at Cape Elizabeth Light in 1855, making the lights brighter and more readily identified. Ten years later an unusual change was made for daytime recognition. The west tower was painted with one broad, vertical red stripe, and the east light was given four horizontal bands of red. It is believed no picture of this color combination is in existence. A giant steam whistle was installed on the station four years later for use in foggy weather, and this necessitated the construction of another separate building, some distance away from the keeper's home, for the installation of a huge boiler and other essential parts of the plant. The ten-inch locomotive whistle gave a terrific blast every minute, lasting eight seconds.

In 1873 the rubble towers were taken down and two stately

cast iron edifices were soon erected in their place, three hundred yards apart. The characteristics of the two lights were then made into one fixed and one flashing light, and a fog siren was installed to replace the locomotive whistle. A short time afterward the keeper's dwelling was repaired and a new house built for the head keeper. In 1884 a first-order mineral-oil lamp was installed in the east tower by Keeper Marcus A. Hanna, who was the first to illuminate the new light. Hanna had been keeper at Pemaquid Point Light in 1869.

Perhaps the most thrilling episode in Cape Elizabeth history occurred on January 28, 1885, when Keeper Hanna saved two of the crew members of the schooner *Australia* of Boothbay, Maine. The weather had been fair but cold the day before, with a light wind blowing in from the northeast. Toward dusk the breeze freshened, and by midnight a severe storm swept in from the sea. Keeper Hanna, who had been sick with a bad cold, was doing his best to conquer his miserable feelings and make sure that the giant fog signal blast was operating at the height of its efficiency.

But his was a hopeless task. The wind increased, the snow fell in unprecedented heaviness, and the waves, although the tide was low, were soon smashing against the ledges around the headland. By three in the morning Hanna realized that no ship at sea could possibly hear the steam whistle, although he kept sounding the blasts every minute of the night. He felt very ill and tried to ward off an intense desire to sleep. Finally, at six in the morning, Assistant Keeper Hiram Staples reported at the fog signal house for Hanna's relief. By this time, according to Hanna, "one of the coldest and most violent storms of snow, wind, and vapor was raging that I ever witnessed."

When he started back to his home from the fog station, Hanna encountered great snowdrifts three to five feet high, and in his weakened condition had to crawl through the deeper drifts to reach his home. Hanna's wife was waiting up for him, and after telling him that he should have known better than to go out on such a night, put him to bed, announcing that she would attend to putting out the lamp in the lighthouse at the proper time. Keeper Hanna, exhausted from his cold and his struggle through the deep snowdrifts, soon fell asleep.

Mrs. Hanna, as many other faithful wives have done in their unsung careers at lonely lighthouse stations, extinguished the lamp in the tower at twelve minutes past seven, near sunrise. On her return from the lighthouse she went out of doors on the lee side of the building, where there is a commanding view of the open sea. It was at twenty minutes before nine that she suddenly saw, through the snow and vapor, the masts of a vessel loom up a quarter mile from shore. Mrs. Hanna rushed to her husband with the exciting but disheartening news.

"There is a vessel ashore near the fog signal!" Hastily leaving his bed, without a thought for himself, Keeper Hanna dressed at once and rushed out of the house. He floundered through the snowdrifts and soon reached the fog signal station, which was about two hundred yards from the wreck. Calling to Staples, Hanna found to his surprise that his assistant had not noticed the wreck.

The unfortunate vessel was the schooner *Australia,* which had sailed from Boothbay Harbor at five o'clock the evening before, bound for Boston. Captain J. W. Lewis had a crew of two men, Irving Pierce and William Kellar, both seamen. When the storm hit them off Halfway Rock Light at eleven o'clock that night, Captain Lewis had chosen to run for Portland, but later accepted the advice of Pierce to stand off instead. Shortly afterward the mainsail blew to pieces, and it was agreed to jog off and on under reefed foresail until morning. Because the temperature was down to four above zero, the *Australia* iced over so heavily that the crew were forced to throw over the deckload to keep the vessel afloat. At eight o'clock they saw Cape Elizabeth Light, and hoisted the peak of the mainsail, trusting they could weather the cape.

The wind and sea, however, united to cause their disaster. The *Australia* soon grounded on the ledge near the fog signal station and the men aboard took to the rigging. Because of their frozen condition, for they were heavily coated with ice, the men were unable to move. Suddenly Captain Lewis was hit by a great wave and washed off the shrouds down onto the deck. With his last bit of strength he managed to climb up again, but the battering he had received made him an easy victim for the next great billow that swept across the schooner. When the wave went down, his men saw him no more.

Seamen Pierce and Kellar clung to their places in the rigging. Each successive sea swept across them, leaving its thin coating of icy water that froze on their helpless bodies. Soon they were unable to move in any way, becoming ice-covered forms turning whiter every minute. The tide was coming higher and higher, and the schooner seemed doomed to break up.

Just as they were about to give up all hope, they saw Keeper Hanna and his assistant approaching. They had gone to a pilot house nearby for a good line to throw out to the schooner. After securing a heavy iron weight to the end of the line, the keepers made their way down to the shore, where the schooner was being pounded to pieces as the tide rose. The vessel had hit the shore, which runs northeast to southwest at this point, heading westward, so that her starboard side was near shore, perched at an angle of forty-five degrees with the shoreline. In this position every sea would smash into the *Australia's* stern, sweep high into the air until even the mastheads were hidden from view, and burst out over the bow and sides as it made its way toward shore.

Captain Hanna reached the ice-covered rocks near the schooner, and after getting a vantage point knee deep in the seething foam, made an attempt to throw the line aboard. The weight fell into the sea ten feet short of its goal. Again and again he tried to land the line aboard the schooner. Each time he hauled back the icy cord, it was stiff and unyielding to the touch, contact with the water having frozen it even in that short period of seconds. After at least twenty attempts the poor lighthouse keeper had to give up, for his feet and hands were wet and freezing, the spray was icing his clothing into boardlike garments that allowed him no freedom of motion, and his sick condition had left him with a sense of weakness. Assistant Hiram Staples had gone back to the fog signal station some time before, discouraged by the many futile attempts to reach the two freezing men aboard the *Australia*. Keeper Hanna decided to get ashore and exercise his body by stamping his feet and pounding his arms, and then return to the schooner for a last attempt. His wife, meanwhile, had aroused the neighbors. Help was on the way.

Suddenly, a towering wave, higher than all the rest, struck the schooner, lifted her bodily from the ledge, and smashed the *Australia* against the rocks nearer the fog signal station. Her whole port side was stove in, and the *Australia* was now over on her beam ends. Keeper Hanna, hurrying to the shore, threw out his line and was overjoyed to watch it land aboard the schooner. The men, however, could not free themselves from the shrouds, to which they were frozen, and the line slid off into the sea.

Hanna, shivering with the cold, now waded waist deep into the sea and made his final attempt. By this time Seaman Pierce was able to break away from the icy coating that enveloped him and was ready. The line dropped at the foot of the shrouds, and with great effort, for his clothing had frozen stiff, Pierce slowly reached for the line, grasped it, and bent it around his waist.

Hanna realized that it would be almost impossible to pull the man in unaided, and cried desperately at the top of his voice for help. No one came, so he decided that he could wait no longer. Pierce signaled that he was ready, and went over the side into the sea. The lighthouse keeper hauled away. Wave after wave battered the frozen man as he was pulled to land. When he hit shore, Hanna was forced to pull him up over the rocky ledge. Later Hanna said he never knew where he obtained the energy to pull and push the "helpless, frozen lump of humanity to a place out of reach of the surf." Irving Pierce was totally blind from exposure to the cold, and his jaws were frozen together. His whole appearance was ghastly. "The expression of his face," said Keeper Hanna, later, "I shall not soon forget."

But there was still another shipwrecked mariner aboard the schooner, which was now going to pieces rapidly. Leaving Pierce for the moment, Keeper Hanna stumbled down to the shore again, adjusted the line, and made his throw. Floating wreckage fouled the line, and he tried again and again. Finally it reached Kellar, who wound it around his icy body and signaled at once for the pull ashore. Although he knew in his heart that he would not have strength enough to pull Kellar out of the ocean, Hanna answered that he was ready and told Kellar to jump into the ocean. The lighthouse keeper made a silent prayer that help would come in time, as his strength was failing fast.

As he began the torturous pull ashore, Hanna was greeted by shouts, and Assistant Staples, together with two neighbors, ran down the bank to help him. They had arrived just in time, as if in answer to Keeper Hanna's prayer for aid. The four men soon had the helpless sailor out of the surf. Lifting the two mariners, they carried them through the deep drifts to the fog signal station.

The frozen clothing of the two victims was cut off their bodies, and cold water rubbed on their limbs. Forcing open their jaws, the others poured stimulants down the throats of the shipwrecked victims. Dry flannels were put on the men, and they gradually regained their senses. The sailors were then given hot food and drink, and were soon able to tell their story. When they mentioned how their captain had been swept overboard, Hanna learned for the first time of a third man aboard the schooner. The captain's body later washed up on the shore near the scene of the disaster.

The snowstorm had been so severe that it was impossible to move the men from the fog signal station until the next day, when they were placed on a bobsled and taken to Hanna's residence. Two days later, as soon as roads were broken through from Portland, the survivors were taken to the city.

When it was announced in the 1920's that the west tower of Cape Elizabeth Light was to be dismantled, many mariners protested the act. The government, however, had already conducted exhaustive tests before the announcement, so carried out its plans. The light in the west tower was discontinued for good. The east tower now has a beacon with 1,800,000 candlepower.

On March 3, 1947, the coal collier *Oakey L. Alexander* broke in two off the coast of Maine, and Captain Raymond Lewis brought the stern with all the crew aboard in to beach her on McKinney's Point near Cape Elizabeth. Coastguardsman Earle B. Drinkwater and his men, after shooting out a line with a Lyle gun, brought the crew and the captain in safely by breeches buoy.

Cape Elizabeth Light is now automatic.

15

Cape Neddick Nubble

Captain Joseph Smith, while inspecting lighthouses along the Maine coast in 1837, became interested in establishing a lighthouse in the vicinity of York River, Maine. Others wanted a light put up at the rocky island known as Cape Neddick Nubble. A compromise was reached and a small unlighted beacon was erected at York Ledge. In 1852 the proposal for a lighthouse at the Nubble again was introduced, and this time Congress appropriated five thousand dollars for its construction. However, after an investigation the plan was condemned and the light was not built. In 1874 the project was revived with a fifteen-thousand-dollar appropriation but nothing was done about it. The next year the same amount of money was authorized, but it was 1879 before definite steps were taken. The lighthouse was finished rapidly, however, once the materials were on the island, and on July 1, 1879, the light was first illuminated.

We visited Keeper Eugene L. Coleman at Cape Neddick Nubble Light on August 18, 1941. He and his wife had come to the Nubble in 1930 from Boon Island, where Coleman had entered the service in 1923. Just before World War II,

Cape Neddick Light had been electrified, and the Coleman family had been interested observers when the equipment was put in. Coleman told us of the day he was rowing across the Gut that separates the island from the mainland, with his wife and a friend. The dory went over and the keeper had a busy five minutes trying to rescue his wife, his friend, and the groceries, but all ended happily except for minor injuries to the groceries.

Keeper Coleman took us to the lantern platform near the top of the tower, where we examined with interest an unusual iron railing, each post of which was a lighthouse.

A view from the tower is one to remember. The great Bald Head Cliff stretches out to the northward, lifting its shoulders high above everything else in the vicinity. Coleman spoke of the various rocky formations in sight—George Washington's profile, the Devil's Oven, and Pulpit Rock. "It is a hopeless place to be in, that Bald Head Cliff," said Coleman, "and many is the fine ship or schooner which has met her fate on the jagged ledges over there." As he spoke of the shipwrecks at Bald Head Cliffs, I thought of the wreck of the bark *Isidore*, and of the gravestone erected at Kennebunkport to Captain Leander Foss of the *Isidore*, whose body was never found.

A century ago the story of the bark *Isidore* was told and retold at hundreds of firesides all over Maine. Those who were superstitious said that there were many warnings that should have been heeded before the vessel sailed. Others claim it was fate and that all aboard were predestined to perish. Be that as it may, it was a weird departure which the *Isidore* made from the harbor of Kennebunkport that November morning more than a hundred years ago. In place of the usual cheers and final shouts of encouragement, a vague premonition of approaching danger seemed to hang over the wharf. Several of the women became so overwrought that they sobbed aloud.

On November 30, 1842, the bark dropped down the harbor and stood to the eastward on the starboard tack. Early that afternoon it began to snow, and the wind freshened considerably. The *Isidore* made one or two tacks to work out of the bay, but when the weather shut in about four o'clock, she was lost to the sight of the watchers ashore. In the morning the snow lay in drifts around the town, and a short time later news came up from Ogunquit that the wreck of a large vessel was strewn along the shore. The *Isidore* had lost her battle with the elements, having hit the Bald Head Cliffs just north of Cape Neddick Nubble.

Then the stories of the strange warnings were remembered. Two nights before the ship was scheduled to sail, a seaman named Thomas King, who had already received a month's pay in advance, had a terrible dream. In his dream the ship was wrecked and all aboard were lost. The dream so affected him that he visited Captain Leander Foss of the *Isidore* and begged to be excused from his contract, but the captain laughed at his uneasiness and told him to be on hand before sailing time. However, King hid in the woods until he could see the masts of the *Isidore* as the bark sailed out of the harbor. Later criticized when he reappeared, he was held in great respect when news of the foundering reached Kennebunkport.

The night before the departure of the bark another seaman dreamed of seven coffins on the shores of the ocean, one of which was his own, according to a voice in the dream. He told his friends about it the next morning before the ship sailed. Of the seven bodies later recovered from the wreck, one was that of the seaman who had dreamed of the seven coffins.

The *Isidore* has become the phantom ship of the Maine

Coast. One day at dusk an Isles of Shoals fisherman saw a bark close-reefed, with shadowy men in dripping clothes who stared straight ahead from their stations on the bark. He and many others say the bark is still sailing the seas with its phantom crew.

As we stood there at the top of the lighthouse, with darkness falling, we could picture the bark hitting the nearby cliffs and going to pieces.

We have often visited Cape Neddick Nubble Light and brought books to the keepers there. The light now gives a 5,000-candlepower red flash three times every fifteen seconds.

What I recall with vividness is the cable trip across the chasm between the mainland and the lighthouse. In 1967 Keeper David Winchester placed his son Ricky in a boxlike container connected by cable to the mainland. He then pulled the box by line across to the mainland. This method was used for Ricky to get to school, and was very successful until Coast Guard officials stopped it as too dangerous.

16

Boon Island

The tall granite tower of Boon Island is located nine miles from the mainland at York Beach, Maine, and is situated on a rocky, jagged ledge that juts out of the sea in such a fashion as to make all landing on the island extremely dangerous. Boon Island has been the scene of many unfortunate shipwrecks, the most famous of which was that of the *Nottingham Galley* in 1710. Captain Deane and his crew of the *Galley* were wrecked on the island and forced to resort to cannibalism before help reached them. The incident is described in detail in my book *Storms and Shipwrecks of New England,* while Kenneth Roberts wrote a historical novel on the same subject.

In 1797, the Boston Marine Society met with General Benjamin Lincoln, Lighthouse Superintendent, to discuss the placing of a beacon at this lone, surf-swept rock.

At a later meeting held on the night of February 6, 1799, General Lincoln learned from the well-informed members of the world's oldest marine society that Boon Island was a barren ledge, with no vegetation growing on it. The island was about seven hundred feet long and less than a third of a mile

94

in width, with the average height of the rocks fourteen feet above the sea. After his interview with the Marine Society captains, Lincoln made the following statement:

"I am of opinion that a building of an Octagonal form, sixteen feet in the large diameter at the base, forty feet high . . . well timbered . . . and then shingled with a coat of white pine shingles should be erected."

The government approved the plans of General Lincoln, and the following July he was present at the "raising" of the beacon at Boon Island. The dangers at the ledge to the builders were many. Time and time again the landing party had to turn back because of rough seas, but three months later the beacon was finished, fifty feet high, at a cost of about six hundred dollars.

The edifice lasted through the following five summers and winters, but the great storm of October 9, 1804, which did so much damage all along the coast, swept right across Boon Island with such intensity that it destroyed the beacon and washed it into the ocean.

The following summer a stone monument was built at the island, and when the beacon was completed, Captain John F. Williams arrived off the ledge to remove the crew of carpenters and the contractor. In some unexplained fashion, Williams' boat overturned, throwing the contractor and two of his carpenters into the sea. Williams saved himself, but the others, unable to swim back to the ship, soon sank beneath the waves to their deaths. Captain Williams sailed to the mainland at once, purchased a new boat, and returned to Boon Island, where he removed the remaining workers in safety.

On June 3, 1811, General Lincoln wrote to Albert Gallatin, Secretary of the Treasury, suggesting that a lighthouse be erected at Boon Island. Part of his communication follows:

"There is no soil or earth on the island, the surface is composed of broken, detached stones of all sizes from several tons to pebbles and are nearer in quality to free stones than granite. . . . It does not appear that the sea ever makes a breach over the island."

Lincoln must have temporarily forgotten the washing away of the Boon Island Beacon in the great storm of 1804 when he stated that the sea never swept over the ledge. Albert Gallatin agreed that a light at Boon Island was necessary, and asked for bids for a tower not more than twenty-five feet high. This information was advertised in the Boston *Independent Chronicle,* and many contractors were eager to erect the tower.

John Hill stated in his bid that a lighthouse, residence, oil vault, and cistern could be built for $14,000, while Noah Porter and Thomas Heath, with their low bid of $2,527 actually received the contract. By winter the tower was completed and the first keeper, whose name is unknown, arrived at the island. A few weeks at the desolate ledge proved enough for him, however, for when the great, curling billows began to sweep right up to the top of the island, he decided that there were other positions ashore which he might obtain. On December 16, 1811, the keeper resigned, and David Oliver, a carpenter who had helped construct the light, took his place.

Oliver soon became weary of the loneliness of his work, and relinquished his place to Thomas Hanna. Also tiring of the loneliness, Hanna "signified his determination to resign," according to Commissioner Smith of the Treasury Department in a letter written on May 2, 1816. Smith appointed

Eliphalet Grover as the new keeper. Grover was furnished with a boat the following year. In 1822 the boat slip was repaired, but storm ruined the new slip, which was later rebuilt at a cost of $300.

About this time Winslow Lewis, the lantern builder and lighthouse expert, published a booklet on American lighthouses. This great lighthouse man described Boon Island as flashing from a height of thirty-two feet above the ocean, and claimed that this fixed light could be seen from a distance of from eighteen to twenty-one miles at sea .This assertion is hard to understand unless we realize that when Lewis figured the distance, he assumed the observer was high above the deck of the vessel in the most advantageous position aboard, usually on the masthead of the schooner or ship. However, the average distance a lighthouse can be seen from the deck of a vessel is many miles less than Lewis estimated.

In 1831 a severe gale swept directly across Boon Island, destroying the tower completely. Simon Pleasonton authorized Seward Merrill to construct a new edifice. The old wooden monument was then torn down, and the ruins of the old lighthouse reduced to such a height that passing sailors would not notice it and become confused.

Much trouble resulted from the fact that Boon Island was under the jurisdiction of Maine rather than New Hampshire, and Simon Pleasonton in 1831 made the change, putting Boon Island under the control of the latter state. At that time the salary of the keeper was six hundred dollars.

Politics came into the picture at Boon Island in the 1840's. In June 1841, Mark Dennet resigned as keeper. He was succeeded by Captain John Thompson, who in September 1843 was removed from office in favor of John Kennard, a former tailor who had been at Whaleback Light. Thompson wrote at once to President John Tyler. Part of his letter follows:

"I have been a seaman from a boy—being now 60 years old, am poor, have a family to support, with little or no means. I voted for your Excellency for Vice president and intended to exert my feeble influence to promote another election for you for President—why I am removed, I am at loss to determine."

John Kennard retained his position, however, and Thompson did not come back to Boon Island until 1849.

Nathaniel Baker became the keeper at Boon Island in 1846. During that year a large schooner, the *Caroline,* was wrecked on the ledges at Boon Island and became a total loss. The crew were saved by Keeper Baker. Three years later petitions were circulated around York, Maine, for his dismissal, with the suggestion that Peter W. Stover be appointed in his place. One of Baker's friends, Alexander McIntire, wrote Secretary of the Treasury William H. Meredith in protest. "Captain Baker is a careful, faithful, and vigilant man—understands his duty and performs it . . . the light can never be in the care of a better man," said McIntire in his letter. Assistant Keeper Benjamin O. Fletcher also wrote to Meredith. Excerpts from his letter follow:

"Captain Baker is a man of strict integrity of character and has always to my knowledge kept a good light. . . . I will state also that this Island is situated nine miles from land in the wake of all the Eastern bound vessels engaged in coasting to the West—and it is very necessary that there should not only be a good keeper on this Island but a good pilot. I believe all parties are satisfied with Capt. Baker, and would not desire a change on any account. Capt. Baker is the third keeper I have been here with and I can truly say that he is far the best man that has kept the light."

Less than a month after Fletcher's letter was received, Keeper Baker was removed from his position at Boon Island.

His place was taken by John S. Thompson, who had been removed in 1843. Augustus Jenkins, Collector of Portsmouth Harbor, in charge of Boon Island, was so upset at this removal and appointment that he wrote to Washington as follows:

"Having visited Boon Island several times to inspect the Light House, it is but simple justice to say of Capt. Baker, that he kept the Light House . . . in good order. . . . In fact, no man could do more to keep a better Light than Capt. Baker, and I considered him one of the best Keepers under my superintendence."

Storms often parted the bell buoy located off Boon Island from its moorings. In 1851 Congress appropriated $150 for another buoy, which the following year was washed out to sea. A more expensive buoy costing $5,000 was then placed on the station at Boon Island Ledge, about three miles eastward of Boon Island Light. In 1856 this buoy broke away from its anchor and drifted by the island, but because of the storm the keeper was unable to attempt to secure it.

A short time later Captain C. H. Thurlow, master of the schooner *Coral*, noticed the buoy adrift at sea, and took the marine beacon in tow. Bringing the twisting and bobbing marker into Portsmouth Harbor, Captain Thurlow asked $800 in salvage, but this request brought a violent protest from the lighthouse department. On January 4, 1859, Captain Thurlow was awarded $100.

On August 21, 1852, an appropriation of $25,000 was made to build a new lighthouse. Still in use, the tower, built of ashlar masonry, is 137 feet high, twenty-five feet in diameter at the base, and twelve feet in diameter at the top of the building. In 1887 the entire tier of masonry two courses below the watch room deck, began to loosen from the rest of the tower, and swayed badly in gales of wind. It was feared that the lantern of Boon Island Light would fall off, and so the next summer the top of the light was firmly secured to the tower with six iron tie-rods.

The name of Keeper William W. Williams appears more often than that of any other man in the history of the lighthouse. For more than twenty-seven years he was stationed at Boon Island Light. Often the weather kept him from leaving the station for weeks, thus preventing him from bringing out special treats for the Thanksgiving and Christmas holidays. On one such occasion he was unable to go ashore to purchase a Thanksgiving turkey he wanted, but a flock of ducks providentially smashed against the tower on the night before Thanksgiving, supplying him with a substitute for the dinner he had planned.

I have in my possession a letter written in 1899 by Keeper Williams describing the Portland Gale of 1898. It was a terrible gale, to be sure, but Keeper Williams agreed with Keeper Reamy out at Minot's Light that the 1888 blow was more severe.

A strange legend is related about one of the keepers at Boon Island Light.

A new keeper came out to the light near the middle of the last century with his bride. The couple spent many months of happiness together on the island, but the keeper fell ill and died. That very night a great gale began to lash the island. The frantic young widow, alone with the body of her husband, realized that she must keep the light on Boon Island shining during the storm. The girl climbed the tower and lighted the lamps. Then she returned to keep her death watch with her lover. Night after night the storm continued, and she faithfully carried out the lighting of the tower lamps. Finally the storm went down. Because of the strain of watching over her dead husband and keeping the light going, the girl lost her reason, and the following night there was no welcoming glow from Boon Island. Fishermen landed on the island the next day to see what was wrong, and found the poor, demented girl wandering helplessly around the rocky ledge, bemoaning her sad fate.

Celia Laighton Thaxter tells the unhappy story, and we quote the last four lines of her poem:

> They bore the dead and living both away
> With anguish time seemed powerless to destroy.
> She turned, and backward gazed across the bay,—
> Lost in the sad sea lay her rose of joy.

17

Other Maine Lighthouses

Maine, because of its rugged coast and numerous peninsulas and islands, has far more lighthouses than any other state its size. Space forbids mentioning all of the beacons and lights of the Maine coast in this book, but we include most of the principal lighthouses.

Avery Rock Light, built in 1875, has a white flash every six seconds. The lantern is in a white, square tower on the former keeper's dwelling. Located at the southern end of the rock, this untended light guards the entrance to Machias Bay.

Nash Island Light is off the shores of the east side of Pleasant Bay. Established in 1838, it was rebuilt in 1873, and is similar in construction to Avery Rock Light. It is a flashing white light every six seconds.

At the southwest entrance to Frenchman's Bay stands Baker Island Lighthouse, which was built in 1828 and rebuilt in 1855. The light in the white tower, shining from a height of 105 feet above high water, is a well-known landmark. Baker Island has a 3,000-candlepower flash every ten seconds. About ten miles to the southwest of Baker Island is Great Duck Island Light, with the homes of the three keepers arranged in orderly fashion side by side in back of the lighthouse. Built in 1890, the white cylindrical tower gives a single red flash every ten seconds with a candlepower of 70,000.

Egg Rock Light in Frenchman's Bay has a red flash every five seconds. The light is sixty-four feet above the water. Off the southern entrance to Northeast Harbor stands Bear Island Light, a white tower first lighted in 1839.

The Isle au Haut Light, located a short distance from shore, is connected with the island by a white bridge. It is a relatively new lighthouse, having been erected in 1907. Goose Rocks Light, built in 1890 on a ledge in the Fox Islands Thorofare, was at one time in charge of Willis Snow of Rockland, Maine. Some distance to the north stands Eagle Island Light in a pretty setting of typical Maine scenery. First erected in 1839, the light shines from a height of 106 feet above the sea.

The tower at Two Bush Island was first lighted in 1897. The island was the scene around the turn of the century of the wreck of the schooner *Clara Bella*. Keeper Norton's dog Smut saved the crew of two men by his barking. Two Bush is the nearest light to Matinicus Rock.

Rockland Breakwater Light was first illuminated in 1888, and was rebuilt when the keeper's dwelling was erected in 1902. It gives a white flash of 450,000 candlepower every five seconds from a height of thirty-nine feet. It is now unattended. On the opposite side of Penobscot Bay, farther to the north, stands Dice Head Light, first lighted by Keeper Jacob Sherburne, who returned from being a shipmaster for "eight kingdoms of Europe" to accept the position as keeper in June 1828.

On the west side of the mouth of the Penobscot River stands the Fort Point Light, so named because Governor Pownall of Massachusetts built a fortification there around 1759.

Franklin Island Light was established in Muscongus Bay in 1807, while Ram Island Light, located on the south side of Fisherman Island Passage, was not lighted until 1883. Burnt Island Light, at the entrance to Boothbay Harbor, has been active since the year 1821.

The Cuckolds is about half a mile southward of Cape Newagen. A relatively new light, it was not established until 1892. It presents an unusual appearance from the water with its granite base supporting both a lighthouse and keeper's dwelling. In September 1925 Keeper Fred T. Robinson saved several persons from a disabled motorboat that had broken down near the lighthouse and was rapidly drifting to sea.

Two years ago we enjoyed our trip to the Cuckolds when we met the young Coastguardsman keeper, his wife, and their new little baby. The light has a a candlepower of 500,000 with a double flash every six seconds.

Ram Island Ledge Light was built in 1905. In general appearance resembling Graves Light in Boston Harbor, it is not to be confused with Ram Island Light in Fisherman Island Passage. Ram Island Ledge is on the north side of the entrance to Portland Harbor. Portland Breakwater Light, first built in 1855, was reconstructed in 1875, and now shines from a height of thirty feet above the water.

Wood Island Light, located to the south of Old Orchard Beach, was first lighted in 1808. It was the scene of a murder some years ago, and is said by many to be haunted by the ghost of the murdered victim. The light has two 500,000-candlepower flashes every six seconds. There are still resident keepers at Wood Island.

Off Cape Porpoise is Goat Island Light, identified by a white flash of 15,000 candlepower every six seconds. The white tower is connected to the keeper's dwelling by a covered way.

PART II

VERMONT AND
NEW HAMPSHIRE LIGHTS

18

Vermont

Although located inland, the lighthouses of Vermont add a touch of beauty to the waters of Lake Champlain. Some of the beacons, such as the famous Juniper Island Light, have been standing many years. Juniper Island Light was built in 1826, and remodeled twenty years later. It is situated in Lake Champlain at the entrance to Burlington's Harbor. For some time before the Civil War the keeper at Juniper Island was Luther Moore, who received $350 a year for his services. Today the light is a fixed white beacon, giving a 490-candle-power beam from its position ninety-three feet above the waters of Lake Champlain.

Other lighthouses in the vicinity include Split Rock Light and the lights in the Whitehall Narrows established in 1838 and 1856 respectively. Watch Point Light, in Lake Champlain, was built in 1891, while Barber Point Light was erected eighteen years earlier.

19

The Isles of Shoals Lighthouse

Comprising a fairyland of islands far enough from the mainland of New England to be called a kingdom of the sea, the Isles of Shoals have attracted the attention of the white man for more than four centuries.

Many famous explorers in history sighted the Isles. It is probable that Verrazano landed on one of them. Possibly Gosnold stopped here as he made his way down the coast, but if such was the case, he made no mention of it in his journal. We can state with certainty, however, that the noble captain, "Admiral John Smith of New England," not only visited the Isles of Shoals but also named them for himself! In this case Smith's desires for lasting recognition were unsuccessful, and *Smith's Isles* were long ago changed in name to the *Isles of Shoals*.

When Christopher Levett came to the coast in 1623, he first touched New England soil at the "Isles of Shoulds." Barren as they are, Levett could not find even "one goode tymber-tree no so much goode grounde as to make a garden." John Smith did but little better, for he stated that the islands were "without either grasse or wood" except for three or four short shrubby old cedars. In 1629 Captain John Mason, proprietor of the Province of New Hampshire and Sir Ferdinando Gorges, proprietor of the Province of Maine, divided the islands, Maine taking Duck, Appledore, Malaga, Cedar, and Smuttynose, and New Hampshire occupying the remaining: Londoner, Star, and White Islands. On the latter island in 1820 the Isles of Shoals Light was erected. Many events of interest occurred on these eight islands before that time.

Religious struggles at the Isles of Shoals have been many. It is believed that as early as 1641 services were held in a meeting house on one of the islands. When Massachusetts extended her jurisdiction over the Isles of Shoals, the Anglican clergyman from Portsmouth, Richard Gibson, against whose marriages and baptisms at the Isle Massachusetts protested, started trouble. He called on the islanders to rebel in favor of the Gorges claim. This led to speedy action on the part of the Boston Puritans, who immediately dispatched a shallop to the scene of operations. The Reverend Mr. Gibson was imprisoned in Boston. Later released, he sailed for England in 1642, it is believed.

The Isles of Shoals were named because sailors who had seen the eight islands in a group called them a shoal or group of islands similar to a shoal of fish—thus the islands became known as the Shoal of Isles. This rather awkward expression was later changed to the Isles of Shoals, and as such it has come down to the present day.

The Isles of Shoals figured prominently in the great summer hurricane of 1635, the same storm which caused the wreck of the *Angel Gabriel* at Pemaquid Point and the loss of the Avery shallop at Thacher's Island, Cape Ann. When caught by the gale, the Reverend Richard Mather and his family, important in Boston history, were aboard the ship *James* on their way to America. On the night of August 14,

1635, the Reverend Mr. Mather made the following entry in his diary:

"This evening by moonlight, about ten-of-the-clock, we came to anchor at the Isles of Shoals, which are seven or eight islands and other great rocks, and there slept sweetly that night, until break of day."

It was the calm before the storm, however, for the greatest gale of the seventeenth century, and one of the four great hurricanes of New England history, began that same morning. Three anchors and cables of Mather's ship were lost in rapid succession, the sails were ripped and torn asunder, and the ship was driven toward Star Island. Luckily, the *James* missed crashing against the cruel ledges of the island by a few feet, and drifted out into deeper water. She later escaped being wrecked because of a shift in the wind, but the entire Mather family always remembered that adventure which began at the Isles of Shoals in 1635. Richard Mather expressed himself as follows: "We shall not forget the passage of that morning until our dying day."

One of the strange results of the great hurricane of 1635 was the loss of the home of Mr. Tucker, the tailor of the islands. The building was washed off into the sea from Smuttynose Island, later coming ashore at far-distant Cape Cod, intact and in such a condition that the Cape Codders hauled it ashore and made it habitable with a few minor repairs. The papers and linen found in the building identified it as belonging to tailor Tucker of the Isles of Shoals, who had barely escaped from the house with his family before it washed into the waves. An aftermath to this tale occurred in 1666 when tailor Tucker jumped into the water and drowned.

During a short period in the history of the Isles of Shoals

women were forbidden to live there. In 1647 Richard Cutt and Ode Culling, fishermen around the islands, petitioned the Court "that John Reynolds, contrary to an Act in Court [which says] that noe wimin shall live upon the Ille of Showles, hath brought his wife thether. Your petitioners thearfore prayeth that the act of Cort . . . may be put in execution to the removall of all wimin from inhabiting ther." The two petitioners lost out, however, and the lady remained with her husband. From that day to this women have had the privilege of visiting and living on the islands off the New Hampshire coast.

After a long period of agitation for adequate protection of ships near the dangerous islands and ledges, the first Isles of Shoals Lighthouse tower was erected at White Island in 1820. It was a stone tower, with the lantern showing approximately ninety feet above the surf. The name of the first keeper is unknown.

The Laighton family came to the Isles of Shoals in 1839. Thomas B. Laighton, candidate for governor of New Hampshire, was defeated by means he considered unfair, and so in 1839 he sold out his business at Portsmouth and obtained the position of keeper of the Isles of Shoals Light. Five years before this he had purchased Appledore, Smuttynose, Malaga, and Cedar Island from Captain Samuel Haley.

With him to the islands Laighton brought his wife and two children, Oscar and Celia and a faithful retainer, Ben Whaling. Thus, as owner of four islands and keeper of a fifth, Laighton could surely lay claim to the honor of being "Lord of All He Surveyed."

Even then, treasure had been found at the Isles of Shoals, for before Captain Haley, resident of Smuttynose, left the Isles of Shoals, he revealed to Keeper Laighton that he had discovered several bars of silver under a flat stone some time before 1820. Realizing three thousand dollars from the sale, he had devoted a portion of the proceeds to a sea-wall, stone wharf, and breakwater which still allows the mariner to enjoy a safe harbor while anchored at the Isles.

At White Island, Keeper Laighton soon mastered the intricate essentials of keeping his lights brightly burning, and in this he was ably assisted by Ben Whaling. In carrying out their duties at the lighthouse, Keeper Laighton and Ben took alternate watches of four hours each, winding the hour-clock that revolved the light. During many of the worst storms, when people could not sleep, Thomas Laighton would gather his family about him, and, shouting at the top of his voice to drown out the sound of the mightly breakers, would read *Little Nell* to his family. Two years after the family arrived at the lighthouse a baby boy was born to the Laightons. They named him Cedric.

While Mrs. Laighton lived in the lighthouse residence she had geraniums and other flowers blooming in the kitchen all winter long, and it was indeed a cheerful home in which a chance visitor found himself. In the cellar of the keeper's dwelling stood the cistern, into which rainwater poured from the roof of the home. Every storm broughts its individual problem of letting in the rainwater but at the same time making sure to seal the cistern before the waves beginning to sweep across the island should pour in their briny water. The salt would manage to seep into the cistern in spite of almost everything the keeper could do.

Notable visitors to the White Island Lighthouse during this period included Richard Henry Dana, author of *Two Years Before the Mast,* and Nathaniel Hawthorne, the great novelist.

During the storm of December 22, 1839, the brig *Pocahantas,* bound for Newburyport from Cadiz, passed so close to White Island during the height of the gale that Celia Laighton and her mother heard the signal gun from the doomed vessel as it swept on to destruction on the sand bar off Plum Island. All aboard perished. Celia herself lit the lights that fearful night. We quote part of her story:

> I lit the lamps in the lighthouse tower
>   For the sun dropped down and the day was dead.
> They shone like a glorious clustered flower,—
>   Ten golden and five red.
>
> The sails that flecked the ocean floor
>   From east to west leaned low and fled;
> They knew what came in the distant roar
>   That filled the air with dread!
>
> Flung by a fitful gust, there beat
>   Against the window a dash of rain;
> Steady as tramp of marching feet
>   Strode on the hurricane.
>
> It smote the waves for a moment still,
>   Level and deadly white for fear;
> The bare rock shuddered,—an awful thrill
>   Shook even my tower of cheer.
>
> * * *
>
> When morning dawned, above the din
>   Of gale and breaker boomed a gun!
> Another! We who sat within
>   Answered with cries each one.
>
> * * *
>
> The thick storm seemed to break apart
>   To show us, staggering to her grave,
> The fated brig. We had no heart
>   To look, for naught could save.
>
> One glimpse of black hull heaving slow
>   Then closed the mists o'er canvas torn
> And tangled ropes swept to and fro
>   From masts that raked forlorn.
>
> * * *

> And when at last from the distant shore
>   A little boat stole out, to reach
> Our loneliness, and bring once more
>   Fresh human thought and speech,
>
> We told our tale, and the boatman cried;
>   "'Twas the 'Pocahantas,'—all were lost!
> For miles along the coast the tide
>   Her shattered timbers tossed."
>
> Sighing I climbed the lighthouse stair,
>   Half forgetting my grief and pain;
> And while the day died, sweet and fair,
>   I lit the lamps again.

Young Oscar Laighton rowed over to Appledore Island one day to discover his first tree, a ten-foot sumach, which gave him much astonishment at the time. "Not even a bayberry bush," said Oscar Laighton, "ever grew at White Island."

The visit of the lighthouse inspector was always an important event in the career of Keeper Laighton. Arriving at the island on the lighthouse schooner, the official would inspect the entire premises while the schooner was unloading the half-year's supply of oil, wood, coal, and a barrel of pork. With great excitement, the Isles of Shoals children watched every load go ashore. The children of the other islands were often invited over to enjoy the event, and among them were the Becker boys and girls. These young people lived across on Smuttynose Island with their father, who was a tenant of Keeper Laighton. Captain Becker had a glamorous niche of his own in the island's history, as he had fought against Napoleon at Waterloo. This German veteran lived for many years at Smuttynose Island with his wife and six children.

Another German who figures in the history of the Isles of Shoals was the murderer Louis Wagner. One night in 1873, knowing that the men were away from the island, he rowed all the way across to Smuttynose Island from the mainland to rob fisherman Hontvet's residence. Caught and recognized by the women, Wagner killed two of the three females on the island. The murderer then returned to his dory and rowed back to the mainland. Later he was captured, tried, and hanged.

As Keeper Laighton was busy with plans for the hotel which he was building on Appledore Island, it was not long before young Celia was keeper in fact, polishing the reflectors and keeping the plate glass windows shining in the lantern room of the lighthouse. At low tide she would row across to Seavey's Island with her young brother Oscar to land at Sandpiper Cove. It was at this cove that Celia composed her classic poem, part of which I quote here:

> Across the narrow beach we flit
>   One little sandpiper and I,
> And fast I gather bit by bit,
>   The scattered driftwood, bleached and dry.
>
> The wild waves reach their hands for it,
>   The wild wind raves, the tide runs high,
> As up and down the beach we flit—
>   The little sandpiper and I.
>
> Above our heads the sullen clouds
>   Scud black and swift across the sky;
> Like silent ghosts in misty shrouds
>   Stand out the white lighthouses high.
>
>   *   *   *
>
> Comrade, where wilt thou be to-night
>   When the loosened storm breaks furiously?
> My driftwood fire will burn so bright!
>   To what warm shelter canst thou fly?

I do not fear for thee, though wroth
The tempest rushes through the sky:
For are we not God's children both—
Thou, little sandpiper, and I?

Keeper Laighton retired from the lighthouse service in 1847 when Celia was twelve years old. He had built a great hotel, which was to be ready for business the coming year. Thus Thomas Laighton's days as a lighthouse keeper were over. The subsequent career of this unusual personality was a successful one. Laighton, appropriately called by Robert Carter the Prince of Appledore, died at his beloved Isles of Shoals in the year 1866.

During the Civil War, because of the activity of blockade runners and southern gunboats, the Isles of Shoals Light received special attention, and was entirely rebuilt of granite in 1865. The walls were made two feet thick. On the western side of the edifice the kitchen extended the full length of the house.

Around the year 1900, a leading Unitarian, Thomas Elliot, suggested to Oscar Laighton that he be allowed to bring out to the islands a substantial group of his fellow churchmen. The following season hundreds of Unitarians arrived at Star Island, where the Oceanic Hotel was then active, and Oscar Laighton presented them with the old stone church for their devotional services. Soon the Unitarian Association purchased the entire island and the hotel as well. The Congregationalists later joined the Unitarians in having religious exercises there. On many occasions the White Island Light keeper participated in the religious services.

The family name of Downs has been important in New Hampshire and Isles of Shoals history for generations. An exciting event occurred at the Isles of Shoals Light one night when John Bragg Downs was acting as keeper. During a wild

March hurricane Downs was alone at the great white tower with a friend who had volunteered to stand watch with him. The keeper, Captain Haley, recently assigned to the post, had gone to "America," as the mainland was then called, to bring out his wife and family. Downs was thus in complete charge of the lighthouse station. When he saw the first signs of an approaching storm, Downs wished that he had not agreed to take over the responsible position.

For nearly a week the northeasterly winds prevailed, and, to make matters worse, at the turn of the tide on the sixth day a great snowstorm hit with furious intensity. Before midnight the giant waves were surging right across the island, forcing the acting keeper and his assistant to flee to the tower itself for safety. Around midnight there was a lull in the storm, and Downs told his helper to take a nap, while the acting keeper prepared to eat a supper of fish and potatoes.

Although he felt strangely weary, the assistant, instead of going to bed, stood by the door watching Downs get ready to eat. Possibly to make conversation, perhaps because of a premonition, he spoke to Downs.

"Well, John, what would you think if somebody was to knock at the door just now?" he asked, shouting above the thunder of the breakers against the rocky ledge.

"Think! I should think it must be the devil himself, for no human being could land on White Island this night and live." Just then, as if in answer to his statement, there came a knock at the door, and both men froze in their tracks. Could it be their imagination, or did they actually hear a noise at the door?

Then it came again, louder and more insistent. Rap—rap—rap, knock—knock—knock, bang—bang—bang. Unmistakably, human knuckles were pounding at the lighthouse door, though as far as the two men knew, no other person was then on the island! What could it be? Acting Keeper Downs hastened to light his lantern and then started for the door. He later admitted that he was frightened at what he might see when the door opened, but he pulled at the handle and stared out into the darkness.

There, almost filling the doorway, was a giant sailor. Bleeding from more than a score of deep, razorlike cuts, the man was wet and cold as he stood before them in the snow storm.

"Brig ashore, sir!" he cried. "Right near the lighthouse tower!"

John Downs and his assistant took the sufferer inside, bathed his many wounds, and dressed him in warm garments.

While this was going on, the sailor told his story of the disaster. The keeper learned that the vessel was a Russian brig, bound for Salem, loaded with hides and tallow. She had come to grief at the southwestern point of White Island.

The captain, supposing himself over a hundred miles from land, was overwhelmed by the disaster. The snow fell so fast that it was impossible to tell where they were, but during a lull a great light could be seen almost directly over them, and it was realized that they had been wrecked near a lighthouse. The sailor had volunteered to lower himself over the bowsprit down into the darkness, to go for help. As the waves receded and he felt himself on a rocky ledge, he let go the line and scrambled for higher ground, but the sharp rocks and barnacles cut and bruised him severely. As he made his way toward safety, time and again the waves hurled him against the rocks; each time he clung desperately to the ledge as the waves swept over him. Then, when the water went down, he would hurl himself toward the next rock and await the sweep of the coming billow.

Finally he reached a ledge above the force of the sea. Resting for a moment, he then looked around for the keeper's home. As soon as he found a light streaming from an unshuttered window, he stumbled and ran for it. Knocking and banging on the door, he was admitted by Keeper Downs.

As the sailor finished his story the three men started out in the storm. They soon reached the rocky shore opposite the wreck, which could now be made out clearly, the brig's bow evidently suspended on a pinnacle of rock. It was easy to see that the vessel might go to pieces at any moment, so Keeper Downs decided he must act at once. Securing a stout line he sent it out to the doomed vessel, where it was made fast. But there was no projecting rock or convenient post where the line could be bent. After frantically trying to figure out a solution, Downs decided to wrap the line around his own body, and have the assistant and the sailor help hold it. Downs then descended into a deep crevice, braced himself, and told his assistant to order the crew to come in on the line, but only one at a time.

The first men to come in were not severely injured, but the last two of the fourteen members of the Russian brig's crew had to be helped and were almost swept off the ledge when their strength failed. It was a torturous effort to get all the men up to the lighthouse, but somehow it was accomplished, and they were cared for at the lighthouse. John W. Downs tells us that his grandfather, John Bragg Downs, was greatly concerned about having enough to eat for the entire ship's company, especially when the storm continued, preventing Keeper Haley's return for more than a week. Downs began to fear, toward the end of that week, that all hands aboard the island, sixteen in number, would starve. Shortly afterward the storm went down and Keeper Haley returned with a large supply of food. That afternoon the fourteen men left for the mainland. It was said that John Bragg Downs often went out on the edge of the island during a storm, and wondered how the sailor could possibly have reached shore from the pinnacle where the brig had been wrecked. But whenever I look down at the ledge from the air and see the tiny crevice where Downs made himself a human anchor to save thirteen doomed men, I marvel even more at this brave man's miraculous achievement.

20

Portsmouth Harbor Light

The first lighthouse to shine in New Hampshire was Portsmouth or Newcastle Light, erected in the year 1771 at Fort William and Mary on Newcastle Island in Porstmouth Harbor. An act of the Legislature, approved April 12, 1771, directed that a light should be established at Fort William and Mary for the benefit of "vessels arriving or being upon this coast in the night time." Of course, this beacon was not in fact a lighthouse, as the lantern was hoisted to the top of the flag pole at the fort. The cost of hoisting and lowering the lantern was paid for by the vessels which were guided into the harbor by the gleam of the lantern on the pole. Little is known about the man who kept the light at Portsmouth in the early days, but it is a tradition that he helped load an ox team which carried powder from Fort William and Mary to the Americans who fought at Bunker Hill.

A regular lighthouse was in operation some time before 1784. The exact date is in dispute, but in that year Captain Titus Salter was appointed keeper and repairs on the lighthouse tower were made.

One of the strangest contracts between the government and

a lighthouse keeper was that signed by Alexander Hamilton, Secretary of the Treasury, and Keeper Titus Salter of Portsmouth Light, on November 18, 1790, three months before all lighthouses were ceded to the government. Hamilton arranged for Salter to "defray all the expence and charge that hath arisen for the support maintenance and repairs of the Light House." Further arrangements were made to cover the period from August 15, 1789, to July 1, 1791; Salter agreed that either he "or some careful Person give proper attendance on said Light House and in the night time from the setting to the Rising of the Sun, keep the same constantly lighted." Only two types of oil were allowed, spermaceti and hake oil. Salter was to receive $555.99 for his part of the agreement.

When the government assumed control of all American lighthouses, Alexander Hamilton appointed Joseph Whipple as Superintendent for New Hampshire.

In 1792 Keeper Salter was told to keep on hand a substantial supply of oil, "no less than One Hundred Gallons of Oyl . . . which shall be Oyl of the Fish called Hake." A year later the keeper was in trouble. He was informed that the President of the United States was dissatisfied with the care Portsmouth Light was receiving, and that the President "thinks it proper that the keeper of the Light House at Portsmouth be informed, that he must reside on the spot where the Light House is, if he continues in that office, and that he will not be permitted to employ a deputy to take care of the Light House, unless upon some special occasion."

Evidently it became known that the keeper of Portsmouth Light had been admonished by President Washington, for one Moses McFarland in February 1793 wrote to the Honorable Samuel Livermore about obtaining the appointment. McFarland stated that he would "attend to every branch of duty with as little expense to the public as that of the light-house alone."

McFarland was given the position of light keeper with a salary of $3.46 a week to support himself and family. Colonel Whipple's first quarterly report for 1795, copied below, is an indication of the hardships that early American lighthouse keepers were forced to endure.

Portsmouth, New Hamp. May 7, 1795

"Sir:

"I enclose you herewith an amount of expenditures on the Lighthouse in the quarter ending the 31st March. Since my last I have received of the contractor for supplying the oil 6 tureen containing 318 gallons the detention of the proper account thereof has delayed this return. . . .

"I request your consideration also of the present pay of the keeper, he has complained for some time past of the difficulty with which he had subsisted on his stipend (180 dollars per year)—his family are his wife and 4 children, 3 of whom are young. The present price of provisions are, for Indian Corn 100 to 117 cents a bushel. For fresh meats 8 to 10 cents pound. I entreat your feeling attention to this object and that you will be pleased to lay the case before the department through which I pray relief may be obtained.

"I am very respectfully Sir your most obtd. servant

JOSEPH WHIPPLE

TENCH COXE *Esquire"*

As a result of the above communication the keeper's salary was raised from $3.46 a week to $3.83 a week!

By 1800 the old lighthouse was falling to pieces, and a new tower was planned. Finished in 1804, it presented a handsome sight, rising to a height of eighty feet. The new light, a wooden octagonal frame building, contained a lantern room with thirteen spherical reflectors fourteen inches in diameter. In Superintendent Whipple's report announcing the completion of the light, he mentions that the keeper's salary, still $3.83 a week, was inadequate.

In 1805 soldiers at Fort Constitution were pilfering the property of the keeper. "Notwithstanding the utmost care," said the report of Captain Gates, the fort commander, "disorder and abuse often occur."

Firing of the guns at Fort Constitution began to crack the walls and smash the windows in the keeper's residence at the light in 1809. Major Swift, the engineer, and Captain Walbach, the fort's commander, requested the removal of the keeper's residence. Gallatin agreed that the house should be moved, but thought that the charges of $691 were too high. Quite a discussion arose over the matter between Secretary of the Treasury Gallatin and Secretary of War Eustis. Eustis, an old New England soldier, said, "I remember the house. It is too near and ought to be removed." It was moved.

About 1809 Portsmouth Light was used for experiments with fountain lamps, which showed an improvement over the simple pan-type lamp in that the oil level was constant around the wicks. This resulted in a great improvement in combustion and subsequent brilliance of light.

A serious fire that at one time threatened the fort itself broke out in the lantern of Fort Constitution Light early in 1826. When the alarm was given, the sergeant and a company of soldiers responded from the fort. The fire had gained so much headway that many of the men suffered damage to their clothing. On February 27, 1826, Stephen Pleasonton, Fifth Auditor, approved the payment of twenty dollars for the damaged clothing, to be divided between the sergeant and members of his company.

The tower built in 1804 must have been a fine piece of workmanship, for as late as 1843, when overcritical I. W. P. Lewis made his inspection, he stated that the light was "an excellent piece of carpentry, and will bear favorable comparison with its more modern neighbors."

However, by 1872 the tower had fallen into decay, along with the lighthouse keeper's residence. A new residence was erected that year, but it was not until five years later that the lighthouse was rebuilt a thousand yards eastward. Constructed of cast iron, it stood only fifty-two feet above the water.

One of the longest careers in lighthouse history was that of Keeper Henry M. Cuskley, who became keeper at Portsmouth Harbor Light in 1915. Previously he had served at Cape Elizabeth from 1897 to 1903, at Libby Islands for the next nine years, and then from 1912 to 1915 at Seguin.

He had sufficient excitement during his service at Portsmouth. One day a destroyer, the *Worth,* under a Lieutenant-Commander Parker, slid up in front of the light and stayed high and dry as the tide went out. The *Worth* was got off that same evening. At another time a submarine also called a little too close to the lighthouse and remained there until a high tide freed her. Portsmouth Light may thus be the only lighthouse that has had both a destroyer and a submarine stranded in its front yard.

We visited Captain Cuskley shortly before his retirement in 1941. Active and alert in spite of his forty-four years in the lighthouse service, Keeper Cuskley showed us around his station. At that time he believed himself to be the oldest man in point of service in the entire first district.

Flying over the tower at Christmastime, 1972, I thought of the thrilling pre-Revolutionary days when horseman Paul Revere came to the area of the tower on December 13, 1774 to warn the Portsmouthites of the powder embargo.

21

Whaleback Light

When flying over Portsmouth Harbor or sailing out of the bay, the observer quickly notices an unusual double building known as Whaleback Light, which rises out of the water from a ledge situated on the northeast side of the outer entrance to the harbor. In reality Whaleback Light is two lighthouses in one. How the strange consolidation of the two buildings was effected is quite a story.

It was in 1829 that the original Whaleback Light was built. A stone pier forty-eight feet in diameter and twenty-two feet high was constructed on the ledge at a cost of $13,810. On the pier was built the lighthouse tower, which cost $6,150.

Trouble began at Whaleback Ledge almost at once, for after a few high seas swept completely over the top of the lighthouse, the structure began to leak badly. The keeper found it impossible to keep dry during a storm, and there actually developed the danger of being flooded out. In 1837 sheathing was placed around the tower so that most of the water was prevented from coming in. But there had been a fundamental fault with the old foundation that was fatal to the whole structure. The original contract had provided that when the lowest stones were laid, the ledge should be leveled off properly to receive the first course. This had not been done. The contractors laid out the stone upon the uneven surface of the rock, filling up the crevices with smaller stones and rocks, which soon washed out in the storms. There was another omission. The original plans had called for bolting the bottom stones to the ledge itself; this was not done. After the stones had washed away, the water swept in underneath, and the entire lighthouse was undermined to a dangerous degree.

The great Colonel Sylvanus Thayer, father of the Military Academy at West Point, who at the time had an engineering office in Boston, was sent down to the lighthouse with a Mr. Parris. They inspected the foundation and found it so far gone that they advised against putting in more money for a breakwater. Colonel Thayer recommended an appropriation of $75,000 for an entirely new building at the ledge, a lighthouse on the principle of Eddystone. Congress did not make the appropriation.

Although the sheathing had accomplished its purpose in preventing the keeper from drowning inside the tower, the vibration when the waves battered against the light was terrific. Chairs and even tables were moved about the lighthouse floor as the breakers smashed high against the sides of the reinforced tower. Stephen Pleasonton himself announced on April 30, 1842, that he was "in daily expectation that the present building has been demolished by the force of the sea."

But as the years went by and nothing happened, the confidence of the lighthouse officials returned, and in 1855 a new lens and lantern were installed. In 1859 a fog bell was put up. When iron clamps were placed around the base of the foundation pier, they snapped one by one as the wintry gales hit the ledge, although a large iron band around the upper part of the foundation was still in position.

Finally in 1869 Congress took the action recommended back in the 1840's by Colonel Thayer, and voted to build a new lighthouse beside the old one, Eddystone style, at a cost of $75,000. The gray tower, completed in 1872, was seventy-five feet high. Built with dovetailed blocks of the best granite, the new Whaleback Light has stood the test of many great storms. The 1829 tower was allowed to remain for several years, but when a new third-class Daboll trumpet with double caloric engines was brought out to the ledge, the abandoned lighthouse was cut down to its foundation pedestal. On this base an iron tower was constructed to house the fog trumpet, and its red-painted sides extended more than half as high as the lighthouse itself.

During the gale of 1886 the sea battered in one of the heavy windows in the five-foot-thick granite walls of the tower, flooding the living quarters of the lighthouse. Captain Leander White of Newcastle, keeper at that time, was almost drowned before escaping to the upper level, where he hoisted one of his bed blankets to the masthead as a signal of distress. It was such a gale that no one could help him, and the blanket whipped itself to pieces. Captain Walter S. Ames saw the distress signal, and just as soon as the gale abated, left Kittery Point for the lighthouse. By this time Captain White was half-drowned and almost helpless, but Ames was able to take him off safely. Presently they reached shore. The window that had caused the trouble was later filled in with granite blocks.

In the great March snowstorm of 1888, which blanketed New York with an unprecedented fall of snow, part of the old foundation of the 1829 tower at Whaleback was demolished, leaving the new tower completely exposed to the sweep of the sea. After a concrete underpinning had been laid, a substantial bulkhead twenty feet high was constructed and bolted to both towers and the ledge itself. With the work practically finished, the ledge was subjected to the worst storm in years, when the November gale of 1888 swept into Portsmouth Harbor from the northeast. As soon as the storm went down, the keeper discovered that several more courses of the old foundation had been destroyed and the derrick and gear were missing. Almost 2,000 tons of large stones from the old foundation had been piled by the sea against the lighthouse ladder. Repairs were made before the winter ended, and the new work when completed was found to serve as a good protection against the average storm that swept in out of the Atlantic.

Captain Walter S. Ames became keeper at Whaleback in 1891. Eight years later a small boat capsized near the lighthouse, and Keeper Ames launched his boat and succeeded in rescuing the occupants. Meanwhile his frightened assistant, John Wetsel, had started the fog trumpet as a signal to the crew of the Jerry's Point Life Saving Station to come out to the scene. Keeper Ames landed on the shore, however, before the life savers could launch their surf boat.

On December 18, 1948, I dropped a Flying Santa bundle at Whaleback Light. As we missed the tower, we circled and dropped another, realizing that the first bundle would be lost in the sea. On January 5, Colonel Eugene S. Clark, eminent marine expert of Sandwich, Massachusetts, was hiking along the Cape Cod beach after a storm. He saw something wrapped in brownish paper floating toward the shore. Retrieving the bundle, he found that it was the package I had dropped almost three weeks before at Whaleback Ledge. The bundle had floated across Massachusetts Bay to land in front of him on the Cape Cod beach, ninety miles away in a direct line. He still has the book he found in the package, *Storms and Shipwrecks of New England.*

Whaleback Light today has a light of 600,000 candlepower. The light has two white flashes every ten seconds. The diaphragm horn gives a group of two blasts every thirty seconds in fog or bad weather.

Of course, Whaleback Light is actually part of Maine, but since it forms a protection for ships entering Portsmouth Harbor, it has been included with New Hampshire lighthouses. Today it is unattended.

PART III

MASSACHUSETTS BEACONS

22

Newburyport and Ipswich

Lighthouses of northern Massachusetts include the three beacons at Newburyport and the Ipswich tower. At Newburyport Harbor the lights have been changed many times, because of shifting sand bars at the mouth of the Merrimack River. There are two range lights located in the harbor itself, and a tower at Plum Island. The range lights for Newburyport Harbor are shifted from year to year.

The first tower at Plum Island was erected in 1788, and rebuilt for the last time in 1898. Of the several terrible shipwrecks to occur in the vicinity of Plum Island, probably the most discussed in later years was that of the *Pocohantas,* mentioned in the chapter on the Isles of Shoals. Other wrecks include that of the schooner *Lady Howard* in 1830 and the brig *Richmond Packet* in December 1839. The captain of the brig, Commander Toothaker, was bringing a large cargo of flour and corn to Newburyport when the gale caught him just off the coast. Driven ashore on a point of rocks, the *Richmond Packet* began to break up.

When the vessel struck, Captain Toothaker jumped overboard with a line and succeeded in reaching the rocks, where he made the rope fast. Signaling to his wife, who was aboard, to come in on the line, he watched her as she prepared to attempt the journey. Suddenly the line snapped, and the captain's wife was cut off from shore. The members of the crew then let her down on a spar into the water, but a heavy sea swept Mrs. Toothaker off and she was seen no more until her lifeless body washed up on the rocks. The members of the crew were all saved. In this storm there were 130 vessels in Newburyport Harbor, and forty-one were damaged.

The gale had struck so unexpectedly that the keeper of Plum Island Light, who had left the tower for a few hours, was unable to reach the lighthouse when he returned. So no light beamed that night at the entrance to Newburyport Harbor.

At present the tower is automatic.

For many years the sand dunes of Essex surrounded an attractive white lighthouse, and photographers and artists came for miles around to take pictures and paint in the vicinity. Unfortunately, a plain skeleton tower replaced the lighthouse in the 1930's, and no longer does Ipswich Light offer a pleasing picture.

The old tower was first erected in 1838, and T. S. Greenwood is believed to have been the first keeper. The light was forty-two feet above the water, and officially listed as being located "on Castle Neck, south side of entrance to Ipswich Harbor." Many wrecks have occurred near this light down through the nineteenth century, and even recently, but the most thrilling of all took place on December 23, 1839, when Greenwood was the keeper.

In the second of the great triple hurricanes of 1839, a Mr. Marshall saw the schooner *Deposit*, which had left Belfast, Maine, a few days before, coming ashore near the Ipswich Lighthouse. Rushing up the bank to the keeper's home, he told Keeper Greenwood of his discovery, and they both returned at once to the beach.

Captain Cotterell of the *Deposit* had felt his vessel grind into the sand at midnight Sunday, and realized that it would be impossible to launch a boat into the roaring surf that was breaking on the beach directly in front of them. Soon the waves were washing entirely over the helpless wreck. All aboard, including the captain's wife, took to the rigging. Throughout the bitter early morning hours the relentless surf surged along the deck, and before daylight two of the crew had died, unable to stand the wind and spray that had lashed at them continually since midnight.

At daybreak when Marshall discovered the schooner, only five of the crew were alive. Keeper Greenwood hastened to the beach with Marshall, and made plans to reach the survivors. The breakers were still hitting the beach in mountainous surges, so there was no chance of launching a lifeboat. Greenwood was about to give up all thoughts of the possibility of rescuing the crew when he heard the piteous shrieks of the poor woman in the rigging.

"I must do something for her," he cried, and ran for his home. A few minutes later he returned to the beach with a long line. Tying one end around his waist, he cautioned Marshall to hold on for dear life to the other end of the two-hundred-foot line. Marshall was to tie it to the lifeboat after the keeper swam out to the *Deposit*. Although Greenwood was a powerful swimmer, it was almost impossible for him to make headway against the wind and waves, especially with the rope around his waist. But thoughts of the poor woman out on the schooner made him continue to fight the breakers, until he finally swam out beyond the reach of the undertow and eventually reached the schooner, climbing aboard over the bowsprit.

Bracing himself in the shrouds, Greenwood bent a line around the rigging and signaled for Marshall to jump into the boat as the waves receded. Marshall watched his opportunity, and slid the lifeboat into the ocean just as a wave was going out. The next billow smashed into the boat, but Marshall, huddled in the bottom, felt Keeper Greenwood pull the craft through the water, and a few minutes later the lifeboat reached the schooner. It had been a remarkable feat. The hardest part was still ahead, however.

Captain Cotterell, almost senseless from his battering from the sea, was lowered into the boat. A great wave swamped the craft, and both men went under. The captain did not rise to the surface, but Marshall soon reappeared and grasped a line lowered by Greenwood, hauling himself aboard the schooner. Captain Cotterell's wife had witnessed the drowning of her husband, and went mad with grief, shrieking and shouting at the top of her voice.

Now that the boat was lost, other rescue methods had to be devised. The storm and sea were beginning to go down, fortunately, and a few hours later the stern of the *Deposit* was barely fifty feet from the beach. Two sailors reached shore by floating in on broken wreckage from the schooner, but Mrs. Cotterell landed by a different method. Keeper Greenwood and Marshall, standing in waist-deep water by the stern of the vessel, shouted to the lady to jump into their arms. She obeyed them, and the next great wave carried them all up on the beach to safety. The three survivors were then taken to the residence of Humphrey Lakeman, a retired sea captain whose home was near the wreck.

The following Wednesday morning was a sad occasion at Ipswich when Keeper Greenwood attended the funeral of those who lost their lives aboard the schooner *Deposit*. No less than sixteen sea captains acted as pall bearers for Captain Cotterell and his sailors, all of whom were very young men.

23

Cape Ann or Thacher's Island

Fourteen months after the Boston Massacre, a bill was introduced in the Province of Massachusetts Bay Council for the erection of a lighthouse on Thacher's or Thatcher's Island, off Gloucester. On April 22, 1771, the bill was passed. Captain Nathaniel Allen of Gloucester, Major Richard Reed of Marblehead, and Captain Richard Derby of Salem were appointed as a committee to superintend the construction of the lighthouse.

The island was purchased from the heirs of Anthony Thatcher, who had been wrecked there in the first great New England hurricane of 1635. As only he and his wife had been saved from the terrible shipwreck off the island, the General Court gave Thacher the island to recompense him in part for his losses.

When the tower was nearing completion, Captain Derby and Captain Allen appointed a Captain Kirkwood to be keeper there on December 21, 1771. During the Revolution Captain Rogers of the Minute Men removed Keeper Kirkwood from the island, as Kirkwood was a Tory. The lights remained in darkness until after the Revolution.

Captain Joseph Sayward was the keeper at Thacher's Island from 1792 until 1814, when James Sayward was offered the position in place of the "old and feeble" Sayward. The salary of $250, however, was considered inadequate by the younger Sayward, who refused the position. Aaron Wheeler became the next keeper, remaining at Thacher's Island for many years.

During the summer of 1825 Keeper Wheeler worked long and hard making an acceptable path from the eastern lighthouse to the northeastern tower. Many great boulders were broken up and moved away; the smaller ones were surfaced down. Before the winter of 1825 Keeper Wheeler completed his task, and the entire three hundred yards between the two towers was cleared. The following spring Simon Pleasonton authorized the payment of $100 to the keeper for his work.

In 1833 Rufus Choate asked for the removal of Aaron Wheeler, but Simon Pleasonton refused, saying that Choate's was the first complaint ever received against the keeper. Wheeler was advancing in years, however, and on January 17, 1834, Austin Wheeler was appointed in Aaron Wheeler's place. (The relationship between the two Wheelers is unknown.) Charles Wheeler was appointed on November 23, 1836, and in 1845 was still the keeper. At that time the government was paying him $450 a year for his care of the twenty-two lamps in the two towers.

Winslow Lewis tried out his experiments with lights in 1807 at Thacher's Island, and the improvement worked so well that it was installed at Boston Light. New lanterns were put in at Thacher's Island in 1841. By 1859 Fresnel lights had been installed in most of the beacons up and down the coast with two exceptions, of which Thacher's was one. Work was started in 1860 on two lighthouse towers at the island, each of them 124 feet in height. Completed and lighted the next year, the tall, slender towers with their new Fresnel lenses were soon known as the Twin Lights of Thacher's Island. Officially, of course, the lights were and still are called the Cape Ann Lighthouse Station.

Keeper Bray, an injured Civil War veteran, was appointed a short time after the war ended. Probably because of the keeper's wounded condition, his salary was made $1,000. After Bray, his wife, and two children had been on the island a year, an incident occurred that culminated in a thrilling adventure.

On the day before Christmas, Keeper Bray noticed that one of his assistant keepers was coming down with a bad fever, and in spite of all that Mrs. Bray could do, the man grew steadily worse. As the head keeper needed another cask of oil, he decided to row ashore early the next day with the sick man, and at the same time fill the cask. When morning came, Keeper Bray and his other helper assisted the sick man down the slip into the boat. As they pushed off, Bray told his wife not to worry.

"I'll get along with the children all right," she shouted to him, and Mrs. Bray watched the two keepers row the sick man toward the mainland, observing them with the spy glass until the boat disappeared into Loblolly Cove. Then she realized that the wind was coming up and the sky clouding over. An hour after sunrise a bitter snow storm had set in, and there she was, alone on the island with her two babies! All sight of the mainland was soon shut out. Before noon the thick, drifting snow had reduced visibility to less than a few yards.

Most women know what their husbands will do under certain conditions. Mrs. Bray realized that her husband and his assistant, after putting the sick man ashore, would leave at once in an effort to reach the island to take care of the lights. But as the hours went by she had to admit to herself that he must have missed Thacher's Island in the snowstorm and was helplessly lost somewhere out in the gale. In her fear she went to the children and talked with them. Her boy Tom was old enough to toddle about. She started to tell him that the two of them were to take care of the two lighthouses that night. Tom was never frightened with his mother, and the other child was still a baby. As she stood there, a terrific gust of wind ripped the front door from its hinges. She rushed to the entry and bolted the inside door so that no snow could seep in.

Bundling the boy into his heaviest garments, Mrs. Bray made sure that the baby was safe in her crib. Then the two started out on their long journey to the north light. Fighting her way through the snowdrifts, with her child clinging to her, the poor woman was terribly tired before she had gone half of the three hundred yards that separate the two light-houses. In her feeling of hopelessness at the enormous task ahead, she thought of the Bible, and searched for some verse of scripture that would comfort her. Just as she reached the northern light, the message came to her, "But the wise took oil in their vessels with their lamps."

Opening the door, she stepped inside with the boy, and they rested from the effort of fighting with the gale. Then she took the boy and slowly ascended the 156 steps of the granite tower. Resting at each platform, the mother and boy finally reached the top of the north tower, 162 feet above the ocean. As she stood there in the lantern room, with the wind howling against the tower and myriads of tiny flakes hiding the view of even the island itself, Mrs. Bray thought of her husband, out in that same storm, lost on the ocean. She chopped away the stiff wicks of the lamp and trimmed them with the scissors. Then she pumped up more oil and made everything ready for lighting. The clock in the tower said two p.m. Realizing that she would have to run both lighthouses, three hundred yards apart and at the same time make sure her children were safe, Mrs. Bray struck a match and put it against the fibers of the wick. Slowly the yellow flame grew larger, until at last it seemed to challenge the whiteness outside the tower. She had already wound up the great clock work arrangement, known as the carcels, which kept the oil pumping for about five hours, so she now made sure everything else was in order, and went down the cast-iron steps with her son.

"Will Papa see the light, Mamma?" asked little Tom as they struggled through the biting gale. "Where is Papa now?" persisted Tom, and his mother tried to comfort the child as best she could, even though her own heart was gravely troubled. If only the storm would let up, she thought.

But the snow continued to fall as the afternoon waned. At dusk she took little Tom with her again while they climbed the other tower beside the home and lighted the lamp. Upon returning to the house, she gave the children supper and soon both were fast asleep. For the first time since her husband had left that morning she was really alone. When seven o'clock came, the north tower light had been burning for five hours. She must leave her babies and take the long journey to the other side of the island, climb the 124-foot lighthouse, and rewind the carcel clock. On her way back she was grateful to find that the roar of the wind did not seem as insistent and that the thinning snow allowed her to make out the northern light.

But she had not figured on the drifting snow. She stumbled and went down in a heap a short distance from her dwelling. The biblical text came to her again—"Then those virgins arose and trimmed the lamps"—she must get up. Making a great effort, she rose to her feet and blundered on through the gale. She felt very grateful to former Keeper Wheeler, who, a generation before, had cut out a walk from the huge boulders between the two towers, for otherwise she could never have made it. After falling again and again, Mrs. Bray finally reached the north tower and stepped toward the latch of the door. It was buried under the drift, but she finally located it and pushed the door open. She stepped inside. The light was still on and the tower was warm and comfortable. It was a relief to realize she had reached her goal.

After a brief rest, she climbed the stairs to the top. Turning the crank slowly, for she was exhausted, she wound up the carcel again and went down the stairs.

All that night the poor woman alternated between the two towers. By five in the morning her strength gave out and in her tired condition she soon fell asleep.

Unknown to her, the snow stopped shortly afterward. Her husband, miles away, had already made out the welcome gleam of the Thacher's Island Lights, and was following a course toward the lighthouses. At seven o'clock, after a hard row, he reached the island and hurried at once to his home. There he found his wife and awakened her. Their reunion was a happy one. Mrs. Bray asked her husband if the lights were still burning and he answered: "If they were not, darling, I would not be here."

As they talked to each other, little Tom woke up with a start and shouted: "Daddy, did you bring Santa Claus with you?" That was the first realization of either parent that it was Christmas Day, so absorbed with their own adventures had they been.

An incident at Thacher's Island that concerned President Wilson occurred in 1919 when he returned from Europe. Third Assistant Maurice A. Babcock, who later became keeper at Boston Light, was standing in the signal house, keeping the fog signal going. Suddenly there loomed up through the mist the outline of the great steamer that was carrying Woodrow Wilson back to America. Headed for the rocks of Thacher's Island with her escorting vessels, she

West Quoddy Head Light, Maine

Pemaquid Point Light

Owl's Head Light

Inside the lens room at Seguin Light

Boon Island Light

Cape Neddick Nubble Light

Portland Head Light

ABOVE: *The author rowing Graves Light visitors back to boat*

OPPOSITE PAGE TOP: *Cuckolds Light, off Boothbay Harbor.* BOTTOM: *Eagle Island Light*

Thacher's Island Lights, Cape Ann, Massachusetts

OPPOSITE PAGE:
Eastern Point Light, Cape Ann

Isles of Shoals Light, off the New Hampshire Coast

Boston Light and the Brewster Islands

OPPOSITE PAGE TOP: *The author (left) in 1941 visiting the last regular keeper of Boston Light, Maurice A. Babcock.* BOTTOM: *Air view of Boston Light in winter*

LEFT: *Boston Light at dusk*

PHOTO BY EVERETT TATREAU

ABOVE: *Minot's Ledge Light, America's most dangerously situated beacon. Photo by the author.*
RIGHT: *Closeup of Minot's Ledge Light*

Deer Island Light

The Three Sisters of Nauset, as these lights were called in 1890

Scituate Light

For many years the author, as Flying Santa, has flown over the light-houses at Christmas, dropping presents.

Flying Santa about to drop a Christmas bundle to keepers at Sankaty Head Light on Nantucket Island, 1972

seemed doomed. At the last minute, however, the captain must have heard the blasts of the Thacher's Island fog horn, and backed the steamer out of danger.

On February 1, 1932, the northern Thacher's Island Light was discontinued, and a motor-driven flash controller was installed in the southeastern tower. The new characteristic was a group of five white flashes every twenty seconds, having a candle power of 160,000. At the same time the station was electrified, the power reaching the island by means of a submarine cable six thousand feet long that connected the lighthouse station to the mainland.

With the elimination of the northern Thacher's Island Light, the last of seven twin lights passed into history. They had all been on the Atlantic coast: Matinicus, Cape Elizabeth, Baker's Island, Chatham, the Gurnet, Navesink, N. J., and Thacher's. Nauset Light at one time had three towers. All of the eight lights were established between 1768 and 1839. Long experimentation had proved that a single flashing light is more quickly identified from a ship at sea than twin or even triple lights. Merely by counting the flash the mariner recognizes the beacon and knows at once where he is.

When we visited the light at Thacher's in 1945, Captain Austin B. Beal was keeper, having taken the place of George W. Seavey, who had just died. Beal's assistants were six-foot-five Harry A. Wilbur and Douglas Sanders. The keeper at the island had to be an all-around man, including cook, machinist, engineman, boatman, and light keeper.

In 1967 Thacher's Island Light, or Cape Ann Light as official charts call it, went through a period of great security when a key witness for the government, Joseph Baron, also known as Barboza, was taken to the island under heavy guard and great secrecy. The so-called gangster remained on the island for a substantial period of time.

The south tower at Thacher's Island now has a white beam of 70,000 candlepower flashing five times every twenty seconds from a height of 166 feet above the sea. Coastguardsmen live on the island to care for the tower and keep the light burning.

24

Lights Around Gloucester

There are four locations on or just off the Gloucester peninsula where lighthouses stand. One of the beacons, Straitsmouth, was erected in 1835 and rebuilt in 1896, but at present is an automatic station and is not attended. The others are Annisquam, Eastern Point, and Ten Pound Island.

Annisquam Light, or Wigwam Point Light, as it was formerly called, is the oldest of all four, having been built in 1801 on the mainland at the entrance to Annisquam Harbor. The tower was lighted for the first time by Keeper George Day on March 23, 1801, and in 1850 Day was still the keeper at what is now Annisquam Harbor Light! In 1897 the tower was rebuilt.

In 1936 Per S. Tornberg became keeper at Annisquam Light and stayed until World War II. Coastguardsmen took over the duties at that time and continue to tend the light at this white tower in one of the most attractive stations along the coast.

Ten Pound Island has a prominent place on the chart of Gloucester Harbor drawn by Champlain more than three and a quarter centuries ago, but it was not until 1821 that a lighthouse was built on the island.

A strange sea animal visited Ten Pound Island during the summer of 1817, according to several reliable witnesses. This sea serpent came up on the ledges on the extreme eastern point of Ten Pound Island, where it rested partly in and partly out of water. On the tenth of August, 1817, Amos Story, who was later to become keeper of Ten Pound Island Light, saw the monster. His sworn testimony is as follows:

"I, Amos Story of Gloucester, in the County of Essex, mariner, depose and say, that on the tenth day of August A. D. 1817, I saw a strange marine animal, that I believe to be a serpent, at the southward and eastward of Ten Pound Island, in the harbour in said Gloucester. . . . I was setting on the shore, and was about twenty rods from him when he was the nearest to me.

"His head appeared shaped much like the head of the sea-turtle and he carried his head from ten to twelve inches above the surface of the water. His head at that distance appeared larger than the head of any dog I ever saw. . . . I should judge I saw fifty feet of him at least."

Amos Story became the keeper of Ten Pound Island Light in 1833. George W. Davis was the keeper in 1849. An old sailor, he had developed deafness at sea and was given the lighthouse position.

The last regular lighthouse service keeper was Edward H. Hopkins, who entered the service in 1913 at Cape Poge, Martha's Vineyard. After remaining there for five years he transferred to Long Point Light, from which station he went in 1922 to Ten Pound Island, Gloucester Harbor.

We often visited Keeper Hopkins and his wife and son at their Ten Pound Island home, and found them a happy family. One Christmas week, when I was about to take off from the East Boston Airport on the annual Christmas flight over the lighthouses, Mrs. Hopkins heard about it over the radio.

"Let's do something special for Ed Snow when he comes over," she suggested to her husband, who was reading a western story by the kitchen stove.

"What can we do?" he asked, and went back to reading his story. But Mrs. Hopkins was not to be denied. She disappeared down the cellar stairs, and came up a short time later with her arms full of old newspapers. She spread them on the lawn beside the house until they spelled the words MERRY CHRISTMAS. Then she nailed the papers to the ground so that the wind would not change the shape of the letters, and waited for the plane.

An hour later I circled the island, and received an unusual thrill upon reading her greeting to me spelled out in the grass. A picture was taken, and when we returned to Boston later that day, it was processed by the Associated Press. On the front pages of the late afternoon papers was the view of the *Merry Christmas* spelled out in the grass as a greeting to the Flying Santa. Keeper Hopkins' son, returning home from school, purchased a copy of one of the Boston papers. He rowed out to the island and entered the kitchen, where his father was still sitting in his favorite chair beside the stove, reading a magazine. The son handed Keeper Hopkins the paper, holding it open so that his father's eye caught at once on the four-column picture of his own lighthouse and home. His good wife took in the situation at once and tiptoed out of the room, but she hasn't ceased telling the story yet of how she did what her husand believed impossible.

Ten Pound Island is unattended today, but has an automatic beacon.

Eastern Point Light was established in 1832 and rebuilt in 1890. An exciting event of 1871 witnessed by the keeper of Eastern Point Light was the rounding of Eastern Point by the

Gloucester schooner *A. E. Horton,* after she had escaped from the Canadian government. Harvey Knowlton had boarded her after the *Horton's* capture in Guysboro Harbor for fishing inside the three-mile limit, and with the aid of six American fishermen, sailed the *Horton* across George's Banks and into Gloucester Harbor. The entire country was electrified at this bold deed.

Perhaps the hardest task of the keepers at Eastern Point was caring for the light at the end of the breakwater that runs out into Gloucester Harbor from the lighthouse. Walking along this breakwater is no easy task during good weather, but in wintry gales it is dangerous work, with the surf sweeping across the granite blocks to form slippery ice coverings that the keeper must negotiate to reach the end of Dog Bar Breakwater.

On our last visit to Eastern Point Light, we were impressed by the efficiency shown by Coast Guard Keeper Robert Foley and his men. The radio beacon operates with the assistance of a 150-foot tower in both fog and clear weather, day and night. A diaphragm horn giving two blasts every twenty seconds is an important function of the station. The light itself has a candlepower of 100,000 and gives a white flash every five seconds. There is also a special radio-direction-finder calibration station here at the Eastern Point Light Station.

25

Lights of the North Shore

Three lighthouses form a triangular guardianship over the waters off the North Shore of Massachusetts: Baker's Island in outer Salem Harbor, Hospital Point Light in Beverly, and Marblehead Light at Marblehead Neck.

BAKER'S ISLAND

Five miles out to sea from Salem stands Baker's Island Light. Although the island has been inhabited from earliest times, not until after the Revolution was it considered a suitable location for a marine beacon. On July 28, 1791, a large group of Salem men journeyed to Baker's Island, where they erected a daytime marker. As the years passed, however, shipping losses continued along the North Shore, and so the Salem Marine Society began agitation for a lighthouse.

Baker's Island Light was authorized by Congress in 1796, and erected without delay. On January 3, 1798, Keeper Chapman illuminated the light for the first time. This lighthouse was similar in design to the edifice we have already described at Matinicus Rock, Maine. The keeper's home was in the same building as the two lighthouse towers, which were at each end of the structure.

In the War of 1812 Keeper Joseph Perkins of the lighthouse saved the frigate *Constitution* from the British Navy. Detecting Old Ironsides as she was beating across the Bay, chased by two British warships, the *Tenedos* and the *Endymion,* and seeing that the captain of the *Constitution* needed assistance, Perkins rowed out to the warship and piloted the ship to safety inside Salem Harbor, her English antagonists thwarted by the vigilance of a Yankee lighthouse keeper.

During the winter of 1817 a great ship, the *Union,* heavily loaded with pepper, crashed on the rocks at Baker's Island. This mishap was charged to the fact that one of the lights had been extinguished under orders from the government. Since the ship was loaded with 3,600 picals of pepper and 900 picals of tin, the wreck proved a costly one to the owners. When another unfortunate vessel crashed ashore shortly afterward, petitions were drawn up to re-establish the second light. Many believed that mariners confused Baker's Island with Boston Light, as both had but one beacon, but the government did not restore the second light at Baker's Island until 1820.

James F. Lundgren was appointed keeper in 1881. Professor Sears, the geologist, and Lundgren's son journeyed out to lonely Halfway Rock one summer to examine the geological formation there, and to their surprise found several badly tarnished copper cents. Returning to the mainland with their coins, they learned that it had been the custom for Marblehead and Salem sailors to toss pennies ashore at the rock to ensure success on their coming voyage.

The great tornado of July 16, 1879, hit Baker's Island, and a bolt of lightning struck and demolished the fog bell tower. This sudden gale caused the death of more than thirty persons in Boston Bay.

When the smaller of the two lighthouses was declared inactive on June 30, 1916, a new and brighter beacon was placed on the higher tower. The present light has an alternating 300,000 candlepower white and 70,000 candlepower red flash every 15 seconds. Four white flashes and four red flashes are seen every minute, with each period of darkness between flashes lasting about seven seconds.

MARBLEHEAD

When Marblehead Light was planned in 1833 there were many conferences and meetings of the citizens before a site was chosen. The land located close to the old fort at Marblehead Neck was finally approved. The property actually belonged to a Mr. Brown, who asked $500 for it. After much bickering, a compromise was reached and the lighthouse built. Congress appropriated $4,500 for the erection of the light and adjacent buildings. To avoid difficulties with the War Department, Fifth Auditor Stephen Pleasonton wrote to Secretary of War Lewis Cass, asking Cass if he would "instruct the commanding officer of the Fort to permit the Lighthouse to be erected on the land attached to the Fort, more especially as it is represented that the Lighthouse will be without the lines of the Fort and will in no wise interfere with the ordinary duties of the Garrison."

If the appropriation had been large enough for a suitable lighthouse, all would have been well, but a small edifice was erected, one which worked in a satisfactory manner until cottages were built in the vicinity; then mariners could not see the light. By 1880 Marblehead Light was surrounded by cottages on all sides, and something had to be done. Three years later a one-hundred-foot mast was set up, on which the keeper hung an auxiliary light. Twelve years went by before further complaints were made, and then it was suggested that there be erected a new lighthouse tower, built high enough to clear all houses in the vicinity. Henry T. Drayton, who had recently been appointed keeper, attended faithfully to his lighthouse duties all during this period of agitation. The new tower was finally approved.

Finished in 1895, the iron lighthouse presented a spindly appearance. The eight cast-iron pilings were 84 feet high, and were capped at the top by the lamp room and lantern, bringing the total height above the ground to 105 feet, or 130 feet above the sea. Formerly white, and in 1933 red, the present light is now fixed green.

At the completion of forty-three years in the lighthouse service Captain Drayton retired. Keeper Drayton had spent the first ten years of his career aboard a lighthouse tender, but for one third of a century had tended Marblehead Light.

When Harry S. Marden retired from the United States Army in May 1938 he was told that Edward Rogers, who had been taking care of the Marblehead Light, was giving up the position. Marden accepted the post as keeper of the property and light. For the next few months he ran the green light at the top of the tower, but when the great New England hurricane of 1938 came sweeping up the coast, the light failed.

Harry Marden was equal to the situation, however, and brought his car up to the lighthouse, connected the batteries with the electric light wires, and stayed up in the windswept tower all that wild night. When morning came, Marden was able to say proudly that his light had lasted through New England's worst hurricane.

In October 1942 Harry S. Marden was called back into active duty in the army at Fort Banks. He was later assigned to Fort Strong, Long Island, where besides his regular army activities, he had old Long Island Light under his control.

Marblehead Light is located at the scene of the greatest sailing races in America. Unfortunately, the tall, spindlelike legs of the lighthouse tower do not fit into the picturesque scenery. Of course, it is to be realized that lighthouses are for utility and not for beauty, but in this case it is especially unfortunate that beauty and utility were not combined.

26

Egg Rock

Egg Rock lies two miles south of Phillips Point in Swamp-scott, and a mile northeast of Nahant. It can be seen rising out of the sea from almost every vantage point from Winthrop to Marblehead. The most exciting times in the history of this island were between 1855 and 1922, when Egg Rock Light flashed its welcome beacon.

The first adventure of interest occurred about the year 1815, when a young Italian, on the eve of his departure for Italy to visit his parents, sailed out to Egg Rock to pick forget-me-nots for his sweetheart. The boy drowned on his return journey from the lonely rock, and the girl died of a broken heart.

It was exactly forty years later that Egg Rock Light was planned, after much agitation for a lighthouse from Swamp-scott fishermen. Massachusetts ceded Egg Rock to the United States Government under Chapter 17 of its Acts and Resolves, and Ira P. Brown was the successful bidder for the contract to build the tower, charging the government $3,700 for the work. Egg Rock Light first flashed out its white signal of welcome on the night of September 15, 1856. Because of possible confusion with other lighthouses, its beam was changed to a red flash the following year.

George B. Taylor was the first keeper at Egg Rock. He reached the ledge in the old fishing boat, *Moll Pitcher,* taking his entire family and all the furnishings for the new house in September 1855.

An enormous Newfoundland-Saint Bernard dog named Milo came out to Egg Rock with the Taylor family, and soon made himself at home with the seagulls and the other wild life of Boston Bay. As the stone masons were finishing the tower, they left a small hole in the little square addition that served as an entry way, and Milo thus had a private entrance to the lighthouse. One day Keeper Taylor took a shot at a great loon, wounding it, but the bird started to fly away and fell into the ocean. Milo ran down on the rocky ledge that leads into the sea and jumped into the water. The loon saw the dog approaching, however, and took off to fly a quarter mile before coming down again. Milo continued his pursuit, and in a short time was less than a hundred yards away. Just as the dog felt sure of his victim, away soared the loon again, necessitating another long swim. This unusual contest was continued until the loon and the dog actually passed out of sight. Before long darkness closed in on the ocean. Milo did not return that night, and the family began to wonder if the dog had drowned in the sea. Late the next afternoon, however, Milo was seen swimming toward Egg Rock, not from the ocean but from Nahant. In the darkness he had missed the Rock, continued to Nahant where he had rested for the night, and left for his home the next day.

It is believed that Milo rescued several children in and around the rock, but all details are lacking. Because his fame spread far and wide, an artist drew a picture of Milo with one of Keeper Taylor's sons Fred, resting between the paws of the giant canine. The picture, known as *Saved,* became famous all over America. At the time of the picture's greatest popularity a sad accident befell the boy who posed with the dog. While passing through Shirley Gut, Fred Taylor, then about eighteen, was drowned.

When the national political situation changed in 1861 Keeper Taylor lost his position at the light to Thomas Widger, who, it was said, had voted the right way. Three children were born at the light to Mrs. Widger during the nine years of their occupancy. One of them, Abraham, came to this world under unusual circumstances. About the time of his expected arrival Keeper Widger rowed ashore to get a nurse. The wind had risen when the journey to the rock was about to begin, and in some way the boat capsized as the party left the beach. Wet and angry, the nurse refused to go out to the light, and the keeper searched in vain for another person to make the trip with him. Finally the keeper's father agreed to go, and they started the next day, December 1, 1865. All this time the expectant mother and her two children, aged two and five, were alone on the island. Before the boat hove in sight, however, her third son, Abraham Widger, arrived. Another son, Thomas, was born on the rock a year or two later.

In Waldo Thompson's *Swampscott* we read of a visit to Egg Rock Light by Dr. William B. Chase, a Swampscott physician, during the time Keeper Widger was in charge. It was in a midwinter gale that one of the local residents noticed the distress signal flying from lonely Egg Rock. The captain of the schooner *Champion,* coming into the Bay, also saw the flag. He hove to in the lee of Egg Rock. Keeper Widger shouted across that they needed a doctor at once. Half an hour later the *Champion* arrived in port, and Doctor Chase was summoned down to the beach. The first dory that was launched capsized in the gale, but Dr. Chase reached the schooner in the second.

Soon they were in the lee of Egg Rock, and both dories were put over so that one could help the other if they were in trouble. The sea was still running high, freezing to ice as it dashed upon the rock. The roar of the surf was terrific as the two dories edged their way toward the foot of the icy steps that led to the top of the island.

Waiting for a favorable moment to slide the dory up on the rocky shore, the sailors ordered the doctor to lie down in the bottom of the boat. Then they rowed furiously toward the lighthouse, landed, jumped out, and with assistance of Keeper Widger, pulled the boat and the doctor high up the rock, but not before a great wave had almost swamped the dory. Later, the doctor said that he had never felt so helpless as he had with his heels in the air and water dashing over his prostrate form. The doctor treated the sick member of the lighthouse keeper's family and then faced the trip back to the mainland. The launching of the dory from the rock was successfully accomplished, but Dr. Chase told the story of his trip to the isolated lighthouse many, many times in later life.

The keeper and his wife were frank in their entries in the journal which they kept at the light. For a day in 1873 we read the following:

"A severe rainstorm. Keeper went ashore to get some groceries and got caught in the storm; was detained away four days on account of the rough seas. The wife kept the light all trimmed and burning bright and clear. Keeper was drunk ashore all the time."

In the journal we read that in May 1873 a large cod was caught on the northeast side of Egg Rock by Ebenezer Phillips. Purchased by a Mr. Lees, who cut it open, the fish was found to have inside its stomach an eighteen-carat gold ring, with the initials H. L.

Another entry told that the keeper discovered a great, black Newfoundland dog on the island with a collar marking of D. B. Short, West Newbury. How the dog arrived at the rock and from whence he came was never learned.

On June 25, 1874, Charles Hooper assumed his duties as the new keeper. The following year two lighthouse inspectors visited Egg Rock. They were George Dewey and Winfield Scott Schley, both naval officers who became famous admirals during the war with Spain.

Around the year 1880 young Frank Taylor and his brother noticed a peculiar signal flying from the island where Keeper Richardson was in charge, and decided to row out and see what was the matter. Richardson's relatives, thinking he might need food, sent him a basket full of provisions. On reaching the island, the boys were told by the keeper that he had lost his boat and could not return to the mainland. He was then so discouraged and worried that he had started to construct a boat at the lonely rock. After staying on the island to keep the captain company for a short time, the boys took Richardson back with them. Keeper Richardson soon obtained another boat in which he rowed out to the rock in time to light the tower that same night.

A story has come down through the mist of years, told by Swampscott fishermen, repeated by Nahant and Lynn residents time and again, until it probably will never be known how much is truth and how much pure legend. One of the keepers between 1860 and 1890, whose name is unknown, had the misfortune to lose his wife by death early in the winter, when the island was surrounded by ice. Dressing her in her best finery, he carried his wife out to the oil shed, where he laid her down reverently in the corner and covered her lifeless form with a wooden protection. Within a day or two the body had frozen solidly, and remained in that condition all that cold winter and until the first signs of spring indicated to the keeper that he could successfully row to the mainland. Carrying the icy corpse down to his boat, he placed it in the stern and rowed ashore. The funeral was held within three hours of the time he landed, for he had to return to the lighthouse before night. After the burial, he visited a home a short distance from his former residence ashore, and asked a childhood sweetheart, then forty years old, to marry him, explaining that not only did she have to give her answer within two hours, but that the ceremony would have to be performed that very afternoon. He was leaving for the island to arrive before darkness, with her, if she gave her consent in marriage, but without her, if she didn't. Somewhat flustered, (for what lady wouldn't have been!) she gave her consent. A trunk was rapidly packed, the preacher who had officiated at the funeral of his dead wife was called in to marry him to his newly betrothed, and the couple were brought down to the shore to push off in the same craft that had borne the body of the keeper's first wife a few hours before. As far as is known, after the bride had become accustomed to the isolated rock, the couple were perfectly happy at their remote island.

Charles Dunham reached Egg Rock on January 5, 1884, and assumed his duties as the new keeper. His comments in the lighthouse journal are perhaps more interesting than those of any other keeper in residence there. Even Dunham never let his pen carry him away, however, for many thrilling adventures were set down with a word or two to stand for a life saved or a great storm that threw the surf and spray a hundred feet into the air. When he took charge of the lighthouse tower he was assisted by his sixteen-year-old daughter Dora, who is mentioned in the first entry:

"March 2, 1884. Dora and I went to Nahant today for corn, oats, and shorts and to get monthly reports and other mail. There was quite a streak of the polar regions about this forenoon in the form of large blocks of ice around the island, and between the station and the shore."

The hours, days, and months without social contact that the faithful lighthouse keeper's wife endured in her tragic loneliness before the telephone and radio came, is indicated by the following entry:

"August 18, 1884. . . . Went to Nahant with wife, her first shore since September 28, 1883."

That same year a severe cold snap on December 19 sent the mercury to six below zero, and from December 16 to 29 no one could leave the island. The philosophical keeper threupon entered the following thought on Christmas Day:

"December 25, 1884—Could not get ashore, and consequently no Christmas presents."

It was a terribly severe winter that continued to bother Keeper Dunham and his family out on the rock. The entries give a telling story of the hardships that were encountered:

"Jan. 17, 1885—Terrific westerly winds in the evening, and jars the clock so that it stops, at any rate it stops, whether the wind does it or not.

"Jan. 18—Clock stopped again this morning.

"Feb. 12—Cistern frozen over.

"Feb. 16—Terrific easterly winds and a very heavy sea. Night the rain beats in at the East chamber windows. Seas break across the island.

"Feb. 25—My birthday, 43 years old, Charles Dunham."

Signs of a coming event were included in the following entries:

"April 28—Went to Nahant for wife's mother from Maine.
"May 20—Went to Lynn for a nurse.
"May 27—Slake lime and make whitewash.
"May 28—Girl baby born on Egg Rock to Mr. and Mrs. Charles Dunham."

The girl was named Ada, and became the third child in the Dunham household, the others being Dora, already mentioned, and Charles A. Dunham, six years old at the time.

Although the winter had been a severe test for Keeper Dunham, the rest of the year 1885 still had much in store for him, including the arrival of a swimmer at the rock from the mainland, a rescue at sea, and a terrific thunderstorm. R. Ashton Lawrence swam from Bass Beach, Nahant, to Egg Rock Light in the unusually fast time of thirty-five minutes that summer. When we consider that the modern speedy crawl stroke was not in vogue at that time, and that his course was one of the roughest stretches of water in Boston Bay, Lawrence's accomplishment must stand as a remarkable feat.

On August 24, 1885, occurred one of the worst thunderstorms in Dunham's memory. He saw the thunderheads in the distance as they slowly advanced toward the rock, but it was late afternoon before the storm struck in all its power. A terrific deluge of rain, combined with a gale of wind, knocked the plaster down from the upper southeast room, and treated the entire area around the light to an overwhelming downpour. Although intense in nature, the thundersquall was of short duration, and just at sunset the air cleared to reveal disabled and dismasted schooners and other craft all around Boston Bay. One vessel in particular was only two miles out to sea southeast of the station. Dismasted and seemingly in distress, the schooner appeared in immediate need of assistance, but two vessels passed by without going to its aid. Dunham did not dare to row out to it, for the hour was "too near lighting time." He worried about the fate of the schooner, but never learned what happened to her.

The great days of the international yacht races are recalled by the lighthouse logbook. Keeper Dunham, high on Egg Rock, was in a perfect location to enjoy these yachting contests, and the names of all the champions of yesterday are faithfully recorded in the journal. The *Thetis, Galatea, Priscilla, Puritan, Mayflower* and *America* are mentioned, and the thrilling cup contests between the *Volunteer* and the *Thistle* as well.

Captain George L. Lyon, veteran Boston Bay lightkeeper, spent twenty-two years at Egg Rock Light, from 1889 until 1911. In 1897, while he was keeper, the entire lighthouse structure as well as the other buildings were destroyed by fire. Workmen quickly began building a new tower, but their shacks also caught fire early one morning. Edmund B. Johnson, seeing the blaze, rang in the local Nahant fire alarm, and the firemen rushed to the shoreline in response. As they had no means of reaching the island, all the fire lads from Nahant lined up on the shore to watch the buildings on the Rock as they went up in flames.

The three-acre rocky promontory was given telephone service around 1900 when Preston W. Johnson of Nahant installed the necessary equipment. The line ran from the Iron Mine in Nahant to the south side of Egg Rock, a distance of about a mile from landing to landing.

During World War I many young men in the Coast Guard were put ashore at the Egg Rock Light Station for their training, and when the war ended there was no regular keeper. The lighthouse tender *Mayflower* left a young boy there each week to take care of the station, and some of the youths found the rock a terribly lonesome place. The local girls of Nahant and Swampscott discovered the situation, and telephoned out to whatever boy happened to be on the station, chatting in a friendly fashion with some boy they had never seen.

One night a youth from Manchester, New Hampshire, was alone at the rock when a great storm hit the ledge, and before ten that evening he was almost frantic with terror. The mighty waves would hurl themselves up the steep sides of the island, sending ton after ton of spray right across the rock itself until the boy, isolated there, felt that he could stand it no longer. In spite of the danger he planned to take the little skiff, which was his only means of leaving the light, and try to row ashore at the height of that terrible gale. Of course, his craft would be overturned and sunk before he could row a dozen strokes, but in his frenzy to leave the island he did not realize that he was planning to row to his death.

As he made his final preparations to reach the mainland, the telephone in his watchroom rang. It was one of the girls calling to cheer him up. After a few minutes of conversation she realized that he was about to commit an act that would end in his death. Trying to reason with him, she explained that he would never reach shore alive. After a two hours' conversation she arranged with another friend to take over, and so it went, with the girls of the North Shore keeping the boy's mind off the storm hour after hour. Finally, with the coming of dawn, the boy decided that he would stick it out.

Soon thereafter the last of the famous Swampscott fishing schooners made its final journey, and according to the government, Egg Rock Light no longer needed a keeper. After a visit of the inspector, the Lighthouse Department decided to place an Aga automatic beacon inside the lens of the old tower, and the last resident left Egg Rock Light.

The automatic light machinery was installed in the fall of 1919. It was only a few years, however, before the government decided that even the automatic light was an unnecessary beacon, and in 1922 came the announcement that the light would be abolished, the tower taken down, and the house on the island offered for sale.

On April 17, 1922, for the first time in two-thirds of a century, Egg Rock was in complete darkness. It was never lighted again. The tender *Mayflower* later made its final trip to the rock to remove the automatic apparatus, and as dusk fell over the bay that night, the *Mayflower* steamed out to sea, thus severing all connections that Egg Rock had enjoyed with the Lighthouse Department.

It is said that the light keeper's home at Egg Rock was sold for five dollars, and that all the purchaser had to do was to take it down off the eighty-foot cliff and get it ashore. Work started in September for the accomplishment of this purpose. A gang of men began the difficult tedious job of transplanting the house to the mainland. Local fishermen, sailing by the ledge, skeptically watched the operations. Several predicted that unless the weather was right there would be no launching at all, and they were correct. By the sixteenth of September the building had been moved about halfway down the precipitous rock when plans were delayed. October came and still the building remained near the base of the island.

A few days later the attempt was made to move the house out aboard the waiting barge. Suddenly the huge Manila rope snapped with a report that could be heard for miles, and the keeper's house slowly rolled over on its side and, gathering momentum as it went, slid into the water with a crash of breaking timbers and smashing window panes. The surrounding coastline was covered with debris for the next few weeks as the lighthouse building was broken up by the waves. The last remains of Egg Rock Light were gathered by the thrifty driftwood enthusiasts and stored in cellars along the shore.

27

Graves Light

Lighthouse builder Royal Luther of Malden, Massachusetts, landed in a small boat at Graves Ledge in Boston's outer harbor during the summer of 1902 to examine the rocks in the vicinity. Northeast Graves, a pinnacle off by itself, had been suggested as a possible location for the planned lighthouse, but after landing there Luther decided against it. He chose the central body of rock as a suitable area for the construction of the tower.

There were many exciting adventures during the two years 1903–1905, when Luther superintended the building of Graves Light. The cutting of the granite blocks began at Cape Ann early in 1903, and actual work at the lighthouse site commenced June 1 of that year. After necessary blasting operations had been completed, a landing stage, timber bulkhead, and platform were set up. The stone schooner *A. J. Miller* was moored off the ledge, ready to take the men aboard should an emergency arrive.

The first Cape Ann granite was landed at Graves Ledge on August 11, 1903. The lowest course, thirty feet in diameter, was laid on a previously prepared surface just four feet above the low tide mark. Work progressed so rapidly that by October 31, when work was suspended for the year, twenty-one courses had been completed to a height of forty-two feet.

While the stone cutting was proceeding at Rockport, the iron work was finished at Boston, and a beautiful first-order lens was almost completed in Paris. By July 1, 1904, forty-four courses rose to a height of eighty-eight feet above Graves Ledge, but the work could not be finished that year.

The following June the lantern was brought out to the tower on a lighter, and by midsummer of 1905 all was in readiness for the station to begin operation. Other work done in connection with the building of the light consisted of the construction of a granite oil house ninety feet south of the tower with a footbridge connecting it to the light. Two thousand tons of riprap protect the wharf from the northeast gales.

On the night of September 1, 1905, Keeper Elliot C. Hadley climbed the lighthouse ladder to illuminate Boston Bay with the most powerful beam in Massachusetts history, 380,-000 candlepower. Graves Light long held the New England record for power. In 1910 Keeper Hadley, who had also seen service at Plum Island and Baker's Island, made the following statement:

"The Graves doesn't get pounded so hard in a Northeast as an Easterly, and Southeast is the worst. . . . I've stood on the bridge and looked up at solid water rushing in toward the ledges. I don't know how far up the solid water comes. I've been knocked down by it on the wharf beside the light, and opening a window to look out more than half-way up the tower, I've had as much as three buckets-full dashed in my face!"

George Lyons, who had served for twenty-two years at Egg Rock, was the next keeper. Other keepers were Captains

Towle, Carter, and P. S. King. Octavius Reamy was appointed to Graves Light in 1924.

Keeper Llewellyn Rogers relieved Octavius Reamy on the latter's retirement from the service. During Rogers' career there were three shipwrecks in the vicinity. In 1936 the *Romance* sank after a collision with the steamer *New York* during a heavy fog, but all aboard escaped safely. The *City of Salisbury,* called the "Zoo Ship," hit a sunken reef off Graves Light in 1938. Although there was no loss of life, the million-dollar cargo was ruined. All that year excursion boats visited the wreck, which proved to be the most spectacular shipping disaster in Boston Harbor history. Late that fall the vessel rolled off the ledge during a northeasterly and went to the bottom.

In the early morning hours of January 21, 1941, the fishing schooner *Mary E. O'Hara* passed Graves Light and headed for the inner harbor. Suddenly there was a crash, and the *O'Hara* slowly sank in forty feet of water. The schooner had struck an anchored barge. The frightened men scrambled up into the icy rigging, and waited for rescue. One by one they dropped off as their strength failed them, until only five remained alive. With the coming of dawn, the survivors were rescued by the trawler *North Star,* but the loss of nineteen men made it the third worst disaster in the history of Boston Harbor.

The rock plovers call at Graves Light in the winter time. Hundreds of them settle on the ledges that at low tide stretch out for a quarter mile, and the keepers find the birds an enjoyable diversion. The plovers feed by driving their long, sharp beaks into the barnacle shells attached to the rocks, and seem to thrive on this simple diet.

If you should ever visit Graves Light, there is much to observe. When you row ashore there, look up at the finely chiseled block of granite over the doorway on which there is the inscription "1903," the date when construction began on the tower. Climbing a heavy copper ladder on the western side of the lighthouse, you reach the first stage, forty feet above the ledge. Here is found the covered cistern, which is thirty-five feet deep and holds hundreds of gallons of water. The tank is filled twice a year with water brought out to the ledge by the tender. The second stage is the engine room, where two semi-Diesel engines that run the fog horn are ready for any emergency. Pity the poor light keepers when the steady racket from the engines makes life almost unbearable during a foggy season. At the third level is the kitchen, neat and clean at all times. The bunk room is on the fourth floor, two double bunks serving to accommodate four men if necessary. The fifth staging, the library and watch room, where the men spend their leisure time, is very cozy. The radio, TV and telephone are connecting links with the mainland. The telephone was installed during World War I. The sixth stage holds the mechanism for the light, while the light itself occupies the two floors above. A wonderful panorama awaits you at the top of Graves Light. The view is unsurpassed on a clear day, and I shall not attempt to describe it.

Graves Ledge was named for Thomas Graves, vice-admiral of John Winthrop's fleet and a resident of Lynn who became America's first foreign trader. The builder of Graves Light, Royal Luther, died in February 1943 at the advanced age of eighty-seven. Graves Ledge Light seems destined to stand for many generations as a memorial to these two useful Americans.

The candlepower at present is 1,400,000 and the characteristic is a double flash every six seconds.

28

Boston Light

America's first lighthouse was established on Little Brewster Island in Boston Harbor. Of course, there were lighted beacons before this across the Boston Light Channel in Hull, and we know of other beacons established earlier at Vera Cruz, Mexico, but the first lighthouse, as we know them today, with an enclosed light in a house, was the illuminated tower at Little Brewster Island.

As early as 1673 there was a beacon at Point Allerton, Hull, for on March 9, 1674, the selectmen of Hull, which includes what is Nantasket Beach today, asked the General Court if certain considerations could be given them for their trouble that year "about the setting up and wardinge off the Beacon erected on Poynt Allerton By order off the Honoured Counsell." In 1678 Captain James Oliver was sent to Hull by the Council to live at the "island" there. At that time the high tides separated Point Allerton from the rest of Hull, as Nantasket Beach was not by then built up to its present height above water.

In 1680 Jaspar Dankers and Peter Sluyter visited Boston. In Danker's Journal we read the following, translated from the Dutch:

"There are many small islands before Boston, well on to fifty, I believe, between which you sail on to the town. A high one, or the highest, is the first that you meet. It is twelve miles from the town and has a beacon upon it which you can see from a great distance, for it is in other respects naked and bare."

One of the first mentions of a lighthouse in America can be found in Clough's *New England Almanac* for 1701, where we read, "Q. Whether or no a Light-House at Alderton's point, may not be of great benefit to Mariners coming on these Coasts?" Twelve years later John George, a merchant, representing his associates in Boston, proposed the "Erecting of a Light Hous & Lanthorn on some Head Land at the Entrance of the Harbor of Boston for the Direction of Ships & Vessels in the Night Time bound into the said Harbour."

When this proposal was read in General Court, it met with immediate response. A committee headed by Lieutenant Governor William Tailer included Eliakim Hutchinson, Andrew Belcher, John Clark, Addington Davenport, Samuel Thaxter, and Major Thomas Fitch. They conferred with George and his associates, and made plans to provide a lighthouse at the entrance to Boston Harbor.

Boston was America's center in the early eighteenth century from a maritime point of view. Many of her merchants and shipowners had followed the sea when younger and were willing and anxious that the port be properly protected by a lighthouse. Almost half a century went by after Boston Light was built before New York was considered important enough to have a lighthouse at the entrance to its harbor.

On May 13, 1713, in the Boston town meeting, it was noted that "the Town of Boston may have the preference before any particular persons" in putting up and maintaining the lighthouse. Six months later the court passed the order for the erection of the light, and the Boston Light Bill was passed July 23, 1715. The exact wording of the act authorizing the first lighthouse in the Western Hemisphere follows:

"Whereas the want of a lighthouse at the entrance to the harbour of Boston hath been a great discouragement to navigation by the loss of the lives and estates of several of his majesty's subjects; for prevention thereof—
"Be it enacted . . .
"That there be a lighthouse erected at the charge of the Province, on the southermost part of the Great Brewster, called Beacon Island, to be kept lighted from sun setting to sun rising.
"That from and after the building of the last lighthouse, and kindling a light in it, usefull for shipping coming into or going out of the harbour of Boston, or any other harbour within the Massachusetts Bay there shall be paid to the receiver of impost, by the master of all ships and vessells, except coasters, the Duty of one penny per Tun, inwards, and also one penny per Tun, outwards, and no more, for every Tun of the burthen of the said Vessel, before they load or unlade the goods therein."

George Worthylake, whose father had lived at George's Island for many years, was chosen as first keeper of the newly established Boston Light. Arriving at Little Brewster Island, Worthylake found all in readiness for the official illumination of the tower. On September 14, 1716, Keeper George Worthylake climbed the high tower of Boston Light and lighted it for the first time.

Worthylake's salary was fifty pounds a year, but he probably made much more as a pilot for vessels entering Boston Harbor. In addition, he owned a flock of sheep that he herded in his spare time. In 1717 Worthylake petitioned for an increase in salary, as the terrible storms the previous winter had prevented him from watching his sheep at Great Brewster Island. Because of this, fifty-nine sheep wandered out on the Great Brewster Spit and drowned when the tide came in and washed them off the bar.

The first dramatic episode in the history of America's oldest light occurred on November 3, 1718, when Keeper Worthylake was returning to the lighthouse from Boston, where he had gone to collect his pay. While off Lovell's Island in the Narrows, Worthylake went aboard a sloop lying nearby. His wife Ann and daughter Ruth were with him.

The Worthylake family boarded the sloop while its master James Nichols was away from the vessel. They were invited aboard by a passenger, John Edge, with whom they "tarried on board about an hour." During this period they ate and "drank very friendly . . . tho not to Excess."

Between ten and eleven o'clock the lighthouse boat put off from the sloop in the direction of Boston Light, and Mr. John Edge was aboard with the Worthylakes. Back at Boston Light Ann Worthylake, daughter of George Worthylake, awaited the return of her family, with Mary Thompson, a friend then living on the island. The two girls watched the lighthouse boat come up to the mooring, located in the lee of the island. Ann instructed the slave Shadwell to row out in the island canoe, or lapstreak boarding boat, and bring in the three Worthylakes and their guest John Edge. This was between twelve and one o'clock.

The usual story has been that the weather was rough and the gale capsized the craft, but in the depositions made before the coroner there is no mention of a bad storm or gale. As far as we can tell, the canoe, loaded with George Worthylake, his wife Ann, their daughter Ruth, John Edge, and the slave

Shadwell, started ashore from the mooring near the light-house, when suddenly young Ann and her friend Mary saw "the s^d Worthylake, his wife & others swimming or floating on the water, with their boat Oversett." The melancholy statement of the two girls ends with the sentence: "the Depo-nents believe [it was] between twelve & one oClock that day when they Discovered the Boat or Canno Oversett & their Dead ffriends in Distress—and further say not—"

Evidently when Worthylake's body was found, the money which he had received in Boston was missing, and various people were questioned as to where it might have gone. The Waters family, then living on Lovell's Island, felt it necessary to make a statement regarding the entire incident:

> George Worthylake
> Ann his Wife
> Ruth his Daughter
> Mr. John Edge
> Shadwell Negro

"William Waters of Lovel's Island & William Waters Junr of Lawful Age Testify & say That on Monday last they saw the Lighthouse boat near a sloop lying in the Narrows; and after-wards they saw the boat put off towards the Lighthouse Island, between ten & Eleven a Clock; and on Wednesday morning Mary Tomson and Anne Worthylake Daughter of George Worthylake belonging to the Island came to Lovels Island in a canno & Informed the Deponents That the s^d George Worthylake his wife Ann & Daughter Ruth & Negro Slave Shadwell together with another Man were Drowned & driven near the shoar and soon after the Deponents with Capt Gould & Wm Walters of Boston, & some others assisted in carrying the Dead Corpses of the persons above-named on Shoar. They the Deponents took nothing from them & believe that none who assisted in pulling them on Shoar took any thing from them and further the Deponents Say not— Signed and sworn before the

Jury this 6th Novr 1718   William Waters
Att^y Samuel Tyley   Coroner   William Waters"

After the inquisition concluded, the bodies of the three members of the Worthylake family were interred in a common grave at Copp's Hill Burying Grounds, with a single triple headstone marking the resting place.

Young Benjamin Franklin was interested in the tragedy at the lighthouse, and wrote a ballad about the disaster. Thirteen years old at the time, Franklin sold his "Lighthouse Tragedy" on the streets of Boston.

Mr. Robert Saunders, who is mentioned as a sloop captain in 1711, was now ordered to go to "Beacon Island and take care of the Lighthouse." Within a few days he also perished in the ocean, and Boston Light gained the doubtful reputation of losing its first two keepers by drowning. Although Saunders was not in service long enough to be officially appointed, we should honor his sacrifice by calling him the second "Keeper of Boston Light."

The merchants of Boston now recommended Captain John Hayes, an experienced mariner, for the position of keeper of the light, and he was appointed by the Court on November 18, 1718. The duties of the keeper were many and varied at this period in the history of Boston Harbor. He was health officer, pilot for the vessels coming in and going out of Boston Harbor, custodian of the fog gun, and keeper of the light.

John Hayes, called by the late Rufus Candage "an able-bodied and discreet person," received at first fifty pounds a year, but when he petitioned for an increase in salary, the court raised his annual pay to seventy pounds. In his petition he mentions the habit of entertaining the mariners on the island to make a little extra money for himself, but says that he "has found the same prejudicial to himself, as well as the Town of Boston, and therefore has left off giving Entertainment."

On June 29, 1719, Hayes asked for a gallery to be built on the seaside of the lighthouse so that he could "come to the Glass to clear off the Ice & Snow in the Winter Time, whereby the Said Light is much obscured." He also asked, "That a great Gun may be placed on the Said Island to answer Ships in a Fogg." The court took steps to prevent ice from forming on the glass of the light, and also sent a cannon to Little Brewster Island. The gun, Fitz-Henry Smith, Jr., suggests, was probably taken from Long Island. In the picture of Boston Light drawn by Burgess around 1729, the gun stood near the tower. The date 1700 is engraved on the gun.*

On January 13, 1720, a bad fire broke out at Boston Light, caused "by the Lamps dropping on ye wooden Benches & snuff falling off & setting fire." Captain Hayes tells us that "ye said fire was not occasioned by ye least neglect of ye Memorialist." Whether or not Memorialist Hayes was to blame, £221 s16 d1 was expended to repair the damage done by the fire. Hayes received his salary only after an interview with the council as to the cause of the fire.

Two years later Hayes had a hard time inspecting all the ships from plague-ridden European ports, and in this manner lost many piloting jobs. The court granted him twenty pounds to repay him for the money lost.

The "Great Storm of 1723" did considerable damage to Boston Light. This gale, perhaps the most severe in the eighteenth century, raised a tide estimated at sixteen feet. This mark of 1723 is probably the highest in the history of Boston. Captain Hayes weathered this terrible gale, but the

---

* The gun was removed from the island and now stands on the grounds of the Coast Guard Academy at New London, Connecticut.

people of Boston feared the lighthouse had suffered. On visiting the island, a committee found that Boston Light had been damaged and the wharf ruined, but authorized expenditure of only £25 for urgent repairs. Substantial renovations were delayed, but three years later £490 was spent to put the island in proper order.

A bad gale blew up on September 15, 1727, while Captain John Bangs was bringing a sloop in past Boston Light, and the storm forced the boat ashore on Greater Brewster Spit. The next morning as the wind blew harder and the storm increased, Captain Bangs sent one of his crew to Captain Hayes at the light with a request that Hayes come out in his boat to help the sloop off. Hayes went to the assistance of the stranded vessel, but, the storm growing worse, efforts had to be abandoned until the tide turned. Hayes was then successful in pulling the sloop off the Spit. Leaving two of Bangs' crew in his boat to follow, he piloted the craft safely into Boston. The two sailors in Hayes' craft ran onto the rocks near South Battery and damaged the vessel considerably. Hayes told the court the boat was "old and crazy" and unfit for future service, but he was advised to get the craft repaired. The government paid all of the expenses except £15, which they charged up to Captain Bangs. Probably the next time John Bangs brought his sloop into Boston Harbor he steered amply clear of that stretch of sand and rocks on which Bug Light now stands.

The infirmities of age finally forced Hayes to retire from active service, and on August 22, 1733, he notified the government he would leave the service when his year was up.

The merchants of Boston now petitioned for the appointment of Robert Ball, who became the next keeper of Boston Light. Once firmly established at Little Brewster, Ball made a careful survey of the piloting business in Boston Harbor, becoming quite upset upon realizing that other sailing craft in the harbor were taking his business away from him. He soon petitioned the General Court for the right to have preference, as the others never worked in the winter while his was a year-round task. The other pilots decoyed the masters of ships coming into the harbor by "wearing a wide vane such as properly belongs to the province boat, and of the same color and livery." The court gave Ball permission to be the "established pilot" of the harbor for the next three years, and allowed him to keep two well-fitted boats, unmistakably distinguished. It further decreed that any person who painted his boat with a similar vane would be fined five pounds, the fine to be given to Ball.

Robert Ball, whose period of service is longer than that of any other keeper, never received a set sum for taking care of the light, but petitioned every year for his salary. It seems to one perusing the records in the Massachusetts Archives that he spent most of his time petitioning the General Court!

In 1751 a bad fire damaged the lighthouse, so only the walls remained. A temporary light was now shown from a spar some distance from the remains of the lighthouse. The light was repaired at a cost of £1,170, and, as the court believed that "the Charge of such repairs should be bourne by those who receive the immediate benefit thereof," a higher duty was instituted.

Robert Ball, in addition to his regular duties at the light, was quite a real estate operator, owning three islands in Boston Harbor at the time of his death. Calf Island and Green Island were then given to his son John while his daughter Sarah received the Outer Brewster. Ball petitioned the court in February 1774 for his pay to November 19, 1773, and it is probable that his nephew, William Minns, was the actual keeper of the light from that time until the British took over the island in 1774.

The name of the man who kept the light while it was

under English rule will, in all probability, remain a mystery.

Early in July 1775, the Provincial Congress wished to have the lamp and the oil removed, as the harbor was then blocked up and the establishment at the island useless. On the twentieth of July, Major Vose, leading a small detachment of American troops, visited Boston Light, where the men burned the wooden parts of the lighthouse. On their way back from Little Brewster Island they were met by an armed British schooner, but they outmaneuvered the English ship and reached the mainland. An eyewitness, quoted by Frothingham in his *Siege of Boston,* says that he saw "the flames of the light house ascending up to Heaven, like grateful incense, and the ships wasting their powder." The Americans had already cut one thousand bushels of grain in Hull, and now returned safely through the American lines with all their spoils.

The British began at once to repair the lighthouse, and the workmen as they labored were guarded by the British marines. But the Americans were not ones to allow the rebuilding to continue, so Washington placed Major Tupper in charge of three hundred men, who, on July 31, started from Dorchester and Squantum for Boston Light. They were successful in landing their armed whaleboats at Little Brewster Island, and the historic Battle of Boston Light began. A writer of the period tells us that:

> When Tupper and his men had landed there
> Their enemies to fight them did prepair
> But all in vain they could not them withstand
> But fell as victims to our valient band.

The guard defeated, Tupper destroyed the work done on the lighthouse and prepared to leave the island. The tide, however, had gone out and his whaleboats were left stranded there. In the meantime, the British had sent their own small boats to the island, and as the Americans finally pushed their boats into deep water, they were attacked by the English troops.

The Americans were helped in this new skirmish by a field piece under the command of Major Crane at Nantasket Head. When the situation looked threatening to the Yankees trying to leave the island, a direct shot from the American gun crashing into one of the English boats turned the tide of battle. After the British retired to the boats, it was found that only one American had been killed, while the English losses were comparatively heavy. Major Tupper brought a badly wounded British soldier to Hull, where he soon died. His gravestone is still pointed out by the older inhabitants of Hull.

George Washington was so pleased with the work of Major Tupper that he commended the major and his men for their "gallant and soldier-like behavior in possessing themselves of the enemie's post at the lighthouse."

After the British left Boston on March 17, 1776, they lingered down the harbor menacing all the towns of the bay. Samuel Adams was quite indignant that nothing was done to make the British leave the harbor and suggested in a letter that the various islands be fortified. Tudor tells us in his diary that eight ships, two snows, two brigs, and a schooner still remained in the harbor. On June 13, 1776, American soldiers landed on Long Island and at Nantasket Hill; the next day they opened fire on the fleet and soon had the British ships at their mercy. The British vessels weighed anchor and sailed down the harbor, but they sent a boat ashore at Boston Light, leaving a time charge which blew up the lighthouse, thus repaying the Americans who had twice damaged the light under British rule. It has been said that Boston Light was the last spot occupied by a hostile force in

Boston Harbor, but the British landed at the outer islands during the War of 1812.

A guard of Americans landed at Little Brewster Island shortly after the light was blown up and recovered much useful material from the debris. The council met in Boston on September 3, and decreed that as "the top of the old lighthouse was unfit for further use, it should be delivered to the committe to supply the cannon with ladles."

John Hancock, the governor of Massachusetts, notified the Legislature on November 8, 1780, that no light existed at the entrance to Boston Harbor, but thirty months passed without action being taken. The Boston Marine Society then addressed a message to the Senate and the House of Representatives, and pointed out that Boston was without a lighthouse to guide the shipping to its wharves, and that such a serious defect would have to be remedied before the people of Boston could expect a return of the days of good shipping. This petition had more effect than Governor Hancock's message of 1780, as the very next month the commissary-general of Massachusetts was directed to erect a lighthouse on the site of the old structure. The sum granted by the legislature, £1,000, lasted until the lighthouse was nearly completed, when an additional £450 was appropriated to finish the job.

The new lighthouse measured seventy-five feet high, with the walls at the base seven and a half feet thick, tapering to two feet six inches at the top. The lantern, fifteen feet high, was of octagonal shape, and its diameter was approximately eight feet. The above information was taken from the article on the light that appeared in *Massachusetts Magazine* for February 1789, written by Keeper Thomas Knox, who had been appointed November 28, 1783.

The famous vessel *United States* made her final voyage in 1784. The last entry in her log book, dated May 26, 1784, reads as follows: "Got Thomas Knox, a pilot, on board, just without the lighthouse, and at 3½ got along Mr. Hancock's wharf at Boston. All well."

Thomas Knox brought his parents out to the light, and both his father and mother passed away in the year 1790. Back in 1761 his father had purchased Nix's Mate Island, and Thomas now became its owner. He finally sold it to the Commonwealth of Massachusetts.

Thomas Knox continued in the service of the Lighthouse Department until 1811, when he was succeeded by Jonathan Bruce. The new keeper brought his wife, Mary, to live at the lighthouse. The couple witnessed the thrilling encounter between the *Chesapeake* and the *Shannon,* June 1, 1813, the battle lasting but fifteen minutes. The well-trained crew of the English ship *Shannon* made short work of the American ship as the first six minutes practically decided the battle. Captain Lawrence of the *Chesapeake* was carried below, mortally wounded, and as he was lowered through the companionway he cried out to his men, "Don't give up the ship." As the deck of his boat was becoming a shambles, Lawrence's crew obeyed for only nine minutes, when they were forced to surrender the *Chesapeake* to Commander Broke of the English vessel.

Johnathan Bruce and his wife stayed on at the light after the war ended. The importance of his position as keeper of Boston Light was somewhat dimmed by the establishment of Long Island Light in 1819.

David Tower was the next keeper at Boston Light. The great December hurricanes of 1839, occurring on December 15, 21, and 27, threw more than a score of vessels onto the shores around Boston Harbor, but Tower was helpless to aid the crews of the Schooner *Charlotte* and the Bark *Lloyd* driven ashore at Nantasket. Less than five years after the triple hurricanes of 1839, David Tower died in service at Boston Light.

Joshua Snow became keeper on October 8, 1844. In that year many improvements inside the light were made. The lighthouse was equipped with a cast-iron circular stairway, having a central iron pipe and a wrought iron railing. "A cast iron deck and scuttle were put in, with iron window frames, a large outside door of iron, and an inside door with frame and large arch piece over it." The improvements of 1844 can be seen today, except where repairs have been made.

Captain Tobias Cook of Cohasset relieved Snow in the last week of December 1844. While Cook was keeper of Boston Light, James Lloyd Homer, the man who wrote as the "Shade of Alden," paid him a visit. He tells us that the light was eighty-two feet above the sea and makes the mistake of believing the steps leading up into the light were of stone. There were two wharves on the southwestern side of the island, according to Homer, and anyone steering his boat between the two piers would be sure of a cordial reception. A rather amazing development at Boston Light was the establishment about this time of a "Spanish" cigar factory, with young girls brought from Boston to work at Little Brewster Island. This business, set up to practice a fraud on the good people up in the city, was soon broken up, and the girls were sent back to Boston to work under less romantic conditions. Homer comments on the incongruous situation of a Spanish factory at Boston Light.

Tobias Cook resigned as keeper in 1849, and Captain William Long of Charlestown became the new official in charge of the light, bringing his family, including a daughter Lucy, out to Little Brewster. Through the kindness of Mrs. Herbert L. Wilber, I have been allowed to read the diary of her grandmother, Lucy Maria Long, which was kept at Boston Light from October 19, 1849, until October 2, 1851. I will quote a few of the entries from this almost priceless relic of Boston Harbor life over a century ago:

"Sunday, October 21, 1849. Pleasant weather in the morning. I went into the Light House for the first time, the rest of the day was spent in rambling among the rocks.

"Monday, October 29.—Pleasant weather, in the forenoon I went in the cutter's boat to carry Antoinette to the Pilot Boat 'Hornet.' In the afternoon I went over to the island, on returning saw the body of a man on the bar, supposedly washed from the wreck of the vessel, lost on Minot's Ledge."

At low tide it is possible to walk across the bar from Boston Light to Greater Brewster Island, and from there well along Brewster Spit; this is the route Miss Long took many times. She tells us that a gentleman came out to the lighthouse on November 10, 1849, to try to induce her to go to Fort Warren to teach the children of the workmen, but she did not accept the offer as she enjoyed the social life of Little Brewster Island too much to leave it. When her father went ashore, Lucy lit the great light herself. Her record of one of these occasions follows:

"Mon. Dec. 31.—A snowstorm, in the morning, George came over to wind up the clock, and I cleaned the light, at night I light the Light."

Other interesting incidents of 1850 are included in the following excerpts:

"Wed. Mar. 6.—Pleasant weather, in the morning two Pilots from the June came and wound up the clock, in the forenoon Mr. Rollund and Mr. Longly came down in the Pleasure Boat Flirt to set some glass in the Lantern, the Steamship America sailed, at night I light the Lights.

"Sunday, May 19.—Pleasant weather, in the morning Mr. Dolliver went to Boston in the Boat June, in the forenoon

William and myself walked on the spit as far as the beacon. At noon Mr. Phillips and Mr. Perry called from the Islands.

"Monday, Aug. 26.—Pleasant weather, this morning Albert came down in his boat."

The above-mentioned Albert was the Albert Small of the unusual lighthouse romance that culminated in the proposal at the top of the lighthouse. This courtship between Lucy Maria Long and Pilot Albert Small went on for many months, in spite of the scores of other young pilots who made Little Brewster Island the mecca of their leisure hours. Day after day we read of as many as six pilots landing at once to enjoy a social hour or two at the light.

One afternoon, accompanied by Sarah Godbold, a six-year-old chaperon, Lucy Maria Long and Albert Small went up to the top of Boston Light, presumably to admire the wonderful view from that well-known vantage point. Albert, however, had an important matter that he wished to discuss with Lucy at this time, and believing the little girl would not realize the full implications of what would occur, led Lucy a few feet away and asked her to marry him. Unfortunately for us, she did not enter a detailed account of the incident in her diary, but we do know that her answer given at the top of Boston Light was "Yes."

Sarah was burdened with a very large secret for such a little girl. As soon as the three returned to the lightkeeper's house she informed the family of all that had transpired, to the embarrassment of the happy young couple, but the parents and the other pilots were quick to come to the rescue of the blushing pair with hearty congratulations. The culmination of this lighthouse romance came on June 16, 1853, when Lucy Maria Long and Albert Small were married.

In 1851 Captain William Long was succeeded at Boston

Light by Zebedee Small, whose pay at this time was four hundred dollars a year. During his regime, the Lighthouse Board of the United States Government was established. Congress had been investigating the conditions in the Lighthouse Department, and in the act that established the board it made restrictive regulations affecting those merchants furnishing supplies to lighthouses. Certain ship chandlers had been detected in giving concessions to the purchasing agents who supplied the lighthouses with food, and Congress was determined to prevent such manipulations in the future.

A visitor to Little Brewster while Small was in charge left an account of his impressions while there:

"Boston Outer Light, with its natural standard or tiny island, seems placed by the hand of nature in the spot for the special purpose to which the hand of man appropriated it. Though greatly exposed to the storms, and facing the severe eastern gales that blow up between the capes from the oceans, it yet is perfectly safe and secure in the hardest weather. Near the base of the light there is placed a gun, which is fired at intervals in foggy weather to warn off the mariners who may have got too near the breakers. A fog bell is also at hand to be rung by the keeper of the light in thick weather. It is difficult to express in words the thrill of delight that nerves the breast of the tempest-tossed mariner of the long voyage, when Boston Light heaves into sight, and its bright steady eye beams forth over the sea."

Hugh Douglass became the next keeper of Boston Light on June 2, 1853. The only important change while Douglass was at the lighthouse was in the rapidity of the light's revolution. In 1842, I. W. P. Lewis referred to the mechanism that turned the light as the "machine of rotation," and the speed of revolution at that time was three minutes. Elaborate changes were made by 1854 when the speed was increased to one minute, thirty seconds. Douglass resigned the year Bug Light was built, 1856.

Douglass was succeeded by Moses Barrett, a native of Gloucester. Boston Light was provided with the Fresnel lamp in the third year of Barrett's term and at the same time the tower was raised to its present height of ninety-eight feet. It was now listed as a second-order station.

Barrett was at Boston Light until late in 1862, and his last two years spent there were full of adventures. When Fort Sumter was fired on he knew that exciting times were ahead. Boatload after boatload of soldiers sailed by the light in the first year of the Civil War; Captain Wilkes took Mason and Slidell by Lighthouse Island to Fort Warren; Belle Boyd, the Rebel spy, was brought into the harbor a little later, and noticed the white shaft on Little Brewster Island on her way to Boston.

The incident that impressed Barrett more than all the events connected with the war occurred on Sunday morning on November 3, 1861, and was the worst tragedy in the history of Boston Harbor. The square rigger *Maritana*, 991 tons, had sailed out of Liverpool on the twenty-fifth of September with Captain Williams in command. She ran into heavy seas coming into Massachusetts Bay and approached Boston in a howling southeaster with a blinding snow falling. About one o'clock in the morning she sighted Boston Light and headed for the beacon that she was never to pass.

The *Maritana* crashed onto Shag Rocks and the crew and passengers were soon fighting for their lives. The sailors cut the masts away. The vessel now showed signs of breaking up, and the passengers and crew were ordered into the weather chains.

About eight-thirty the great ship broke in two, and Captain

Williams, standing on the quarter-deck at the time, was crushed to death. Seven people floated to Shag Rocks on the top of the pilot house, while five others were successful in swimming to the same ledge. After the hull of the ship had broken in two, fragments of the wreckage started to come ashore on both sides of the island, and the watchers on Lighthouse Island saw a body in the surf. By afternoon the sea and the storm had quieted appreciably, and Captain Barrett's signal to Hull was acknowledged. The bodies of the unfortunates now started to wash up on the beach, and that of Captain Williams was among the first. At two o'clock Pilot Boat No. 2, the *William Starkey,* sent a dory ashore at Shag Rocks and rescued the survivors of the tragedy. The boat was manned by Captain Samuel James of Hull, a member of the famous lifesaving family.

It was not until the following March that the last member of the crew was found and buried at Little Brewster Island. In the spring of 1862 the wife of Captain Williams came down to the island to receive her husband's watch and other keepsakes that the keeper had been saving for her, and sat with her children on the rocks under the lighthouse. She spent hours looking out at Shag Rocks, the ledge that had broken her family apart forever.

Charles E. Blair became keeper of Boston Light on November 20, 1862, and saw the captured crews of the Confederate ships *Tacony* and *Atlanta* on their way to Fort Warren. Six of these prisoners escaped on the night of August 19, 1863, and two of them sailed by the island on their way down to Maine, where they were captured. Blair returned to the mainland on July 18, 1864, and was replaced by the celebrated Thomas Bates.

Bates took charge of a rescue on January 31, 1882, at the time the *Fanny Pike* went ashore on Shag Rocks. She went to pieces quickly, but Captain Bates rowed out to the little ledge and took the crew off safely. Assistant Keeper Bailey and Charles Pochaska, a young fisherman who lived on Middle Brewster Island, helped him make the successful but dangerous trip.

Bates spent many pleasant nights at the lighthouse, and Assistant Keeper Edward Gorham, with his accordion, helped along the musical program that they all enjoyed on Sunday evenings. Bates, admonishing the others to sing louder, would tell Gorham to "bear down" on his accordion as they sang *When the Roll is Called up Yonder* and *Crossing the Bar,* every sailor's favorite. After almost thirty years of service Thomas Bates died on the island on April 6, 1893.

Alfred Williams assumed charge until the official appointment was made on May 3, 1893, when Albert M. Horte was made keeper of Boston Light. Horte was keeper less than a year, relinquishing his post to Henry L. Pingree, whose son, Wesley, became interested in Albert M. Horte's sister Josephine. Wesley Pingree and Josephine Horte were later married, spending their honyemoon at Deer Island Light.

About this time the Massachusetts Institute of Technology was experimenting on various types of foghorns in their endeavor to develop one that would be able to penetrate the tricky "Ghost Walk," located about six or seven miles east of Boston Light. Twenty or thirty boys were sent to live on the island, to try out various devices.

Early one morning in 1897, as Pingree's son Wesley was walking down to start the fire for the fog signal, he was amazed to see the steamer *Portland* in between Shag Rocks and the Outer Brewster. She backed out without striking, but a glance at the map will give the reader an idea of the craft's precarious situation.

Keeper Henry Pingree left Boston Light on November 1, 1909. His successor, Levi B. Clark, witnessed the terrible gale on Christmas Day, 1909, when the five-masted schooner

Davis Palmer hit on Finn's Ledge and went down with all hands. She was heavily loaded with coal, and the captain, Leroy M. Kowen, had hoped to dock before noon. His wife, living in Malden, had Christmas dinner cooking when she heard the terrible news. Part of the wreckage of the vessel washed ashore at Boston Light.

During the week of September 3, 1910, the Squantum Air Meet took place, and Claude Graham-White made his memorable flight to Boston Light from Squantum. Assistant Keeper Jennings waved down to the flyer as the airplane roared by just below the top of the light. An eyewitness of the event, Dr. William M. Flynn of Dorchester, tells us that there was a line of motor boats and naval launches stretched all the way from Squantum out to the light, as many thought that Graham-White would surely drop into the water at some point in his trip.

Charles H. Jennings was appointed to take charge of the beacon on Little Brewster Island on May 1, 1916, and served during the hectic war days when the U-boat scares alarmed the coast. Before the war began, the two hundredth anniversary of the lighting of the beacon on Little Brewster Island was observed, on September 25, 1916.

Perhaps the most thrilling experience in which Jennings participated was the rescue of the men on the *U.S.S. Alacrity,* which was wrecked on the ice-covered ledges off Lighthouse Island on February 3, 1918, at three-forty-five in the morning. Captain Jennings, awakened by the sound of gunfire, aroused the assistant keepers, Lelan Hart and Charles Lyman, who rushed down to the shore. They saw the doomed ship and endeavored to reach it by firing the gun of the Massachusetts Humane Society. Four attempts were made, but each time the rope parted. Jennings now brought the dory down to the shore, and, assisted by sailors Hero and Harvey of the Naval Reserves, pushed the dory over the ice and into the surf.

Twenty-four men were clinging to the wreck of the *Alacrity* and their position was precarious. If they fell in between the ice cakes, they could not keep afloat and, if they stayed on the boat, she might soon slip off the ledge and sink. Jennings and his two assistants finally reached the wreck after a perilous trip, flung a line aboard, and began the rescue of the half-frozen sailors. Four times the men ran the gauntlet of ice, rocks, and raging surf until they finally succeeded in saving all twenty-four of the men. For this heroic deed Jennings later received a letter of commendation from William C. Redfield, Secretary of Commerce.

J. Lelan Hart succeeded Jennings as keeper of Boston Light. Hart's first knowledge of the islands of Boston Harbor was obtained during the shipwreck of his boat, loaded with lime, at Outer Brewster Island. The vessel was a lime coaster, *A. Heaton,* owned by A. C. Gay of Rockland, Maine. As the vapor whistle at Boston Light had been out of order, the ship crashed onto the rocks in the dense fog. The lime caught fire, and Captain Hart's ship burned to the water's edge. Fortunately, the captain and members of the crew escaped to safety by rowing to Boston Light in the life boats.

Maurice Babcock succeeded Lelan Hart in 1926. Babcock and his wife and family spent the fifteen succeeding years at the light.

On the second day of December 1934, a memorial list of the twenty-five keepers of Boston Light was unveiled in the lighthouse itself by Fitz-Henry Smith, Jr. The Coast Guard boat *Pueblos,* which took the party out to Lighthouse Island, had previously stopped at Spectacle Island to pick up Keeper Lelan Hart, and had put in at Lovell's Island to allow Keeper Charles Jennings to join the group.

In 1941 the Coast Guard took over the duties previously performed by the Lighthouse Service. It was my privilege to accompany Keeper Maurice Babcock, the final representative of the old Lighthouse Service, as he climbed America's oldest beacon for the last time. It was a sad journey we made that afternoon, and as we reached the lantern room he looked fondly at the lenses and the lighting apparatus with its gas mantle, all of which he would never see again. Then Maurice Babcock, twenty-fifth keeper of Boston Light, stepped out on the platform that surrounds the tower and looked out to sea. Neither of us spoke, but we each knew what was in the other's mind—the old days of the lighthouse service were gone forever, never to return.

On the retirement of Keeper Babcock the new man in charge at Boston Light was Ralph Clough Norwood. After many years as assistant at the light under the Lighthouse Service, Keeper Norwood was made a Coastguardsman when that branch of the government took over. An expert oarsman, he thought nothing of rowing twenty or thirty miles along the coast.

Boston Light, extinguished during World War II, was again in operation on July 2, 1945, its 100,000 candlepower flash sending out a warning from the focal point 102 feet above the sea.

On September 14, 1966, the two-hundred-and-fiftieth anniversary at the light, I quoted Homer's *Iliad* in reference to the "watch-fire's light." Elliot L. Richardson, now U.S. Attorney General, stood at my shoulder as I gave the quotation in Greek. He later gave the main address to the gathering.

The flash is now 1,800,000 candlepower at Boston Light, the oldest lighthouse in America.

29

Minot's Ledge Light

Historic Minot's Light is the most dangerous beacon in America. A visit to the tower is a never-to-be-forgotten experience. One may compare it with the first airplane ride, or an inlander's initial glimpse of the mighty ocean.

It had been a comparatively calm day the first time that we climbed Minot's Light, but with the sudden change of weather conditions for which New England is noted, we found ourselves watching the roughening seas with great personal interest. We were then standing on the lower turret of the 114-foot tower. Far below us the sea was gathering for a mighty surge. The wind, quiet in the forenoon, had been increasing in intensity until it was then almost gale force.

Away in the distance great waves were breaking, and on the ledges off the shore white foaming crests were in sharp relief to the scene we viewed from the top of Minot's Light. Then, with the sound of a muffled cannon roar, the billow struck. The immense granite tower quivered as the ocean momentarily reclaimed the ledge for its own, while we experienced a great but terrifying thrill when tons of water engulfed the base of the structure.

Such was our introduction many years ago to the most dangerous lighthouse in America. That morning we had arrived at the ledge. Because the sea, breaking against the tower, made landing a hazardous undertaking, we stood off until the loop of rope was lowered. Then the keepers hoisted us, one by one, up against the outside of the tower in the impromptu sling, until we gripped the ladder high above the waves.

The gale soon attained such velocity that the skipper of our boat was obliged to seek less perilous waters. Meanwhile, we were marooned on top of Minot's Light. Because of the shelving ledge, the waves at half-tide are usually more spectacular than when the tide is high. The wind increased and the billows were breaking with such savage fury that by early afternoon we were looking upon the sea in one of her angry moods. As we watched the waves sweep by, each of us was seized with a childlike helplessness.

A fortunate shift in the wind later that afternoon quieted the waves to some extent, allowing our skipper to return to the ledge. The keepers then lowered us into our waiting boat, and as we sailed away, our captain gave three farewell blasts on the whistle. While the assistant keeper waved in answer to our signal, the head keeper sounded three hammerlike strokes on the gigantic fog bell in the lighthouse, and we realized our visit was over. We had joined the favored few who have watched a gale from the top of Minot's Light.

John Smith was the first to mention the Indian tribe of Quonahassit, from which the name Conyhasset, as well as Cohasset, is derived. Minot's Ledge itself is one of the Quonahassit Rocks. Captain Smith had a narrow escape from death while visiting in what is now Cohasset. Because of a quarrel between the natives and his sailors, the Indians ambushed him on his way out of the harbor. His boat, approaching the open sea near Hominy Point in Cohasset, became the target for many arrows shot by the red men. Smith retaliated by firing his gun at the natives, and in his account says that he killed one of them and injured another. They continued out to sea without further trouble. Many believe that Smith Rocks off the shore have some connection with this incident.

These ledges off the rock-bound coast of Cohasset will always be dangerous reminders of the perils of the sea. It is probable that, since the earliest times, few years went by without a wreck or fatality on the Cohasset reefs. One of the early shipwrecks along the coast was that of the sloop owned by Captain Anthony Collamore, a noted citizen of Boston in the seventeenth century. When he sailed from Scituate to Boston with a load of wood on December 16, 1693, Collamore cut inside of Minot's Ledge and the boat hit a sunken reef. The sloop went down and all on board were thrown into the water. One by one they sank beneath the waves and were drowned.

Another tragedy at the ledge was added to the list of shipwrecks on December 6, 1818, when a northeast storm hurled the bark *Sarah & Susan* against Minot's Rock. Loaded with hemp and iron, the bark split in two, fore and aft, the superstructure breaking away from the keel and bilges. The crew of thirteen clung desperately to the wreckage as the vessel drifted toward the shore, but four were drowned before help came. The others were rescued by volunteers from Cohasset.

Inspector I. W. P. Lewis visited a majority of the lights along the Massachusetts coast during the time that he was representing the government in this section. On many of his trips he passed close to the Conyhasset Ledges, and visited Scituate Light several times. In 1843 he listed the wrecks which had taken place in the vicinity from 1832 to 1841, counting more than forty on neighboring reefs in that period. Lewis declared that there was greater need for a lighthouse on Minot's Ledge than on any other part of the New England coast. "The loss of lives and property have been annual, and will continue to occur until a light is established and the one at Scituate suppressed," was his statement.

Because of the activity of the Boston Marine Society and Inspector Lewis' report, the government finally took an interest in the possibility of a lighthouse at Minot's Ledge. Cohasset citizens and many others favored the construction of a stone tower, similar to the Eddystone Light off the coast of England. It was decided to send a competent engineer to Minot's Ledge and await his report on the technical side of the problem.

Down in Connecticut, at the entrance to Black Rock Harbor, Captain William H. Swift was now chosen to visit Cohasset and give his opinion on the possibility of building a light off the shore. After his arrival in Cohasset, Swift asked Captain Daniel Lothrop, a prominent underwriters' agent, to make a list of the shipping losses from 1817 to 1847. On April 15, 1847, Captain Lothrop presented him with an impressive compilation of ships, barks, brigs, ketches, and schooners lost in the general vicinity of Minot's Ledge.

In addition to the list of complete disasters, there were fifteen other vessels that suffered partial damages to the sum of $21,000, making in all a total shipwreck loss of $364,000. At least forty persons were drowned in the shipwrecks. With such an outsanding loss of lives and money in the short space of thirty years, we realize why there was so much agitation for a beacon to guide the mariners past these treacherous reefs.

After visiting various locations around the Cohasset shore, Captain Swift decided that Minot's Rock was the only suitable place for the proposed lighthouse. He argued against a stone tower, however, because there was not enough of the exposed surface of the rock available for the base of such a structure. Nevertheless it is only fair to point out that later, after Swift's lighthouse had crashed into the sea, exactly the same location was used for the erection of the new stone tower.

Captain William H. Swift of the Topographical Department believed in the theory of the iron pile light. This principle states that a lighthouse built on iron piles offers less resistance to the waves that pass harmlessly through the uprights than a stone tower against which the waves break with the full power of the sea behind them. He strongly urged this open-work style, and it is possible that his extreme enthusiasm decided the issue. Another point in the government's final decision was that iron was suitable economically. We must realize that Minot's Light was built by the Topographical Department, headed by a group of very sensitive individuals who were quick to take offense at any suggestion of Fifth Auditor Stephen Pleasonton, superintendent of American lighthouses.

It is impossible to overemphasize the extreme danger of Swift's undertaking. Conditions at the sea-swept ledge at Minot's Rock were at all times hazardous. Barely twenty-five feet wide, the ledge exposed at low tide was dry only two or three hours a day, and it was on this narrow rock that Swift planned to erect a seventy-five-foot structure. He was faced with difficulties that would have discouraged the ordinary engineer. The men could work only on very calm days when the tide was at its ebb.

After several reconnaissance trips had been made, the workmen landed machinery on the ledge from a schooner. Usually, unless it was too rough, the boat remained near the rock. When the daily work was finished, the men went aboard the schooner for the night. In this way much valuable time was saved. If a storm threatened, the craft sailed into Cohasset Harbor to await less tempestuous weather.

Swift made his plans carefully. Nine holes were to be drilled, twelve inches wide and five feet deep. Eight of them were to be placed in a circle whose diameter approximated twenty-five feet, while the ninth was to be located in the center of the circle. Iron piling ten inches in diameter would later be cemented into each hole, after which braces would be constructed to strengthen the piling.

The story of drilling through the solid rock out on the isolated ledge is one of constant struggle against the elements. A triangle was set on top of heavy spars and supported a platform high above the rock. On this platform the drilling machinery was installed. The cutting edge of the drill was in the shape of a Z, and fitted to a 600-pound iron shaft thirty feet long. The machine was technically described as having a wheel and axle furnished with tooth and pinion, and a crank or windlass at each end. The contrivance was placed on a frame of strongest oak, and required the combined strength of four men to operate. A cam and flywheel were attached to the axle, and with each revolution the drill went up and down about eight inches. When in operation the drill usually made about fifty strokes a minute. Four men worked twenty minutes each shift on the drilling machine.

Engineer Swift asserted that the holes were fashioned perfectly. But it was not entirely a simple job of mechanics. The triangle and drilling machinery were swept from the rock by two different storms during the first summer of 1847. On several occasions the workmen were thrown into the water by great waves that swept unexpectedly across the ledge, but none was drowned. It was indeed remarkable that no lives were ever lost in the building of either the old or the new lighthouse.

All summer long the workmen labored on the exposed ledge, and by October 25, 1847, when they ceased operations for the year, thirty-four men had worked at the rock. A daily average of twenty-one men toiled in danger on the ledge.

When the last wintry gust had departed and the spring sun

warmed the icy water, the men returned to their unfinished work on the ledge. New spars, this time forty-five feet long, were installed to support the triangle upon which the men worked. By the middle of August the nine holes had been drilled in the solid rock to a depth of five feet, and the first load of iron piling soon arrived.

By September 21 all nine piles were placed. Because of the uneven surface at the ledge, the length of the piling varied from thirty-five and one-quarter feet to thirty-eight and three-quarters feet. The outer piles slanted toward the center so that they met at the top in a circumference whose diameter was only fourteen feet. About nineteen feet above the rock the piles were braced horizontally by three-and-one-half-inch iron rods. Another series of horizontal braces was put in nineteen feet above the first series. Eight feet below the top of the piling there was a third set of braces, made of two-and-one-half-inch square iron rods.

The fundamental principle involved was to allow the sea to break through the tower without giving it too much resistance. Braces planned to strengthen the lower part of the tower were never put in, as it was believed they would lessen rather than increase the general security of the edifice. Later, the structure actually broke off where these braces had been planned to go.

A cast-iron spider, or capping, was now hoisted up to the top of the piling. It consisted of eight arms, one for each outside iron support, and weighed five tons. With the capping of the spider, the hardest part of the work was over, and only the keeper's quarters and lantern remained to be installed.

The keeper's quarters and the lantern room were erected, and the expensive French lantern with its fifteen reflectors was installed. Twenty-one inches in diameter, the silver-plated reflectors intensified the rays of the oil lamps. These individual lights were arranged in two circular rows, one above the other, appearing from the sea as a single unit of illumination.

The lantern room itself, built in the form of a polygon with sixteen faces, was eleven feet wide, six and one-half feet high, and was topped by a cast-iron ventilator. The sixteen plates of glass were forty-four by twenty-four inches, and three-eighths of an inch thick. Minot's Light was a fixed beacon, which flashed out an arc of 210 degrees around Massachusetts Bay.

The framework at Minot's Light had been slightly damaged, causing a delay in the lighting of the beacon. It has been said that the tower was first lighted on December 13, 1849, but in the words of the keeper, Isaac Dunham, the lamps were lighted for the first time on January 1, 1850, officially.

Although the passage of almost a century has somewhat obscured the story of Isaac Dunham's ten months at the first beacon, we are nevertheless able to mention many incidents that occurred there in 1850. We know the names of at least two of the men who assisted Keeper Dunham in his duties. They were his son, Isaac A. Dunham, usually confused with his father, and Russell Higgins of Eastham. As Keeper Dunham was at the first lighthouse at Minot's Ledge for a period of time almost twice as long as that of any other man, his remarks carry considerable weight. Until a few years ago, it was believed that all of the actual records at the light were lost when it fell into the sea on that wild April morning. The first logbook, however, left the light with Keeper Dunham, and was part of the estate of his granddaughter, Mrs. R. A. Elliott.

On the inside cover of his logbook Dunham wrote his name with the date December 1849, evidently the month he first came out to the light. The initial entry in the diary seems to prove conclusively that January 1, 1850 was the date for the first lighting. We shall quote from time to time directly out of the pages of Keeper Dunham's record, written while in the lonely tower on the ledge:

"January 1st 1850   Daily Journal
1   Drawn oil for the lantern
            and Light up the Light House
1   on Minots Rock for the first time
Tuesday   on the night of January the first
            1850."

At about half past four the morning of March 12, 1850, Keeper Dunham heard someone call "Halloa" at the foot of the lighthouse ladder. It was Captain Wilson, who had come to take Mr. Hemmenway back to the mainland. Since Assistant Higgins was on duty, Dunham decided to go back with Captain Wilson for some articles that he needed. While he was ashore the wind shifted to the east, and Dunham felt that a snowstorm was brewing. A light snow was falling and the wind was coming up as he launched his dory for the long row to the light. By the time he arrived at the rock, a thick snowstorm from the northeast had set in. Fortunately, however, the waves had not had time to make up, and Dunham landed safely at the ledge. In his logbook he reports:

"It came on to blow 5 minutes after we got the boat hooked on so that I could not have got on alone.

"Tues. 19th . . . Quite a fleet of vessels out of Boston.

"Sun. 31st Clensd the Lantern for Liting up For this months ends. and I thank God that I am yet in the Land of the Living—and that I have been preserved during the last winter and I hope and pray to be.—"

* * *

March was the last month of winter, but April turned out to be as severe as any winter month:

"April
"Fry 5 This day and the last night will long be remembered by me as one of the most trying that I ever experience during my life.

"the wind N. E. to E. blowing very hard with a sea running mountains high—it must be that we were in the hands of a merciful God for witch I am thankful that we are yet spared—have cleaned the light up.

"Sat. 6 The wind E. blowing hard with an ugly sea which makes the Light House real like a Drunken Man—I hope God will in mercy still the raging sea—or we must perish. We have made out to clean the lantern up.—

"God only knows what the end will be. At 4 P.M. the gale continues with great fury. It appears to me that if the wind continues from the East as it now is that we cannot survive the night—if it is to be so—O God receive my unworthy soul for Christ sake for in him I put my trust. . . .

"Mon 8th the Wind W.N.W. blowing very fresh which will kill the ground sea. Thanks be to God for this blessed wind. . . .

"July 2 . . . Higgins came on to the Light House. Very rough and had to swing from the Light House on a rope and drop on the Boat. it would have frightened Daniel Webster."

Keeper Isaac Dunham was so terrified by his experience during the April gale that he later wrote to the government requesting that the tower be strengthened and not allowed to succumb to the ravaging sea. This communication incurred the displeasure of the builder, sensitive Captain Swift, who professed the greatest confidence in the structure. Since the summer went by and no action had been taken, Isaac

Dunham resigned as keeper of Minot's Light on October 7, 1850. Captain Swift found another who believed in the safety of the lighthouse tower when he interviewed Captain John W. Bennett, an English sailor of twenty-five years' experience. Bennett, after his appointment, openly belittled the man who was leaving the service. This scoffing attitude did not make Dunham's lot a happy one. John W. Bennett's repentance came later, however, when his own words closely paralleled those of Dunham during the terrible gale.

The new keeper, known as a brave and energetic man, arrived at the Rock on October 7, 1850. Retiring Keeper Dunham, surfeited with memories of many terrible storms, did not relish Bennett's charges that there had been false statements circulated concerning the safety of the lighthouse. Dunham knew only too well how true those statements were, but he comforted himself with the thought that Bennett would soon change his mind.

Keeper Bennett hired a new crew of assistants from Cohasset, an Englishman by the name of Joseph Wilson and a Portuguese named Joseph Antoine. Arrangements were continued as they had been during Dunham's regime with two keepers always remaining at the light. A visitor to the rock at this time mentioned to Bennett the fact that the braces were constantly being sent to the Cohasset blacksmith shop for straightening and strengthening.

Bennett, nevertheless, was still undecided about the tower. In a letter dated October 9, 1850, Keeper Bennett wrote to the *Boston Journal:* "I desire to withhold my own opinion until I have snuffed a good strong north-easter. . . . Much remains to be done to secure it [the Light] from accident."

Keeper Bennett went on in his letter to suggest that the tower be braced by sinking iron rods into adjacent ledges, but the plan was later found to be impracticable.

A howling northeast storm in the late fall of 1850 completely changed Mr. Bennett's mind about the safety of the tower, and he notified Superintendent Philip Greeley that the light was in danger. A committee was assigned the duty of inspecting the structure at close hand. Unfortunately, the committee arrived during a perfectly calm sea. Observing the water lapping gently against the iron supports and noting as well the nine sturdily constructed iron pilings, they agreed that even in a severe storm the water would break harmlessly through the open iron work. The committee then returned to Boston, and in the comfort and security of the big city, decided against strengthening the light in any way, because, they affirmed, the great lighthouse was capable of weathering "any storm without danger."

On Sunday morning, March 16, the inhabitants of Boston witnessed the beginning of another terrible storm. An extremely high tide overflowed the wharves and piers of the city, causing considerable damage to the cellars of warehouses. Streets were flooded by the rising sea, and Boston became an island when the areas around Boston Neck were inundated. But out at Minot's Ledge, eighteen miles from the city, conditions were much more serious.

The keepers were awakened at two o'clock that morning by the rising wind and heavy snow pelting against the lantern. With the coming of dawn a wild scene presented itself to the two men. As far as their eyes could see, the ocean was in great turmoil. By night the storm had become a gale, and when dawn of the second day broke it was not safe to stay in the lantern room. The two men climbed down the ladder leading to the storeroom, located under the keepers' quarters, as they feared the upper part of the lighthouse would go over.

Here a room had been built at the top of the piling for the storage of fuel and food supplies. The two frightened men cowered in the storeroom under the light for four days and nights. At frequent intervals a lamp chimney or reflector smashed to the floor two stories above them, and one of the keepers attempted the perilous climb up the ladder inside the structure to repair the damage. As they tried to reach the lantern room they were often knocked off the rungs by the tremendous force of waves that caused a violent pitching of the tower. Sleep, of course, was out of the question, and uncooked meat and dry bread their only sustenance.

By the afternoon of the fourth day the wind went down somewhat, and when the tide turned, the tower was not subjected to such heavy seas as in the morning. When darkness came the ocean had quieted appreciably, and although the great waves hit with occasional high surf, the storm was over. By morning the lighthouse tower had ceased its racking and straining and the keepers rejoiced at their good fortune. Soon after the abatement of the storm, Assistant Keeper Wilson flew the boat flag, as he was more than anxious to enjoy his long-overdue leave. When the relief craft came out, he set sail for the mainland, leaving Principal Keeper Bennett and his assistant, Joseph Antoine, at the light. A few days later Wilson visited Boston. During his stay in the city a friend asked him whether it would be difficult to hire another capable man for the position in the event Keeper Bennett left the lighthouse.

"Yes, sir," he replied. "I shall stay as long as Mr. Bennett does, and when we leave the light, it will be dangerous for any others to take it." The young man, only twenty, was feeling rather happy that the winter was over. He was looking forward to being at the light the coming summer, with the warmth and sunshine making up for the winter of terror he had recently experienced. But the summer never came for Assistant Keeper Wilson.

While he was in Boston he was also asked what he would do if the light should fall. He answered that he was quite confident of reaching the shore. In view of what actually happened three weeks later his remarks take on special significance. His final statement was that he would stay at the light as long as the tower stood. When the time came that is exactly what happened.

The head keeper, John W. Bennett, spent the next few days at the light tightening and strengthening the braces. He found the dory smashed beyond all hope of repair, however, and made arrangements to go to Boston to purchase a new one as soon as Assistant Keeper Wilson returned from his leave. A relatively calm spell was enjoyed the first week in April, but around the eighth of that month easterly winds began to blow. Bennett decided to leave the light when the east wind diminished somewhat, and on the morning of Friday, April 11, he flew the signal for the boat to come out. Leaving the weakened structure in charge of the two assistant keepers, Joseph Antoine and Joseph Wilson, Head Keeper Bennett sailed away from the lighthouse never to return. And it was the last time he saw either man alive.

Arriving on the mainland, Keeper Bennett proceeded to the Custom House in Boston, where he interviewed Collector Philip Greely concerning the purchase of his new boat. The next day he returned to Cohasset and made an effort to reach the light, but the easterly had increased, so that a heavy sea was running at Minot's Ledge. Late Monday the wind had developed into a gale, which intensified to hurricane force by Wednesday morning. The exact course of the storm on Wednesday, April 16, 1851, was east-northeast.

The storm raged all along the coast from New York to Portland, Maine. The feeling was general that the storm brought a higher tide and greater gale than any since December 1786.

The city of Boston actually became an island during the Wednesday high tide as the water came across the neck, cutting the city off from the mainland completely. The evening *Transcript* for April 16, 1851, reported:

". . . This is believed to be the highest tide ever known in Boston. It began to recede slowly about 12 o'clock. Thousands of spectators flocked down to the wharves to witness the grand spectacle which the waters . . . presented.

"Great apprehensions are felt in regard to the lighthouse at Minot's Ledge. The weather is still too misty to distinguish if it is still standing."

At the time this article was written, however, the light was still fairly upright. The two heroic keepers had continued to carry out their tasks in spite of the great odds against them. They kept the bell ringing and the lamps burning for the ships in distress outside the ledge. Their worst night was about to begin. The storm seemed to have spent its fury, but as is so often the case, the great seas grew even higher as evening came to the men at Minot's Ledge.

No one will ever know the exact circumstances of the tragedy that befell the two brave keepers out on the rock. The following explanation is offered as a possibility. It is, however, an account in which all the known facts are put together in a sequence that may be considered reasonable.

We know that several families living at the Glades in Scituate saw the gleam of Minot's Light about ten o'clock that fateful Wednesday night. Thus we may naturally assume the light was still standing at that time. The two men, realizing their danger would be greatest around high tide at midnight, prepared a message for the outside world in case they failed to survive the storm. Casting the bottle containing the message out from the lighthouse, Wilson and Antoine now made their plans for what proved to be their last night in this world.

The wind had abated considerably, but the great tide was slowly rising, sending wave after wave through the upper framework of the weakened structure. There was still that terrifying surge of hundreds of tons of foaming surf just below them. The doomed tower, rocking perceptibly back and forth, seemed about to crash at any time. Higher and higher the billows swept, until almost every wave smashed against the keepers' quarters, sixty feet above the ledge. Probably around eleven o'clock that night the central support snapped completely off, leaving the top-heavy thirty-ton lantern tower to be upheld by the already weakened outside piling.

The great five-and-one-half-inch rope hawser, which had been fastened into position by Keeper Bennett, ran from the top of the tower to a seven-ton granite rock located about two hundred feet in the lee of the lighthouse. Keeper Bennett used this cable to get on and off the tower whenever a turbulent sea was running.

Many believe that this cable, pulled by a huge rock as the boulder in turn was pushed toward shore by the sea, was a contributing factor in the destruction of the edifice. Keeper Bennett usually slackened the hawser when a storm came up, but it is a question whether this was beneficial to the lighthouse. If the rock started moving, the slack would soon be taken up, and until this happened the force of the waves against the cable would be greater, since the rope was not taut.

With the central support cracked off, the tower became more and more dangerous. The cable attached to the rock probably had the same effect that a rope would have, tied to the top of a high tree after it is almost chopped through, with the granite block creating a pull like men trying to bring the tree down. Inch by inch the granite block moved toward the shore, gradually increasing the strain on the eight remaining iron supports. Without question the lighthouse slanted at an angle of twenty degrees from the perpendicular by midnight. The previous afternoon a man with a telescope, standing on the beach at Cohasset, was peering anxiously in the direction of the ledge. He detected a decided list toward shore when he occasionally saw the structure through the mist, and felt that the lighthouse was doomed.

Just before one o'clock on the morning of April 17, 1851, because of the combined forces of wind, sea, and straining hawser, the great Minot's Ledge Lighthouse eased over into the sea. One by one the pilings broke, snapping like pipe stems, until only two or three remained. There the tower rested for a time.

The keepers realized that the end was near. Wishing in some way to communicate with their loved ones ashore, they seized the heavy hammer and began to pound furiously on the great lighthouse bell. We know that this signal was heard, for many residents at the Glades later recalled the sound of the bell that came over the water to them even above the roar of the surf at one o'clock that wild morning.

With the tower so bent over that the storeroom and capping received the full force of each breaking wave, the remaining supports soon gave way, and the great tower plunged beneath the ocean waves. The government had made a costly mistake. The sea reclaimed the ledge for its own.

But what of the two keepers?

Letting themselves down by the hawser into the water, the two men, each with a life preserver strapped to his back, dropped into the boiling surf. We believe that Antoine and Wilson did come down the hawser, for the stay was later found, and from its appearance it seemed probable that the lanyard connecting it to the lighthouse had been let loose. It had been tied in such a way that only human hands could have loosened it.

The body of Joseph Antoine was washed ashore soon afterward at Nantasket. The writer believes it possible that young twenty-year-old Wilson tried to live up to his expressed determination of reaching land.

A short distance from the Glades lies Gull Rock. Here it was that Joseph Wilson was washed ashore, more dead than alive, terribly chilled and bruised by the battering of the icy waves. He crawled up to the top of the rock, and discovered he was not on the mainland. This disappointment, after his long swim from the lighthouse, was too much for Wilson, and he sank, exhausted, in a cleft of Gull Rock far above the reach of the outgoing tide. He probably died before morning of exhaustion and exposure. This is not all conjecture, however, for when the body of Joseph Wilson was discovered the position and condition indicated that the young man reached the rock alive.

When Keeper Bennett had been prevented from going out to the tower, he went to his home on White Head, near the Glades. As the storm increased, the water swept across the shore and surrounded his residence, forcing the keeper to leave his home. Restless and uneasy about the fate of his fellow workers out on the lighthouse, he wandered along the beach. Around four o'clock the next morning, perhaps at the very time when his assistant, Wilson, was near death on Gull Rock, John Bennett began to notice debris coming ashore. He went down to the edge of the sea, and to his amazement Bennett recognized some of his own clothing that he had left at the lighthouse. Wreckage was also coming in. His worst fears were realized when he saw that pieces of timber were actually from the light itself.

The gale that caused the destruction of the lighthouse off Cohasset has since been referred to as "Minot's Light Storm of 1851."

Captain William H. Swift visited the ruins of Minot's Light on April 22, 1851, and made a sketch of the ledge with the broken piling. He also drew the lighthouse tower itself, as it lay in the water with only a part of the side showing. He probably experienced the bitterest moment of his life when he stood on the rolling deck of the boat and sketched the symbol of his costly failure.

The Boston Board of Underwriters now ordered the steam towboat, *R. B. Forbes,* to anchor off the rock and serve as a lightship. A temporary lighting apparatus was installed on the *Forbes,* and plans were made for a new lantern on the ship later in the year. But the storms were not yet over for the season. On April 20 the lightboat was in such danger that she had to leave her station off the ledge and return to Boston Harbor until the gale went down.

After a short period the *R. B. Forbes* was replaced by the old Brandywine Shoal Lightship, which had been anchored since 1823 inside the entrance to Delaware Bay. As a lighthouse had been built in the vicinity, the Treasury Department sent the ship up the coast to Minot's Ledge, where the vessel was moored outside the rock. Captain John W. Bennett, the former lighthouse keeper, was retained in charge of the 110-ton lightship. During an official inspection aboard the vessel on July 8, 1851, it was found that the ship was in bad condition, and unfit for further duty. Nevertheless, it was not until several years later that a new ship was placed off the ledge.

The federal government recognized the importance of rebuilding the lighthouse at Minot's Ledge, and Congress appropriated a substantial sum of money for the purpose. The construction of the edifice was under the jurisdiction of the United States Topographical Bureau. When the bureau advertised for bids for the lighthouse, sixteen were received.

Before a decision could be reached, however, the new Lighthouse Board was created. General Joseph G. Totten, at one time chief engineer of the United States, presented plans for a great stone tower to be built at the ledge. General Totten's design was accepted although Captain Barton S. Alexander is said to have proposed certain radical features that were incorporated in the final design. At least we know that several of his innovations are present as the tower stands today.

After the final drafts were completed, the plans were brought to Cohasset, where two master model-makers were assigned the task of constructing a miniature of the lighthouse. Richard Bourne and Zaccheus Rich worked on the model for two winters, completing it in the little shop that stood for many years at the head of Cohasset Cove.

The Lighthouse Board in Washington was naturally anxious to avoid a repetition of the first catastrophe and ordered Major Ogden, an engineer, to visit the ledge and examine the surface of the rock with care. After a lengthy analysis of the seams and stratification of the ledge, Ogden finally approved of the original location where the former light had stood. Orders were now released for the actual building of the lighthouse.

The most important of several considerations still remaining was the selection of a highly qualified engineer for the construction of the lighthouse. In April, 1855 Barton S. Alexander, a tall, husky captain in the United States Engineers, was chosen to superintend the building of the stone beacon. He was described as "one of those men we sometimes meet who are always clear headed, never in a hurry, but have the faculty of doing a great deal in a short space of time."

In making plans for the actual work at the ledge Captain Alexander found that three conditions were necessary for successful operations. A smooth sea, a dead calm, and low spring tides were essential. The tides were right only "six times during any one lunation, three at full moon and three at the change."

The top of the rock was three feet six inches above the plane of low water. As the plans indicated, the granite blocks were to be laid under low water in seven different places.

All was now in readiness for the work at the rock. Although Captain Alexander tried to land at Minot's Ledge on May 1, 1855, it was not until the twelfth of that month that the swell had diminished enough to make this possible. Alexander's first survey showed that the ledge would have to be cut down to receive the foundation stones of the lighthouse. The space available was so limited that there was no opportunity for the placing of a regular cofferdam.

Realizing that there would be many days when work at the ledge was impossible, Captain Alexander arranged to have Government Island, now connected to the mainland at Cohasset, used for cutting and assembling the granite. The same gang of men would do both jobs, and in that way work full time.

The first active work was undertaken at the rock on June 20, 1855, when the old stumps of the first tower were wrenched from their sockets. A large part of the structure that was still under water a few hundred yards away also had to be removed so that boats could more easily approach the ledge. Captain Alexander writes in his notes about the building of the light that on visiting the ledge for the first time he decided to remove all trace of the former disaster as soon as possible because of the unfavorable effect on the morale of his workmen. A daring Scandinavian named Peter Fox volunteered to go down and locate the fragments of the wreck. Diving under water with a light tackle, he hooked it around a piece of the old tower and swam up to the surface with the line. Then the other workers brought up the heavy iron by means of this line until the entire wreck was removed. It is said that the old tower was broken up and made into nails at an East Bridgewater factory.

At daylight on Sunday morning, July 1, Captain Alexander started out to the ledge with a small group of picked men. They clambered over the rocky surface, where Alexander called them together for a brief word. He mentioned the failures and delays that were certain to occur, but he asked them all to be patient and persevering. In a few moments, he announced, work would be under way that would not end until the completed tower was lighted, "whether it be two years or ten."

Thus, on July 1, 1855, the sound of hammer against chisel echoed through the early Sunday stillness, and the actual work on the stone tower began. But many long and weary months were to elapse before even the first block arrived at the ledge. The surface of the rock itself had to be carefully prepared to receive each of the seven granite blocks required for the foundation.

The first task was to cut a bench mark near the highest part of the rock, from which all subsequent levels were measured. Next they made a level surface to provide room for the tools and an area for the men to stand on.

Permanent iron shafts about twenty feet high were set in eight of the holes in which the old lighthouse piling had been placed. The ninth, or central hole, was left open to form a cavity for the base circle. Later the well for the drinking water was built from the central hole up through the middle of the tower. The iron piles were bound together by wrought-iron frames, with a spider or capping placed at the top of the shafts. For each post ropes were then criss-crossed, low enough for the men to grab when the waves broke over the ledge. The scaffolding also served as a derrick in laying the lower stages of masonry and as a bolt to secure the light to the rock formation. After the entire iron framework was painted a bright red, work was abandoned for the year. The men hoped that no wrecks would take place along the coast that winter, now that New England's bleakest season was at hand. They were doomed to disappointment.

A severe storm hit Massachusetts Bay on January 19, 1857, throwing the bark *New Empire* against the Cohasset outer ledges. She later went ashore near White Head. When the gale had gone down a little that afternoon, Captain Alexander looked out to sea, and was dismayed to find that his framework structure had disappeared. It was the one time that his spirit seemed to be broken. Having personally supervised the construction of every wrought-iron section placed at the ledge and knowing the great resistance of the combined superstructure, Captain Alexander was discouraged.

"If tough wrought iron won't stand it," he said, "I have my fears about a stone tower."

Something had happened during that storm, however, that gave renewed hope to Captain Alexander. He found that the bark *New Empire* had actually struck the temporary tower and demolised the iron scaffolding at the ledge before she came ashore at White Head. Keeper Bennett had often feared that such an accident would destroy the former lighthouse, and now a wreck had occurred that snapped off the wrought-iron framework erected where Bennett's tower had stood. Bound for Boston, the *New Empire* was loaded with cotton, and it was in this cargo that conclusive evidence was later discovered that the ship had crashed into the structure.

When good weather finally came in 1857, Captain Alexander visited the ledge again. He found that he had all of the work to do once more, because of the crash of the *New Empire*. Not only had the wrought-iron structure been smashed to pieces but the upper surface of the rock itself had been damaged and broken. Another set of dowels had to be inserted into the cavities, and this time the piling was planned to reach a height of twenty-five feet, or the place where later the twelfth course of masonry was laid. Month after month the workmen hammered and chiseled at the upper surface of the ledge, at times working in two or three feet of water. Finally Captain Alexander announced that the ledge was ready for the first granite block, and plans were made to send it out from the mainland. Here again difficulties were encountered, for there was only one strategic "dock" nearby where the stones could be unloaded, and the sailboat pounded its bilges against the ledge there even though the keel rested in deep water. The vessel was unable to approach the landing with more than one of the two-ton blocks aboard.

On July 9, 1857, the first stone was laid at Minot's Ledge for the new lighthouse tower. General Totten had planned the form of every granite block in the structure, but because of the wreck of the *New Empire* and of the discovery of several blind seams in the ledge, the stones had to be altered. A plan soon was devised by which the foundation blocks, laid more than two feet under the surface of the lowest tide, could be cemented to the rock-face of the ledge. Temporary cofferdams around small portions of the rock were thrown up by using two or three hundred partially filled sand bags. Whatever water seeped through was quickly mopped up with giant sponges.

The method adopted for securing a bed of mortar under the granite blocks and in the vertical joints was to spread a large piece of thin muslin on a platform at the ledge. A substantial layer of mortar was then applied, and the stone lowered down on the surface of the mortar. Next, the vertical joints of the stone were covered with mortar, the cloth folded up and smoothed along the joints, and the superfluous parts cut away. After remaining five or ten minutes the mortar began to set, and then the stone, with the mortared muslin adhering, was lowered into position. The mortar oozed through the cloth, and formed a good adhesion with the rock surface below.

The masonry was locked and dovetailed in such a way that the impact of each wave made the edifice stronger rather than weaker. As is mentioned elsewhere, there were seven stones in the lowest course of granite masonry. All the first level of granite blocks was laid under water at dead low tide. In the second course there were twenty-nine stones, twelve of them partially under water when placed into position.

Angles and corners were three inches in length and each course was two feet thick, with every stone weighing about two tons. The first three courses bore no resemblance to ordinary masonry. Most unusual curves and corners were carved out of granite so that the blocks would fit the ledge. The foundation stones were secured to the rock by two-inch galvanized wrought-iron bolts, in addition to the eight great piles twenty-five feet high that ran up from the original holes of the old tower. Each stone had to be cut to fit its neighbor above, below and on each side. Strap iron between the courses kept the stones apart while the Portland cement was hardening.

The total appropriation for the lighthouse had been $330,000, and a small surplus was realized when the actual construction was finished. Part of this money was intended to be used for the preparation of a volume about the building of the tower, complete with sketches, pictures, diagrams, and personal reminiscences. The book was never published, but some of the information intended for the volume is included here.

Figures on the hours spent at the rock, for example, were to go in the volume. The men worked on the ledge 208 hours in 1858. By the end of 1859 the thirty-second course, sixty-two feet above low water had been reached. Three hundred and seventy-seven hours were needed to reach this height. The next year, on June 29, 1860, the final stone was laid. The granite work was complete. It had been five years, lacking one day, from the time the first workmen with Captain Alexander had landed on the rock. The rest of the summer of 1860 was spent putting in the lantern and lens, and early in August the cupola was fastened in place. Fred C. Green tells us the lantern was hauled from Boston by oxen.

The new lighthouse was actually finished by the middle of August 1860, and on Wednesday evening, August 22, the lantern was illuminated for the first time in history. Of course, it was merely a trial lighting and had no permanent historical significance.

With the completion of the world's most hazardous stone lighthouse, the government now began its search for a suitable keeper. Joshua Wilder was chosen for this important post late in the fall. Very little is known of his background. The custom of having two men to assist the head keeper was continued, and A. W. Williams and William S. Taylor were chosen first and second assistants respectively. The men landed at the ledge on November 13, 1860, in time to prepare the light for its inaugural flash two nights later.

November 15 dawned, pleasant and free from high winds. The keepers labored throughout the day, in order to have everything in readiness for the important evening ahead.

As the last glow of the setting sun was fading in the western sky, Keeper Joshua Wilder stepped into the lantern room high in the tower of Minot's Light and looked out over the darkening landscape. The sight that met his eyes was thrilling and extremely gratifying. Scores of bonfires were burning along the South Shore to celebrate the first lighting of the new granite tower.

A moment later the first beam from the new tower flashed through the dusk. The goal of many strenuous days, months, and years of constant struggle had finally been achieved. Then, in answer to the bright, steady beam from the high stone tower out in the sea, Roman candles and sky-rockets shot up into the sky from various points along the Cohasset and Scituate shoreline. Keeper Wilder was happy to see that people ashore were doing their part to honor the triumph of man over the destructive forces of the ocean. Minot's beacon again flashed its friendly warning to the ships of all nations entering Boston Bay, but this time the lighthouse was to stand for many years.

With less than a year of service, Joshua Wilder resigned on August 16, 1861. No reason has come down through the years to account for this rather abrupt termination of Wilder's activity. James J. Tower became the second keeper of the new lighthouse.

With him he brought out to the beacon Thomas Bates, who was later to distinguish himself as a life saver at Boston Light. One afternoon, the head keeper was rowing out to the lighthouse when in some inexplicable way the craft tipped over, and he was thrown into the water. From the tower high above, Thomas Bates saw the accident. Although he was alone at the light, the assistant keeper took a desperate chance and won. Working feverishly, he let go the blocks holding the lifeboat to the davits eighty feet above the sea, jumped into the boat, and let the cables run through. The boat, approaching the water at express speed, smashed into the sea so that the hooks disengaged themselves. Bates was now able to row over and save the life of Head Keeper Tower. It is easy to see what a disaster this incident could have become. If the line had tangled or jammed it might have meant the death of both men. It was perhaps because of this noteworthy deed that on July 12, 1864, Assistant Keeper Bates was promoted to the position of head keeper at Boston Light, the oldest lighthouse in America.

Milton Herbert Reamy assumed the position of head keeper at Minot's Light on January 3, 1887. His was the longest career at the famous rock. Beginning in the service as assistant keeper at Duxbury Pier Light in 1878, Reamy became head keeper at the Gurnet in 1880. Now at the age of thirty-five he was appointed to take charge of America's most dangerous beacon—Minot's Ledge Lighthouse.

Keeper Reamy remembered the great "Gale of '88" more vividly than any of the other storms during his period of service. Even the 1898 *Portland* storm did not wreak so much havoc in the immediate vicinity of the lighthouse. Joseph E. Frates, Keeper Reamy's assistant, told him that one particular wave that struck the tower on Sunday, November 25, 1888, made his hair actually stand on end. The tower remained firm, however, for Captain Alexander had built his lighthouse well. The wave caused a strong vibration at the time, but Keeper Reamy declared that nothing but an earthquake would ever shake down the lighthouse.

All during Tuesday morning, November 27, wreckage drifted by the rock, and Keeper Reamy kept watching the flotsam being swept along by the tide. The first object he was able to identify was a steamer's top mast, which was painted black six feet down from the peak. Cabin steps were next sighted, then panel work, casks, boxes, life preservers, and broken fragments of the superstructure. All of the articles seemed to be floating from the vicinity of Jason's Ledge. Keeper Reamy feared that the steamer *Allentown* with eighteen on board had gone down after striking the dangerous reef a mile to the northeast of the lighthouse. He was later asked if he had heard a whistle that fateful night when the *Allentown* was lost.

"I did not," he answered, "and it would have been impossible to hear a whistle if it had been within ten feet of the light, owing to the tremendous roar of the waves as they dashed *over the light*." The writer has italicized, for it is the first recorded testimony to the effect that the sea actually went over the top of the 114-foot structure.

"How did the light stand it, Captain?" a reporter for the *Boston Globe* asked him when he came ashore later.

"She stood it well; there was some vibration and it leaked under the windows. The chimney that we used on the lamp Sunday night was cracked, and that was all the damage I know of."

Fifteen ships were wrecked between Scituate Harbor and Boston in that 1888 hurricane. Life preservers and marked life boats soon came ashore in Cohasset to prove that the *Allentown* actually had foundered near Minot's Light, and the *Edward H. Norton* went ashore on the First Cliff, Scituate, with the loss of all fifteen of her crew.

Keeper Milton Reamy was notified in 1894 that there would be a new lantern of the flashing type installed at the tower sometime that spring. Workmen arrived in April, and for several days were busy removing the old lamp and adjusting the new revolving lens and lighting apparatus. By May 1, all was in readiness for the flashing beacon. At that time the government decided to give Minot's Light a new characteristic, a one-four-three flash. The familiar –, ––––, ––– requires thirty seconds to complete and spells out "I LOVE YOU" to lovers along the shore.

Octavius Reamy of Cohasset succeeded his father as keeper of Minot's Light in 1915. The combined services of the two men total about half a century. Octavius Reamy's first visit to the light had been in 1897, when he took the position of "Additional Keeper."

Two years after Reamy became the head keeper at Minot's Light World War I broke out, and Reamy watched the American destroyers steaming out of Boston Harbor on their way to the war zone.

The winter of 1918 was one of the coldest ever experienced at Minot's Ledge Light. Ice formed at the foot of the tower until it bulged out three feet at the base of the ladder. The shelf of ice was so substantial that the keeper climbed down the rungs of the ladder and stood on the solid mass. It was the only time, Keeper Reamy believed, that the sea was frozen over all the way from Minot's Light to Point Allerton, six miles distant.

Octavius Reamy left Minot's Light on May 11, 1924, when he was transferred to Graves Light off Winthrop, Massachusetts.

Per S. Tornberg was appointed the new keeper. One wintry day, when ice formed on the lower part of the ladder, Tornberg launched the dory to examine the rungs at the base of the tower, fearing that they had been damaged. He let the craft down until it hit the water, then loosened the stern falls. While the bow falls were still attached, he heard a roaring sea coming for him behind the tower. Tornberg could not escape the waves, and the sea simply picked him up and pushed the keeper down against the ledge. Tornberg was able to fight his way up the ladder, but never again tried to investigate the base of the tower in winter time.

In 1936 Keeper Tornberg was succeeded by George H. Fitzpatrick, who stayed at the light except for short intervals until 1945. In 1947 the last boat crew of Coastguardsmen abandoned the tower, and the beacon became an automatic one.

Although the station has a double system of flashing its warning light of 1 — 4 — 3, on several occasions each in turn has failed and during the interval of failure mariners at sea were entirely without help.

More than a dozen rungs from the bottom of the ladder at the tower have been removed, which makes it impossible, at the present time, to climb the ladder without a grappling hook.

Every important location up and down this romantic coastline has its legends and ghosts stories, and Minot's Ledge

Light is no exception. Some of the stories that are included here may be more than mere legends, but because of the difficulty of placing time and persons they cannot receive the stamp of absolute fact.

The first story is about the work at the tower. Since cleaning the lens and the lamps is an integral part of the job at a lighthouse, anything out of the ordinary about this duty is likely to attract attention. One morning, a short time after the Civil War, the head keeper at Minot's Light suddenly realized that something strange had happened. The lamp and the lens had been brightly polished that morning, although the assistant keeper, whose task it was to shine them, was still asleep. When it was time to awaken his helper, the head keeper asked him about the cleaning of the lamp and lens. The assistant was as surprised as his superior to learn that the work had already been done. The following week, it was the assistant's turn to notice that the same procedure had been repeated, although neither man had performed the task. Whether or not there is another explanation, the ghosts of the two keepers lost when the old lighthouse crashed into the sea received full credit for the polishing of the lens and the lamp of Minot's Ledge Light.

For many years mariners sailing past the lighthouse have been insisting that they heard strange voices and see ghostlike figures clinging to the lower section of the ladder. It is said that the Portuguese fishermen, who had usually taken their compatriot, Joseph Antoine, out to the light to serve his turn, in later years saw the ghost of their friend many times while passing the rock. This belief became so strong that, according to Keeper Fitzpatrick, many Portuguese fishermen do not dare to venture close to the new stone tower today. It is said that the ghost of young Antoine has usually been heard and seen just prior to northeast storms when the spectre puts in an appearance apparently to warn his countrymen of the dangers of the ledge. Many sailors of a former generation are said to have seen him grasping the lower rungs of the lighthouse ladder, with the gathering surf sweeping over him, as he cried out, "Keep away, keep away."

Another story concerns the strange tapping at the tower. In the former lighthouse it was the custom of the head keeper to signal his assistant by rapping on the stovepipe that went up through the various floors, in order to inform him that the watch was over. The assistant would rap to reply that he was coming. But in the new lighthouse an electric bell was installed to call the assistant.

One night, as the midnight watch was drawing to a close, the head keeper heard a strange tapping from below, and tapped with his pipe on the table. There was another reply from below. Amazed at the tapping, he thought perhaps it was his assistant, and waited a few moments, but nothing happened. Finally, he rang the bell for his assistant to relieve him, and in due time the assistant appeared. The head keeper told his story, and the assistant denied all knowledge of tapping. The affair was never explained to the satisfaction of either of the men.

A keeper at Minot's Light once remarked, "The trouble with our life here is that we have too much time to think." Rumor has it that around fifty years ago a new assistant keeper thought too much and cut his own throat. Unfortunately he bled to death before the head keeper discovered him.

Some of the world's highest waves have crashed against the sides of Minot's Ledge Light. In the Christmas storm of 1909 Keeper Reamy watched a wave 170 feet high soaring over the top of the tower. I have flown above the lighthouse during many storms, making pictures from the air of these great awe-inspiring waves.

We sometimes wonder what the thoughts of the men stationed at the tower were during the long, wintry nights when violent gales swept in from the Atlantic, sending seething white-capped waves surging up around the sides of America's most dangerous beacon. Perhaps, as the granite tower shook with the impact of the tremendous billows pounding against the outside of the 114-foot structure and the lighthouse was engulfed in foam, the men thought of those two keepers of the old tower, who on that memorable night stood side by side in the face of almost certain death to keep their last faithful watch that ended in eternity.

30

Other Boston Bay Lights

Additional beacons around Boston Bay include several other lighthouses that have materially assisted the mariner seeking a Massachusetts port. They are the Narrows or Bug Light, the two range light stations at Lovell's and Spectacle Islands, Deer Island Light, Long Island Light, and Scituate Light.

NARROWS OR BUG LIGHT

The Narrows Light was built in 1856 on the end of Great Brewster Spit, at the entrance to the Boston Harbor Narrows. The lantern was about thirty-five feet above the water, and warned ships away from the rocks at Harding's Ledge. When the captain brought Bug Light in range with Long Island Light, he knew he was clear of Harding's, and could safely enter the harbor. One of the earliest keepers at Bug Light fled here from the Great Lakes, where it was said he murdered a sailor with a barrel stave. In 1893 Captain Freeman became keeper of the light, and Mrs. Frank Tenney kept house for him. Mrs. Tenney's son lived with them, and in

1908 he attended English High School in Boston, rowing over to Fort Warren every morning to take the boat to the city.

Both Arthur and Tom Small of that interesting lighthouse family of three brothers served at Bug Light. One day when Tom sailed for Bug Light from Boston Light, his sailboat capsized. The Hull life savers came out to rescue him, but the visibility was so poor that they gave up and started to return. On their way they passed Arthur Small, rowing out in search of his brother. It was the middle of winter, far below freezing.

"He's gone, Small, it's no use," they shouted at Arthur. But Keeper Small kept rowing out to where he believed the tide would take his brother's sailboat. In the meantime Tom had been clinging to the bottom of the craft, his heavy woolen mittens frozen to the keel helping him to keep his grip.

"I had always heard that a rescued shipwrecked sailor gets a drink of rum, and that's what kept me hanging on," he told the writer afterward. About the time that he had decided no one would save him that night, he heard and answered his brother's frantic shouting.

Five minutes later Tom was in Arthur's dory, and Arthur was vigorously rowing him back to Boston Light, where the life savers from Hull and the other keepers were waiting. There was a mighty shout when Arthur hove in view with his brother aboard, and soon Arthur left for his own lighthouse, his mind at rest in the knowledge that Tom was tucked safely in bed. Incidentally, Tom Small, the rescued shipwrecked sailor, did NOT get his drink.

The Small brothers were separated during World War I, and after it was over, Judson Small, the third brother, brought a stranger out to Bug Light with him to visit Arthur. Watching Arthur at work, the stranger exclaimed, "You're a hell of a mechanic." Arthur did not realize that it was his own brother Tom, grown fully mature during his years in the service, and decided he had a fight on his hands. As Arthur belligerently walked over to the pretended stranger, Judson Small stepped between them and introduced Arthur to his long-absent brother, Tom.

One terrible wintry day, when the bar was heavily iced up, an Italian fishing boat drove ashore and was wrecked. Arthur tried to reach it, but the tide was high. Finally he was able to wade near the wreck and threw a line out. One man grabbed hold and Small pulled him in. Then another was brought ashore, but the third man was too far gone and perished on the boat. Still ahead was an almost impossible job, however, that of getting the two Italian fishermen up into the lighthouse, but Small finally accomplished it and saved their lives.

Tom Small was the last keeper of Bug Light. On June 7, 1929, the building caught fire and was totally destroyed. The lighthouse board voted against rebuilding the structure, replacing it with an automatic bell and light. Today the sea gulls and the shags are the only signs of life at old Narrows or Bug Light.

LOVELL'S ISLAND RANGE LIGHTS

In 1902 plans were made for the erection of two range lights on Lovell's Island, Boston Harbor, for the accommodation of mariners coming up the South Channel of Broad Sound. Completed the next year, the range lights were placed in the charge of Keeper Alfred G. Eisener.

Keeper Eisener was a poet and writer. One of his books is known as *Dan, or the Gale of '73*. We shall hear more about Eisener in the story of Cuttyhunk Light. Eisener was succeeded in 1919 by Charles H. Jennings, who transferred from

Boston Light. While digging in his backyard one day Jennings uncovered the site of the treasure of the old French man-of-war *Magnifique,* and about seven thousand dollars was removed from the ground soon afterward.

The severe northeasterly storm of March 5, 1931, did considerable damage at Lovell's Island Range Lights, submerging the entire station under six feet of water. The keeper was forced to use a dory that evening to light the towers. During the gale a kerosene oil tank was washed from its foundations.

With the coming of World War II, the U.S. Army at Fort Standish, located on the same island, ordered the lighthouses taken down. They had been extinguished in 1939. All that remains of the lighthouse station at Lovell's Island today is the abandoned oil shed.

DEER ISLAND LIGHT

Deer Island Light, whose beacon first illuminated the area off Deer Island in 1890, has a fixed white light fifty-three feet above the sea that changes to a red two-second flash every thirty seconds, as the government describes it. In actuality, the steady white light lasts twenty-eight seconds, and the red flash is of two-seconds' duration.

There have been three romantic or tragic events in the history of the lighthouse. Keeper Wesley Pingree and his wife Josephine spent their honeymoon there in 1895, while Frank P. Sibley formerly of the *Boston Globe,* married Miss Florence Lyndon, daughter of the keeper at Long Island, as a result of a courtship carried on while Sibley was an acting assistant keeper at Deer Island Light just across the channel.

In the winter of 1916 Keeper Joseph McCabe left the light one Sunday to help his fiancee on the mainland address wedding invitations for their coming marriage. While he was ashore, the temperature dropped rapidly, and a bitter gale sprang up. When McCabe returned to Deer Island, he found his dory frozen to the beach, and so he borrowed a pair of rubber boots and started to walk along the bar toward the lighthouse. Jumping to a large rock, he slipped and fell into the ocean. Philip Pingree and others launched another dory and rowed to the spot, but they never found the body of Keeper Joseph McCabe.

The last civilian keeper of Deer Island Light was Fred Bohm, who came across the harbor from the Spectacle Island Range Lights.

Keeper Bohm was on duty at Deer Island Light during the dangerous period when German submarines were lurking off the Massachusetts coast. His task was a difficult one during the first year and a half of World War II, for he not only was responsible for the care of the light, but patrolled the shore for a considerable distance, both on the harbor and ocean waterfronts near his station. One day a boat carrying four of his men on duty at the light capsized in a rough sea. The Coastguardsmen clung to the submarine netting just off the lighthouse for two hours until they were rescued.

Other keepers at Deer Island Light were King, Burdge, and the Small brothers. Tom Small, while at Deer Island Light, had a ladder-climbing cat that would leap into the water, bring up a fish, and climb back up the lighthouse ladder with the catch in her mouth.

The light is now automatic.

SPECTACLE ISLAND RANGE LIGHTS

Erected in 1903, four range lights stood on Spectacle Island for a number of years, but with the straightening out of the channel, the two inner range lights were torn down. Today no lights remain here to guide the mariner into the harbor. Keeper Creed was stationed at Spectacle Island for more than twenty years, and was succeeded by J. Lelan Hart, who came to Spectacle Island Range Lights in 1926. Others at Spectacle Island were Fred Bohm and Keeper Jaspers.

The island itself is a haunted one. The last keeper was said to have been murdered here at the outbreak of World War II, while at least six other murders have occurred on or just off the island. The last one was that of Lynn Kauffman, whose lifeless body washed ashore here at the foot of the cliff under the lighthouse reservation in 1959.

Long Island Head Light

Boston Harbor's second lighthouse, Long Island Head, was first lighted by Keeper Jonathan Lawrence in October 1819. Known for many years as the Inner Harbor Light, it has been placed at three different locations at the head.

Experiments were carried on at Long Island Light in 1820 by two inventors, Melville and Black, for the important purpose of heating lighthouse oil in cold weather. They were so successful that Fifth Auditor Stephen Pleasonton offered to purchase their invention for the sum of $4,300, but whether the three men ever came to terms is not known.

Keeper Lawrence died in service at Long Island Head in October 1825, and Charles Beck was appointed to fill the vacancy. Beck was still keeper in 1845, when James Lloyd Homer visited the island. Homer observed that Keeper Beck ran the signal system for the pilots, hoisting a black ball to indicate more pilots were needed down the harbor. As late as the year 1851, Charles Beck was still active at Long Island Lighthouse.

On January 8, 1918, Edwin Tarr, keeper of Long Island Light since 1908, died while sitting in his chair looking out over the water. Tarr was the light's last keeper, as the station was soon made an untended beacon. Thus the first and the last keepers of Long Island Head Light, Jonathan Lawrence and Edwin Tarr, died in service on the island.

SCITUATE LIGHT

At the beginning of the nineteenth century, with the increasing maritime activity at Scituate, the government decided to erect a lighthouse at Cedar Point at the entrance to the harbor. There had been many wrecks in the vicinity, and it was thought that a lighthouse at Cedar Point would materially reduce the losses at sea. The week of September 19, 1811, saw the completion of Scituate Light. Simeon Bates became the first keeper of the light at the northern chop of Scituate Harbor.

Keeper Bates performed his work well. The shipwrecks continued to occur, unfortunately, because the sea captains became confused between Boston Light and Scituate Light. Schooners, barks, brigs, and ships crashed with disheartening regularity on the dangerous rocks around Minot's Ledge, located to the north.

With the coming of the War of 1812, the keeper's two daughters, Rebecca and Abigail Bates, performed a remarkable feat of saving Scituate from possible destruction by a British warship. One day early in September 1814, the British man-of-war *La Hogue* appeared off the coast and anchored near the point. The two girls, alone at the light except for a younger brother, sent the boy to the village to warn the inhabitants, and then watched five longboats from the man-of-war start for Scituate.

Rebecca ran down the tower steps, grabbed a drum that belonged to a guardsman who should have been on duty at the light, and handed her sister a fife. Then, as the steady, measured strokes of the oars of the British sailors were heard nearing the spit of land where the lighthouse stood, Rebecca began to beat the drum and Abigail to play the fife. Louder and louder sounded the martial strains, until the British oarsmen passing the lighthouse stopped their rowing. Could the Americans be massing to overcome them?

The ship's commander aboard the *La Hogue,* hearing the music, ran up a flag signifying danger and ordered a gun to be fired for the longboats to return. At this unexpected turn of events, cheers came from the assembled citizens at Scituate, while at Lighthouse Point the girls collapsed on the beach, exhausted from their efforts.

As darkness fell over the coast, the girls watched the *La Hogue* preparing to leave the harbor. There was a gun flash. A single shot, evidently aimed at the lighthouse tower, described its parabola in the air, its screaming passage ending in the water more than fifty yards short of its target. The *La Hogue* then hoisted sail and was soon hull down, bound for another port.

In 1830 the light keeper had considerable difficulty going to and from the lighthouse by land because of the objections of a person named Barker, who owned the adjoining property. Finally the county commissioners agreed that they would lay out a road over Barker's land after the owner decided to sell it. The road is still used today to pass to and from the light.

During the summer of 1834 Keeper Bates died. When Zeba Cushing was appointed in his place, the authorities took pains to impress upon him "the necessity of residing constantly in the house provided for the keeper and of strictly performing the duties enjoined by it."

In 1834 the Scituate Light tower needed repointing, and the work was completed with "Roman cement and whitewashed, the window sills repaired, and the lantern pointed."

The same year it appeared that Scituate Light might be abandoned if a ledge light were built at Minot's Ledge.

On the above subject Stephen Pleasonton wrote:

"Instead of building a new Keeper's house the present year I would prefer to have the old one repaired, as I am somewhat in hopes that Congress may be induced to make an adequate appropriation for building the contemplated light on Minot's Ledge, during the next Session."

Scituate had two lights, one above the other, in the tower in 1849. The keeper, James Y. Bates, was appointed August 24 of that year at a salary of $350. In Imray's *Coast Pilot,* published in London in 1852, Scituate Light was described as a red, fixed beacon, located on "Cedar Point, North Chop, opposite South Chop, or so called First Cliff, entrance to harbor over a gravel bar with 12 feet of water at middling tides."

In 1860 the new lighthouse at Minot's Ledge was completed. On the night of November 14, 1860, Keeper Thomas Richardson lit the Scituate lamps for the last time, as the following evening Keeper Wilder out at the new Minot's Light tower was scheduled to illuminate his tower for the first full night's glow. The career of Scituate Light had ended.

As the years passed, the many loyal citizens of Scituate agreed that Scituate Light should be preserved as a memorial. Remembering some of the old keepers of the light, Simeon Bates, Reuben Bates, and James Young Bates, they suggested to the Bates Family Association that a tablet, placed on the tower, would be a fitting reminder of the connection of the name of Bates with the lighthouse history. In 1928 a fine tablet was placed on the side of the lighthouse, which is now completely restored and renovated. The Bates family and the historically minded citizens of Scituate have reason to be proud of their appropriate memorial, old Scituate Light-house at Cedar Point.

THE GURNET AND DUXBURY PIER

Massachusetts has two minor peninsulas extending north and south into the sea between Scituate and Plymouth near Brant Rock, Marshfield and Green Harbor. The northern one, which includes Humarock Beach, terminates at Scituate's Fourth Cliff. The other, of which Duxbury Beach is a part, reaches far to the south along the great stretch of sand dunes which end at the Gurnet.

On a high bluff at the southern tip of the Gurnet, looking out across lower Massachusetts Bay, stands Gurnet Light. First established as a station back in 1768 by the Massachusetts Legislature, the lighthouse is on historic land and much of interest has taken place there. During the Revolution, the light itself was hit by a cannonball. And long before, in 1606, Champlain landed here and made an interesting sketch of Plymouth Harbor for his chart of the coast.

For many years the Pilgrims called the land "the gurnett's nose" according to lighthouse historian Willoughby. Winsor, the antiquarian of Duxbury, tells us there were about "twenty-seven acres of good soil" there. Incidentally, the name *Gurnet* probably came from one of several similar headlands in the English channel, many of them called the Gurnet after the fish of the same name, which is caught in great numbers along the coast of Devonshire.

In the legislative records of the Governor's Council in the Province of Massachusetts for 1768, we read that a lighthouse was planned in that year to be erected on the eastern extremity of the long strip of land known as the Gurnet at the entrance to Plymouth Harbor.

An unusual arrangement was made with John and Hannah Thomas, owners of the land where the lighthouse was to be built, whereby the province would be allowed to erect and maintain a lighthouse on the Thomas property for the modest sum of five shillings a year! The mention of a Keeper Thomas and later, his widow, would indicate that the Thomas family were appointed to run the light as part of their agreement with the province.

The lighthouse, constructed at a cost of 660 pounds, was thirty feet long, twenty feet high, and fifteen feet wide, with a "lanthorn" at each end of the building, each lantern holding two lamps. It was here at Plymouth's Gurnet Light that, for the first time in America, the system of having two different "twin" lights was begun.

During the Revolution an unusual incident took place. The three towns of Plymouth, Duxbury, and Kingston had erected a fort on the Gurnet. In the midst of an engagement between the fort and the British frigate *Niger,* which had gone aground on Brown's Bank, a wild shot from the ship pierced the lighthouse itself. The vessel soon got off and escaped. This incident of the cannonball hitting the lighthouse has been mistakenly attributed to two other Massachusetts lighthouses. At Boston Light there is a small circular window in the tower, which local enthusiasts have claimed, erroneously, was caused by a cannonball. And on Thacher's Island off Cape Ann, some persons have insisted that one of the twin lights there was struck by a cannonball. As a matter of fact, Gurnet Light Station is the only Massachusetts light known to have been hit by an enemy cannonball.

A terrible shipwreck occurred near the Gurnet Light during the last week of 1778, when the armed brigantine *General Arnold* was caught in a blizzard. Although less than a mile from the friendly gleam of the Gurnet Light, Captain Magee anchored his vessel rather than risk the treacherous waters of Plymouth's inner harbor without a pilot. The vessel dragged anchor and finally hit on White Flats. Before the survivors could eventually be rescued, seventy-two of the crew died, most of them by freezing to death in the below-zero temperature. Because of the ice-blocked harbor, the keeper of the Gurnet Light was unable to go to their aid, nor could the men of Plymouth reach them. Fnally, a causeway was built out over the ice from Plymouth to rescue the survivors.

In 1783 the Legislature ordered that "William Drew, Esq., be and he is, hereby appointed to repair and put in proper order, the lighthouse on the Gurnet, near Plymouth, and lay his accounts before the General Court for allowance and payment." When Massachusetts ceded the Gurnet Light to the federal government, in 1790, the keeper, Mrs. Hannah Thomas, was still active and receiving her yearly rental of five shillings, plus two hundred dollars in pay.

During the great December snowstorm of 1786 a coasting sloop bound from Boston to Plymouth in charge of Captain Samuel Robbins was caught off the Gurnet in what was probably the worst snowstorm of the century. When the gale began, Captains Robbins, who had with him the Reverend Mr. Robbins of Plymouth and fourteen others, tried to return to Boston Light. It was discovered that his compass was out of order, and several hours were spent in a futile attempt to reach safety. Then the storm shut in with terrible fury, wrecking vessels all along the coast.

Off the Gurnet, Captain Robbins watched the wind rip his mainsail to pieces, but managed to keep out of trouble until dawn brought partial visibility. Not being able to see land, he held a council. As the waves were getting higher hourly, the helpless crew finally agreed that their only chance was to try to run the vessel ashore some place and pray for the best. Everyone gave up hope, for death seemed inevitable. "Heaven appeared for us!" one passenger said later.

Soon they were in the giant breakers, and the helmsman

mistakenly shouted out, "Nothing but rocks!" Just then the ship struck a sand bar, slid over, and shuddered to a stop sixty yards from shore. Her boom fell down among the passengers when she hit, but fortunately only one man was hurt. The ship's boat was put over, and by means of a long warp, every passenger and crew member was landed safely in three trips to the sandy beach. This was a remarkable feat, for giant breakers were surging along the Gurnet shore ten and twelve feet high, with the powerful undertow trying to claim each survivor as he made the beach.

After their miraculous escape, the shipwrecked men looked about for shelter, but there were no people living anywhere in the vicinity. They were actually several miles from any habitation. After a long search a group of them found a hunting shack a mile to the north of the place where they landed. In it they discovered a loaded gun by means of which they started a fire. Two others of the party had taken a southerly course, bound for the Gurnet Lighthouse, miles to the south. Finally they reached the home of Keeper Burgess, who at once dispatched his assistant to the gunning hut to suggest they all walk to the Gurnet Light. When he reached the gunning shack five of the shipwrecked mariners were so exhausted that they decided to stay where they were for the night, but nine grateful men took the long walk along the Gurnet sand dunes with the assistant keeper, and reached the light after a hike of at least five miles. Here they rested until the roads were broken through and help finally reached them.

Young John Thomas of the Gurnet Light visited General Benjamin Lincoln in Boston in 1790. His late father had been General Thomas in the Revolution, and his mother was the official keeper at the Gurnet, the boy doing the work. General Lincoln, who had accepted the surrender of Cornwallis at Yorktown, had a long talk with the boy. Young Thomas at the conclusion of his conversation was officially appointed the keeper of Gurnet Light and remained at his station until 1812, when he was relieved by Joseph Burgess.

On July 2, 1801, the Gurnet Light was completely destroyed by fire, but all materials, including the oil, were saved. The merchants of Plymouth and Duxbury quickly erected a temporary beacon at their own expense. In April 1802 Congress paid the merchants $270 for their efforts in completing the beacon, and appropriated $2,500 for a new lighthouse. General Lincoln journeyed to the Gurnet and paid the Thomas family $120 outright for the land where the lighthouse was to be built. The new light first shone in 1803.

Joseph Burgess, believed to be the son of the old keeper, was appointed to the Gurnet Light on October 16, 1812. In 1851 he was still the keeper.

When Captain Edward W. Carpender made his tour of inspection along the Atlantic coast, he arrived at the Gurnet on November 1, 1838. After his examination he expressed himself as dissatisfied with the lighting arrangements at the lighthouse off Plymouth. He believed that many shipmasters confused the Gurnet Lights with Barnstable Light, as the space of thirty feet that separated the two towers at the Gurnet was not enough to keep them from blending together when seen from the deck of a ship out at sea. Several years earlier a ship had been lost a short distance north of the Gurnet because the captain claimed only one light was burning. The real trouble, of course, was that his bearing was such that the two lights appeared as one.

Carpender believed that the solution was to build a new tower that would have two lights on it, one 110 feet and the other 65 feet above the roaring waves. Willoughby in his book shows that the same difficulty would be present—a vessel far out on the ocean would only see one light because of the curvature of the earth. At any rate, Carpender's scheme was never adopted, for the same arrangement of lights was still at the station when I. W. P. Lewis made his visit in 1843.

Lewis said on the completion of his tour of inspection that the lights were in a condition of partial ruin, a conclusion in which Captain Josiah Sturgis of the Revenue Cutter *Hamilton* concurred. Sturgis wrote in 1842 that the towers were old and so decayed that they were "unworthy of repairs." Even the cautious Stephen Pleasonton had a comment to make on the lighthouse towers. Although he was a sworn enemy of I. W. P. Lewis, Pleasonton told the chairman of the House Commerce Committee that he was "much afraid they will fall to the ground in the course of the summer."

The Gurnet Light was rebuilt in 1843. The structures were distinctive, their two high octagonal towers having the general appearance of Nix's Mate Beacon in Boston Harbor. By 1871 the lights then in the twin towers were compared unfavorably to the lights of an ordinary dwelling house. A short time later the power of Gurnet Light was increased.

The Gurnet Light was an important beacon during the long period when Plymouth Harbor was a thriving seacoast port. Then commerce dropped off, and Plymouth lost most of its sea traffic. In 1914, however, the Cape Cod Canal brought the lighthouse back into importance as a coastal beacon between Boston and New York.

In 1924 the Northeast tower of the Gurnet Lights was discontinued, completing a period of 156 years when twin lights had been the Gurnet characteristic.

There is no question but that the mariner can more readily identify the present alternate single and double flashes that beam out over the sea from the tower 102 feet above the waters off Plymouth than the old fixed lights from the twin beacons. The flash is now 700,000 candlepower.

DUXBURY PIER

The brown tower at Duxbury Pier in Plymouth harbor, erected in 1871, is locally known as Bug Light. The 700-candlepower red light flashes three times every ten seconds from a height of thirty-five feet above the water. Duxbury Pier is located on the north side of the main channel, which leads to Duxbury, Kingston, and Plymouth.

Without question, Keeper Fred Bohm's record as a life saver here is an outstanding one. In one year he rescued ninety persons, including thirty-six Girl Scouts.

Keeper Bohm's most unusual rescue came at suppertime one night when the wind was blowing a fifty-mile gale. Hearing terrified screams, he ran out on deck and saw a woman trying to swim toward the light from an overturned boat.

"I launched my boat and rowed toward her," Bohm told me later, "but before I could reach her she had gone down, caught in the devil-tail sea weed the place was full of. I threw off my clothes and jumped over after her. I swam and then waded into shallow water with her unconscious in my arms. Getting her up into the lighthouse, I noticed that her bathing suit was gone. She was in bad shape, and did not respond to first aid. I worked on her for four hours. Finally her eyes began to open, and she gained consciousness."

"Where are my clothes?" were her first words.

"I don't know, but you are lucky to be alive," was Keeper Bohm's reply to the girl whose life he had saved. By midnight the girl was safe ashore, wearing borrowed clothing.

31

Sandy Neck and Billingsgate Lighthouses

SANDY NECK LIGHT

At the west side of the entrance to Barnstable Harbor there stands a privately owned lighthouse, which once was a guardian beacon for vessels off the Barnstable shore. The lighthouse station was first established at this point in the year 1827, after the wreck of the *Almira* in January of that year.

At first the lantern was built up from the roof of the keeper's dwelling, and was sixteen feet above the residence. Sailing directions for 1845 suggested running "directly for the light until within a cable's length of the beach," after which the vessel should "follow the shore around the point."

A new lighthouse was built in 1857, and still stands at the entrance to Barnstable Harbor. Until the station was discontinued, the 180 candlepower fixed light illuminated the harbor from a height of forty-eight feet above the ocean.

In the office of the *Register Press* at Yarmouthport, Massachusetts, is the log book or journal of the keeper of Sandy Neck Lighthouse, dating from October 4, 1873, until the year 1899. The journal, started by Keeper Edward Gorham, begins as follows:

"Saturday October 4 1873 Steamer Verbena anchored off the bar at about seven o'clock.

"Sunday morning October 5 Got under weigh and came up harbor to anchor.

"Monday morning October 6 Captain Gibbs inspected light and landed two tons of coal."

The terrible ice that trapped so many schooners and vessels in the winter of 1875 is graphically described in the keeper's journal. Several of the crews from schooners stranded in the bay were brought to the lighthouse. The ice was almost impassable from late in January 1875 until the middle of the following March.

BILLINGSGATE LIGHT

Because of agitation by Captain Michael Collins, Billingsgate Light was erected on Billingsgate Island off Cape Cod in 1822. The first light had eight oil lamps with crude reflectors. There was a brick dwelling for the keeper, with an attached brick tower for the light. Around the time of the Civil War, Billingsgate Point washed away to such an extent that the lighthouse was in danger of falling into the sea. After temporary measures had been taken, the light continued to function.

In spite of current opinions to the contrary, there was a sizable fishing village at Billingsgate for many years; in fact a picture taken around 1870 shows eight houses or buildings in addition to the lightkeeper's home.

In 1915 the sea began to undermine Billingsgate Light again. Ropes were used to prevent the tower from falling while men climbed up to remove the lens and lighting apparatus from the old beacon. When the tower was finally abandoned, the light shone on each night without a single interruption. One evening it appeared from the cupola of a private house and later from a temporary structure erected near the old beacon.

The light continued to gleam from the temporary structure, which was reinforced and made permanent. In 1922, however, exactly one hundred years after its first establishment, Billingsgate Light was discontinued.

32

Lighthouses Around Provincetown

Several lighthouses are grouped around the entrance to Provincetown Harbor, located on the finger of land which extends in a curved direction from the "bended arm of Cape Cod." Glistening white in the sun or gleaming brightly at night, they form a pleasing vista which the sea voyager enjoys as he sails into Cape Cod Harbor. Long Point Light, at the tip of the inner finger, is first in view, after which Wood End Light and the light at Race Point appear.

LONG POINT LIGHT

At the inner extremity of the long stretch of sandy terrain that curls up to a northernmost point well inside Cape Cod Harbor, stands Long Point Light, illuminated for the first time in 1827. In early days, it was technically described as being on Long Point Shoal, inside Cape Cod, in Latitude 42° 02′ 45″ North, and Longitude 70° 07′ 45″ West. Identified in 1845 as a "Stationery Light, erected on keeper's dwelling, twenty-eight feet above the sea," it was visible thirteen miles. Three years later Fifth Auditor Stephen Pleasonton ordered

Long Point Beach to be "close spiled," as he feared the sand was threatening the lighthouse.

Once there was an unusual settlement around the light. In 1818 the first building was erected there, and before the 1850's a thriving village of two hundred people was established out on the sand shoal. Fishermen made up the largest part of the population, but a series of salt works with their attendant windmills soon put in operation brought workmen for that industry to the village. The salt works proved unprofitable when cheaper deposits were found near Syracuse, New York, and the exodus of the inhabitants from Long Point began just before the Civil War. Several of the more substantial homes were taken by barge across the harbor to Provincetown.

During the Civil War, blockade runners were very active off the coast. When rumors reported the Confederate warship *Alabama* cruising in the vicinity, the authorities decided that two forts were needed at the entrance to Provincetown Harbor. Long Point was chosen as the site for the forts; the laborers arrived at the lighthouse and within a few months had erected substantial batteries. After seeing the forts, the citizens of Provincetown named the two earthen mounds, Fort Useless and Fort Harmless. For years afterward, the obliging caretaker, Sergeant Rosenthal, annually fired off Fourth of July salutes from the forts across the harbor.

In 1875 a new tower was built, but the old lighthouse attached to the keeper's home remained for several years. That very winter a terrific ice floe twenty feet high pushed up on the Long Point Shore, and was the wonderment of hundreds of visitors.

In 1933 Keeper Thomas L. Chase was in charge of Long Point Light during the last week in May when the fog signal broke down. It was impossible to repair the machinery for several weeks, and two days later a heavy "pea-soup" fog came rolling in. As scores of vessels were scheduled to pass the lighthouse, Keeper Chase realized that the signal must be given, mechanism or no mechanism. Arriving at the bell house, he arranged the cord so that he could give it a hard tug every thirty seconds, and pulled out his watch for timing. It was then 10:45 p.m. Wednesday, May 24, when he began his tiresome task, and all during that long night the fog continued. Every thirty seconds Keeper Chase would give a lusty tug, and the 1,000-pound bell sent out its vital message to the sailors at sea. The hours slowly passed, but not until daybreak did the fog thin out. By eight o'clock Thursday morning, the fog had dissipated, so that he was able to rest from his weary task.

After a few hours' sleep he tried to adjust the mechanism himself, but failed. Shortly after dark the fog rolled in again, and the poor man, his arm badly strained, decided to try his left hand with the bell rope. At two a.m. the fog vanished, making it possible for the conscientious keeper to go to bed. Some parts for the fog mechanism reached Provincetown on Saturday, and Keeper Chase took his "dune jumping" Ford to town, obtained the parts, and returned to the light to begin his repair task. A friend interviewed him while he was fixing the bell.

"What will happen, Tom, if the fog rolls in before you have finished? Both your arms are gone, and how will you keep the signal going?"

"Well," replied the keeper, "I've got it all figured out. Although I feel like a baseball pitcher who has twirled a couple of double-headers without rest, I'll still be able to take care of the fog. I'm going to lie down on the dunes, tie the bell rope to my legs, and keep the fog signal going in that fashion until my arms get thawed out again."

Long Point Light is now an unattended automatic station with a flashing green light.

WOOD END

Wood End Light is a white, square tower, built in 1873, a little over a mile from Long Point Light. Wood End forms the extreme southerly elbow of the curving arm north of Cape Cod Harbor. Its comparatively recent establishment makes it the youngest of all lighthouses in the vicinity, but the location is an important one.

During the period between sunset and sunrise a flashing red light illuminates the sea for a distance of twelve miles around the Wood End tower. Flashing four times each minute, the light's 10,000 candlepower beam is bright for one second, then follows a period of fourteen seconds of darkness. The white tower is built right up from the low beach at Wood End. Technically, the lantern is thirty-nine feet above the ground, while the focal point of the light itself is only forty-five feet above the sea.

Henry David Thoreau speaks of a shipwreck at Wood End in his *Cape Cod*. The storm was the same which caused the great shipwreck off Cohasset, that of the brig *Saint John*. Thoreau interviewed one of the shipwrecked sailors then still at Provincetown, who stated the following:

"Before we left the wharf we made the acquaintance of a passenger whom we had seen at the hotel. When we asked him which way he came to Provincetown, he answered that he was cast ashore at Wood End. . . . He had been at work as a carpenter in Maine, and took passage for Boston in a schooner laden with lumber. When the storm came on they endeavored to get into Provincetown Harbor. 'It was dark and misty,' said he, 'and as we were steering for Long Point Light we suddenly saw the land near us,—for our compass was out of order,—varied several degrees [a mariner always casts the blame on his compass],—but there being a mist on shore, we thought it was farther off than it was, and so held on, and we immediately struck on the bar. . . . The sea washed completely over us, and well-nigh took the breath out of my body. I held on to the running rigging, but I have learned to hold on to the standing rigging next time. . . . We all got safe to a house in Wood End, at midnight, wet to our skins, and half frozen to death.' He had apparently spent the time since playing checkers at the hotel, and was congratulating himself on having beaten a tall fellow-boarder at that game. . . . As we passed Wood End, we noticed the pile of lumber on the shore which had made the cargo of their vessel."

The keepers of Wood End Light have seen many shipwrecks since the establishment of the station. More than fifty shipping disasters have occurred in the vicinity of the lighthouse since 1875. The schooner *John M. Ball* hit Wood End in 1890, followed in 1896 by the *Nellie M. Snow*. A year later the British schooner *Clifford* was pushed ashore in a driving northeaster, while in 1898, the year *Portland* sank, the *Lester A. Lewis* was wrecked at Wood End. Three vessels hit shore near the light the next year, the sloop *Active,* and the schooners *Joseph Warren* and *Ada J. Campbell*. In 1901 the yacht *Adventure* and the schooner *Zepher* hit the beach, while the next year the British schooner *St. Bernard,* and the American schooners *Manomet* and *Marjory Brown* were lost at Wood End.

Since Wood End Light is no longer attended by keepers, the Race Point Coast Guard Station sends a patrol to check the area.

RACE POINT LIGHT

One of the worst stretches of sand for shipwrecks along the entire Cape Cod Coast is known as Race Point, but it was not until 1816 that the government built a lighthouse there to protect shipping. Far more than a hundred vessels have met their fate at Race Point since the lighthouse was built, but for everyone one lost it has been estimated that a dozen were helped to safety by the beams of the light.

Less than twenty years after the light was built, a fishing settlement had acquired enough dignity at Race Point to be designated as a separate school district on Cape Cod. In 1839 a bridge was built across Hatch's Harbor to give the residents a shortcut to Provincetown. This bridge is now a dike. The fishing village and the schoolhouse have vanished from Race Point, and the light keepers and their families are the only ones who remain.

Samuel Adams Drake has given us the best description of this part of the Cape:

"After crossing the wilderness, I came to the shore, the sea roughened by it, but not grand. There was but a little drift, and that such 'unconsidered trifles' of the sea as the vertebrae of fishes, jellyfish, a few tangled bunches of weed, and some pretty pebbles. Looking up and down the beach, I discovered one or two wreckers seeking out the night's harvest; and presently there came a cart in which were a man and woman, the man ever and anon jumping out to gather up a little bundle of drift-wood, with which he ran back to the cart, followed by a shaggy Newfoundland dog that barked and gamboled at his side. . . . I followed the bank by the verge of the beach, and the tide having but just turned. Before me was the light-house, and the collection of huts at Race Point. A single vessel, bound for a Southern port, was in sight, that, after standing along, gunwhale under, within half a mile of shore, filled away on the other tack, rounding the point in good style. . . .

"I passed a group of huts, used perhaps at times by fishermen, and at others as a shelter for shipwrecked mariners. The doors were open, and, notwithstanding a palisade of barrel-staves, the sand had drifted to a considerable depth within. Here also were pieces of a vessel's bulwarks, the first vestiges of wreck I had seen. . . ."

One stormy wintry morning around 1875 the *John Rommell, Jr.* struck near the lighthouse. Great waves then pushed tons of ice aboard the helpless craft. The ice broke through the wooden decks and the *Rommell* was soon forced sideways toward the beach. The undertow pushed the loose sand around the vessel, until she was hopelessly marooned. The lighthouse keeper saw members of the crew holding fast to the rigging. Then when the tide went out they climbed down and made the shore. One sailor, weighted down with his frozen clothing, dropped dead on the beach, but the others survived the shipwreck.

More than one hundred vessels have been wrecked here since the early records of Provincetown began. During a thirteen-year period from 1890 to 1903 there were twenty-eight known shipping disasters at Race Point. They include the *Robert Byron, Addison Center, Alice B. Phillips, Boyd & Leeds, Gov. J. Y. Smith, Carl D. Lothrop, Henry A. Paull, C. W. Morse, Ethel Maud, Thomas Brumidge, Eliza Levansaler, Gertie S. Winsor, Fortuna, Lizzie Griffin, Mary C. Hartz,* and *Susan R. Stone.* Wreckage from the *Addie E. Snow,* the *Pentagoet,* and the *Portland* washed ashore here during the *Portland Gale* of 1898.

William H. Lowther was placed in charge at Race Point Light in 1915. James W. Hinckley, from Barnstable, came into the service in 1920, as assistant to Keeper Lowther, and upon Keeper Lowther's leaving the station, assumed charge of the Race Point Light.

When Keeper Hinckley first went on the station he often

carried fifteen pounds of groceries two and a half miles from Provincetown to the lighthouse. Finally he bought a horse. Because it wasn't easy for the horse to make speed over the dunes, it was still a 75-minute trip from Provincetown, but by 1935 a specially-built car with balloon tires had cut the running time to half an hour. Hinckley spoke of the difference in temperature in Provincetown and at the light, claiming it was seven degrees warmer at the Race Point Light, but admitting that the wind blew there as at no other place almost all the time. His words follow:

"The wind often touches a mile a minute. Some of the gusts will throw you several feet, and it's hard going. The sand is bad enough, cutting into your skin, but a combination of sand and snow is almost unbearable. That's when those Coast Guard boys who walk the beach earn their money. This is the only light, after leaving Boston Lightship that ships have to guide them around the head of the Cape. In thick weather you haven't a thing to tell you where you are until you hear my whistle. We give two blasts every minute that can be heard 12 to 15 miles out to sea."

On Christmas Day, 1937, Keeper James W. Hinckley retired from the service. It was his seventieth birthday. Interviewed at the time, he spoke of the women he called the "lighthouse widows," and expressed the hope that someday the government would give a pension to the wives of the lighthouse keepers who, in his opinion, "do just as much as the men."

Race Point Light no longer has resident keepers but is maintained by the Race Point Coast Guard Station a considerable distance away. The white tower sends out a flashing white light of 400,000 candlepower from a height of forty-one feet visible for a distance of twelve miles.

33

Cape Cod or Highland Light

Reverend James Freeman, in 1794, writing for the members of the Massachusetts Historical Society, mentions the "high land of Cape Cod, well known to seamen." Freeman goes on to say that more vessels were cast away at the High Land than on any other part of Barnstable County, Cape Cod. "A light house near the Clay Pounds should Congress think proper to erect one, would prevent many of these fatal accidents." This suggestion of Dr. Freeman, together with agitation by the Boston Marine Society, finally induced the government to take the action that resulted in the erection of Highland Light in 1797.

Today, its peacetime beam of 300,000 candlepower makes it one of the most powerful New England lighthouses. Shining full twenty miles out into the ocean from its height 183 feet above the water, the single flash every five seconds is a welcome sight for all mariners at sea.

In the early days of the beacon's history, it was feared by some that Cape Cod Light might be confused with Boston Light, whereupon a rotating eclipser, or screen, was placed in the lantern room. This eclipser slowly revolved about the light, transforming Cape Cod Light into a flashing beacon. Isaac Small, in charge at Cape Cod in 1800, is believed to have been the first keeper to work this mechanism. Seven years later the eclipser was described by a visitor, Edward Augustus Randall, who journeyed to Highland Light to inspect the apparatus. Randall was quite impressed with the semicircular "skreen" that rotated about the lantern, the complete revolution taking eight minutes, but his final decision, which time has proved an error in judgment, was one of disapproval:

"By this machinery, the light is made alternately visible and invisible, and presents various phases, like the moon; and this is the distinctive mark; but the practical result is not as favorable as must have been contemplated, before the plan was admitted into use.

"We see, that as the skreen is continually turning, the light is *full* only for a single moment in the course of each revolution; it is also totally eclipsed but for a single moment; but during all the time between, it is no more than obscure and imperfect light. . . . There are circumstances enough, at sea, to obscure the best lights, without any contrivances on shore, to assist this misforfune! A light that should appear, not steadily, but by incessant flashes, would be useful; but this cannot be the case with one, the fulness of which returns so slowly."

Constant Hopkins succeeded Isaac Small as keeper in 1812, but passed away five years later. John Grocier was appointed the new keeper of Cape Cod Light by S. II. Smith, Commissioner of the Revenue.

Captain Edward Carpender, inspector of lighthouses, visited Cape Cod Light in 1838 by revenue cutter, and found the keeper attempting to "make a hasty rub-up" in anticipation of an inspection. Carpender observed that the tower was of brick, thirty feet high, and the lantern was 160 feet above the sea. Fifteen lamps provided the illumination. They were arranged in two rows, eight in the lower and seven in the upper row, each lamp having a fifteen-inch reflector. These fifteen lamps covered an estimated area of about three hundred degrees, the land to the south of the tower not being lighted.

The next visitor of importance was Henry David Thoreau, the naturalist and author, who stopped at Truro's lighthouse in 1849, 1850, and again in 1855. Thoreau observed that Highland Light was forty-three miles from Cape Ann Light, and forty-one from Boston Light. Interested in the erosion here, he asked the light keeper how fast the cliff was washing away. The keeper's recollections went back as far as 1789, or before the light had been built. Some years great sections of the cliff washed out, while in other times very little seemed to go. In 1848, many rods of soil went into the sea, and the keeper did not believe the tower would last much longer unless it were moved. The cliffs are still a safe distance from Highland Light, however. Thoreau's remarks follow:

"Among the many regulations of the Lighthouse Board, hanging against the wall here, many of them excellent, perhaps, if there were a regiment stationed here to attend to them, there is one requiring the keeper to keep an account of the number of vessels which pass his light during the day. But there are a hundred vessel in sight at once, steering in all directions, many on the very verge of the horizon, and he must have more eyes than Argus, and be a good deal farther sighted, to tell which are passing his light. It is an employment in some respects best suited to the habits of the gulls which coast up and down here, and circle over the sea. . . .

"The keeper entertained us handsomely in his solitary

little ocean house. He was a man of singular patience and intelligence, who, when our queries struck him, rang as clear as a bell in response. The light-house lamp a few feet distant shone full into my chamber, and made it as bright as day, so I knew exactly how the Highland Light bore all that night, and I was in no danger of being wrecked. . . . I thought as I lay there, half awake and half asleep, looking upward through the window at the lights above my head, how many sleepless eyes from far out on the Ocean stream—mariners of all nations spinning their yarns through the various watches of the night—were directed toward my couch."

The year after Captain Carpender inspected the station, Cape Cod Light was made over. New 21-inch reflectors were installed, together with deck, chandelier, and a different type of lantern. In 1852 other improvements were planned, which included the elevation of the tower and the setting up of the new improved Fresnel type of lanterns. But several years went by before this later change was carried out.

Enoch S. Hamilton became the keeper of Highland Light on December 15, 1850, and received exactly $16.17 for his pay for the rest of the year. His regular pay, however, for a complete month, was $87.50. From the original diary or light-house journal of Highland Light, as the station was then officially called, we learn that during his first month at the new station, January 1851, Keeper Hamilton burned sixty-nine gallons of oil. Two years later, the consumption for January 1853 was seventy-two gallons, showing a fairly consistant burning of the lamps.

The vast number of schooners, ships, and vessels of all types passing the light almost baffles the imagination. Keeper Hamilton's duty, as Thoreau has told us, was to count the number of craft that passed his station at America's front door. From July 12, 1853, to July 23, 1853, a total of 1,200 vessels were visible from Keeper Hamilton's vantage point at the top of Highland Light.

The worst shipping disaster while Keeper Hamilton was at Highland Light was the loss of the *Josepha,* or *Josephus,* as it is commonly called. A remarkable tale, it has been related scores of times until the actual facts have been somewhat distorted. Below is the story copied from Keeper Hamilton's own handwriting.

April 29, 1852

"P. Greely Esqr

"Sir permit me to address through you the English Consul. Mr Gratton desired me to furnish him with a statement of the circumstances attending the loss of the English Barque Josepha. She left Bristol the 19th of March and the 20th of April she struck on a Sand Bar about half a mile to the North of the High-Land Light House and about 300 yards from the beach. The fogg was very thick at the time and during most of the afternoon. Immediately after information was communicated to those in the vicinity of the Light House and circulated in this part of the town quite a concourse of people assembled on the shore to witness the disaster and render all possible aid. At this time the sea was running so high it was dem impossible to board her. I was almost the first one down on the shore opsite the wreck and return immediately after the rockets of the Humane Society. I had the Life Preservers also carried down. I was asked for the boat that belong to Government. I immediately gave it to them with the intention if the rocket carried the line over the vessel it could ply between the vessel and shore. A rocket bursted, that created more excitement. The boat was then hauled down and J. Collins & D. H. Cassidy got in to the boat and pulled for the vessel. When about fifteen yards from the ship the current was running so strong to the north that it drifted them to the leeward of the vessel. The boat being capsized they were drown after clinging to the boat a few moments. While some of the men were preparing to fire the rocket others went for the life boat which was of the distance of a mile from the wreck. When the life boat arrived the men Collins and Cassidy had perished. The tide coming in the sea being very rough and growing more rough every minute it was not deem safe to launch her so all hope of saving those on the wreck was lost at this time!

"It commenced growing dark. Fires were kindled that those on the wreck might be assured that we had not left them. We knew they had not perished for we could distinctly hear their cries so heart rending. At intervals we divded ourselves into company, to walk the beach and render assistance to any of the crew that might be carried ashore on pieces of the wreck. Parts of it being already strewn along the shore. Everything from the wreck tendency to drift to the North. Therefore the men continued to cruise along the shore down to the North of the wreck till 11 oclock and afterwards. Previous to this they had herd crashing of the wreck 5 or 6 times as they heard no voices found no bodies come ashore they concluded all must have perished.

"At 10 oclock I left in company with Rev. Mr. Lord to trim my lamps for the night and immediately after attending to my duties Light House keeper we returned to the scene. On arriving at one of the fires we found one of the unfortunate seamen named George Chetney on his knees side of the fire for he could not stand. We asked him if there were any other saved. He said one more down towards the shore. We hastened down in the direction he pointed and found one named John Jasper. He had crawled from part of the wreck toward the fire to a bank of sand about three feet high but was so exhausted that he could not climb up on it and so exhausted he could not speak. Neither of them had any hats. John no boots and only one sock. We brought him up to the fire then carried him by main strength up a bank of yielding sand and gravel a hundred feet high and return for the other.

"By this time the one we left at the fire had received so much benefit from it the brands of which we had brought together that by putting his arms around our necks he was able to walk along the shore some distance to where the bank was little lower up. It leaving him sheltered from the winds we returned for John laying beside a hole.

"When we arrived about 2 hours after going down to the wreck we got them into the house by the fire. Exchanged their wet clothes for some warm and dry. While removing the clothing of John we found him much bruised. His hands felt badly swollen. After rubbing them with out hands and coarse clothes he revived somewhat. Mrs. Hamilton gave them some warmed refreshments and they were put to bed. In the morning the family physician was called to John and he seemed quite feverish. His hands and feet continued to be much swollen. Unable to sit up for two days though continued to improve. I will now give a statement of the events that occured on board the vessel as given by the survivors after they had sufficiently recovered to narate the disaster.

"The vessel struck on the bar about 3 oclock P.M. [I]mmediately after the vessel grounded and had wore around a heavy seas struck her on the starboard side carrying away the masts. Then they got out—and lowered her over the starboard side of the deck. Another sea came and took away both the long boat pen— The deck then gave away from the stern to the foremast. Then the main and mizzenmast went overboard. The larboard side of the vessel fell in on the iron. The men at this time were up in the fore rigging. When the foremast gave away two of them were washed overboard and the remainder clung to the starboard side of the vessel. The third or fourth sea she broke apart. alltogether. 14 men were washed off. The two remaining ones were providentially nearer the stern and after regaining their hold by endeavoring to make themselves fast to this piece of wreck they were however washed off two or three times but were fortunate enough to regain there hold. The forerigging became entangled in the freight and left them one hour and half. Then a heavy sea cleared the rigging. They came directly ashore nearly opposite the light on the beach. Of the men that were lost I will add Mr Collins was 47 years of age. He leaves a wife and three children. Mr. Cassidy was 23—he leaves a young wife. He had been married only a few weeks.

"Any additional information that may be desired will be gladly furnished. I should have answered your letter sooner had not your letter been directed to Truro P. O. instead of North Truro and thereby was detained a day or two.

[ENOCH HAMILTON, *Keeper*]"

For years afterward John Jasper, as captain of a trans-Atlantic liner, dipped his flag to Keeper Hamilton at Cape Cod Light, and the good keeper would remember the shipwreck of the *Josepha,* when Jasper was one of only two men of the crew saved from the great waves of Cape Cod.

Keeper Hamilton told stories of the hardships of the former keepers, before the lighthouse was rebuilt, when the thin, ordinary panes of glass were shattered time after time during a severe storm, necessitating the placing of boards to keep out the rain and snow. Once, when almost three-quarters of the panes were shattered, very little light sifted through to the fishermen and sailors out in the seething ocean, straining their eyes for the light which meant survival or disaster.

The captain often stayed in the lantern room on stormy nights when the great gales swept in from the ocean to shake the foundations of the light itself. It was his duty to keep the glass clean and the light shining clear. The keeper, high in the tower, felt that his was a grave responsibility when the snowflakes banked against the lantern room, keeping the vital rays away from the sailors out on the ocean. He knew that anxious men were depending on him, and his sense of duty would not allow him to leave the tower.

In the summer other troubles presented themselves. Myriads of moths almost shut out the beams as effectively as the snowstorms. During the spring of 1855 the keeper found nineteen small yellow birds lying dead around the lighthouse.

Keepers around 1850 had to be careful to turn down their wicks in the morning, for when the sun rose, it would often set fire to the wicks by means of the reflectors. One keeper in particular at Cape Cod Light would forget to turn his wicks way down. The sun, on one of the coldest days of the year, actually set fire to the lamps, and the keeper glanced up at the tower at noon to find them all burning.

In 1857 the present tower was built, sixty-six feet above the ground. Other improvements, which totaled fifteen thousand dollars, were completed, but as the years went by Cape Cod Light was considered entirely inadequate for the great number of ships that needed its guidance. Finally, in 1901, arrangements were made to equip the tower as a first order station. On October 10 of that year the new lens, revolving on a mercury float, gave out a flash of 192,000 candlepower. Gradually the intensity was increased to one of half a million candlepower.

On October 27, 1932, Cape Cod Light's oil lamps were replaced by a single 1,000-watt electric bulb of 2,500 candlepower. The great bull's-eye lenses magnify this lamp to 4,000,000 candles! Thus Cape Cod Light, the highest of all lights on the New England mainland, was also the most powerful.

At present, Cape Cod Light has been reduced to 300,000

candlepower, but because of the curvature of the earth and the fact that it is 183 feet above the water, it is visible for twenty miles.

Keeper William Joseph told me more than a quarter century ago that although he watched with interest the trawlers, steamers, and naval craft as they went by Cape Cod Light, it was indeed a far cry from the old days when the keepers would record every day the passing of hundreds of sailing craft.

On the other hand, he admitted, because of the mechanized fleets of sailing craft and fishermen, marine disasters off the light were reduced to a single marine tragedy every year or so. When we realize that the generation living at the end of the eighteenth century saw three out of five New England sailors perish as sea, we know that the life of the mariner is now a much happier one.

34

Lights of the Lower Cape

South of Cape Cod Light there have been three lighthouse stations on the back or outer side of the cape. They were at Nauset Beach, Chatham, and Monomoy Point. All have been radically changed since they were built. Nauset Beach Lights have been changed from three beacons to one; Chatham from two to one; and Monomoy's single tower has now been extinguished.

NAUSET BEACH LIGHT

Nauset Beach Light was established in the year 1838. At that time a unique plan was carried out by building three lighthouses instead of one on the cliff looking out to sea. Fifteen feet high, 150 feet apart, the three stone towers presented an unusual appearance to the mariner sailing along the coast. They were soon christened the "Three Sisters of Nauset." When Inspector Carpender reached Nauset Light on his tour of duty he remarked that a single revolving beacon could have saved the government much expense, and it would have been better identification for ships at sea. Inspector I. W. P. Lewis called the three light towers a "curious trio of lighthouses," adding that they were poorly constructed.

Ralph Waldo Emerson visited Keeper Collins at Nauset Light some years before the Civil War. "Collins, the keeper," said Emerson, "told us he found resistance to the project of building a lighthouse on this coast, as it would injure the wrecking business." Collins' attitude of helping to prevent shipwrecks did not make him friends with several of the residents of Nauset, and there were those who wished him discharged. A letter which I discovered in the files of the Lighthouse Department in Washington includes certain statements of importance in this matter. Referring to Collins, the letter says in part that "Collins . . . keeper of the Nausett Lights . . . ought of right be removed but no one in this town [Eastham] has done anything to effect his removal . . . I feel it a duty to do something to cause removal and as no other person from this place has applied for the situation, I feel prompted to do it myself . . ."

After the government had made tests that proved conclusively that one beacon which flashed was better than three steady lights, two of the "Three Sisters" were sold, moved from the reservation, and used as summer cottages. The third remained as the Nauset Light. When Chatham Light was altered from two beacons to a single light in 1923, one of the cast-iron towers was moved to Nauset, where it still stands, and the third "Sister of Nauset" was also made into a summer residence.

George I. Herbolt was keeper of Nauset Light in 1930. Captain Veidler, an actor of former years, became keeper on Herbolt's termination of office, and several years ago prepared an unusual greeting for me when I flew over Nauset Light with his Christmas package. As we banked over the lighthouse, I noticed that a welcome had been spelled out in the area just behind the lighthouse. The greeting read:

SANTA HELLO. The greeting was constructed by placing scrub pine branches in the form of letters. Keeper Veidler, his son and his wife had worked all morning long arranging the spelling so that we could read the words from the air.

At the death of Keeper Veidler, Keeper Eugene L. Coleman and his wife, Amanda, came to Nauset Beach. They enjoyed being stationed on the mainland after serving at both lonely Boon Island and Cape Neddick Nubble.

Nauset Beach Light shines from a height of 114 feet above the sea with a beam of 400,000 candlepower. Its characteristic retains the old idea of three lighthouse towers with its three flashes every ten seconds. The present forty-eight-foot tower, now a colorful red and white, was moved here in 1923. There is no resident keeper.

CHATHAM LIGHT

A little more than ten miles to the southward of Nauset Light stands the last remaining representative of the famous Chatham Light Station of Cape Cod—a single cast-iron tower with a light that flashes two times every ten seconds from a point eighty feet above the sea. The original Chatham station, established in 1808, was a building with two towers, and the constructor who erected it had much trouble before his work was completed. He had planned to erect it from stones nearby, as he did not know about the scarcity of stones at Cape Cod. When he discovered his predicament he found himself unprepared to transport the rocks to the scene of the building. The discouraged constructor finally reported on June 26, 1806, as follows: "There are no stones to be had so the lights will have to be made of wood."

Thus, the two original towers were built of wood.

It was a momentous occasion for the people of Cape Cod when Chatham Light was finished and a keeper was to be chosen. While going through the old files in the National Archives Building in Washington, I came across an amazing petition containing more than 125 names headed by Nathaniel Freeman, asking for the appointment of Samuel Nye to the position of keeper. There were several other shorter petitions. Many who could not write put down their marks.

On September 19, 1808, Boston Port Collector Benjamin Lincoln wrote Secretary of the Treasury Albert Gallatin that he expected the construction of the new station would be completed in about six weeks, and suggested that the petitions be sent on to President Thomas Jefferson for approval. October 7, 1808, President Jefferson appointed Samuel Nye the first keeper of the Chatham Lights on James' Head. At that time the lights were stationary in character and about seventy feet apart. The lights were both about seventy feet above the sea.

In 1832 the keeper at Chatham Lights, Samuel Stinson, was reported on several occasions in neglect of his duty, and finally was warned by the local superintendent, David Henshaw. Resigning shortly afterward, Samuel Stinson asked to be reimbursed for an addition to the dwelling which he had constructed, but as the addition was built wholly on his own responsibility, Stephen Pleasonton, Fifth Auditor of the Treasury, denied Stinson's application. About this time, new brick towers were erected.

In 1843 Pleasonton decided that Chatham Lights should be painted white instead of being whitewashed, and so paint was used for many years afterward. Whitewash, however, is still used at many of the Massachusetts stations today.

Collins Howes, who had lost a leg in an accident, was appointed keeper in 1841 and removed four years later when President James Polk came into office. Howes was succeeded by Simeon Nickerson, who died in October 1848. On the inauguration of President Zachary Taylor, in 1849, former

Keeper Howes wrote to the Secretary of the Treasury asking to be reappointed. Meanwhile, when Nickerson died, his destitute widow was given the position as light keeper at Chatham, and many friends sprang to her aid when they heard Howes was maneuvering to get his old position back. As a result of the controversy Mrs. Nickerson retained the position and was keeper at Chatham Light for many more years.

The southern tower of the Chatham Lights was rebuilt in 1863, and a new type of lantern installed. But more trouble was on the way. The ever-shifting Chatham Bars were again causing radical changes in the coast line, and by the year 1875 the entire outer beach was vanishing. A comparison of charts between the years 1860 and the present time gives an amazing idea of how Chatham has changed its shore line.

In 1877 conditions were very serious, and the old tower and station began to topple over into the sea. The lighthouse station and two new towers, made of cast iron, were established across the street from the old site. One hundred feet apart, they lighted the mariners' way for many years.

In 1879, after a terrific easterly gale had swept the coast, schoolboys walking along the shore noticed that the underpinning of the old lighthouse had entirely washed away to reveal several clay pits, two or three feet deep. Close examination of the pits by the boys disclosed several ancient coins. How they were placed under the foundation of old Chatham Light has never been explained, but the usual opinion of the local inhabitants is that some old pirate buried his booty there long before the lighthouse was erected.

In 1923 the government took down the north tower of Chatham Light and removed it to Nauset, where it stands today.

At Chatham Light is a federal radio beacon.

MONOMOY LIGHT

Plans were made in 1823 to erect a lighthouse at the tip end of the dangerous Monomoy Point, which extends southward from Chatham, and construction of the lighthouse began the same year. The location, then known as Sandy Point, was approximately eight miles southward of Chatham Light. About 1840 the seas cut the point off from the mainland, making it an island. Shifting sands filled in the inlet later, and the island became a point again. A single wintry storm can change the entire contour of this dangerous sand spit, which runs out from Cape Cod proper, and no mariner in these waters can feel safe until he has put Monomoy Point behind him.

When he visited Monomoy Point in 1838 Inspector Carpender had much to say about the lighthouse and its site:

"This memorable light stands on Sandy Point, 8 miles from Chatham, a long, low beach that reaches right off into the very heart of the whole coasting navigation. . . . This point of land has received an accession of several hundred yards from the sea, making it probable that, in the course of a few years, when the land shall have formed a little higher, it will be advisable to remove this light farther to the southward."

I. W. P. Lewis found the lighthouse in a ruined condition when he made his visit in 1842. The tower was rebuilt in 1855 and again in the 1870's. In the government *Light List* for 1922 Monomoy Point Light is listed as having a red tower, with a covered way leading from the keeper's dwelling. The tower was forty feet high, and had a fixed white light with a red sector that was visible from 255 degrees to 267 degrees, the edges of the sector indicating the position of the whistling and bell buoys at the entrance to the Pollock Rip Slue.

When in 1923 the Chatham Twin Lights were reduced to a single light, more attention was paid to Monomoy Light. The decision was eventually made that Chatham Light effectively guarded Monomoy as well as the seacoast directly in front of Chatham, so Monomoy Light was discontinued. The land on which Monomoy Light stands is now privately owned.

The area around old Monomoy Light was the location where the starved passengers of the horror ship, the *George & Ann,* were landed in 1729. Although the vessel was not wrecked, as were so many others in the vicinity, her voyage was a prolonged journey of over four months from Dublin, Ireland.

A terrible sickness befell the passengers and took the lives of more than one hundred people. But in spite of this decrease in number there was not enough food to go around. Contrary winds delayed Captain Rymer, the master of the vessel. The prevailing westerly winds continued day after day. Finally Nantucket Sound was reached. By this time the passengers had grave suspicions that the captain was attempting to murder them all by starvation and thus acquire their possessions.

One day in October, Captain Lothrop, sailing southward in a Boston Packet, sighted the horror ship, which was then flying distress signals, and came alongside. The frantic passengers, crazy with fear and starvation, were by this time reduced to fifteen biscuits and a few pints of water. They begged Captain Lothrop to pilot them to the nearest land, which was Monomoy Point, and threatened to drop Captain Rymer over the side if he would not agree to their plans. Rymer finally gave in, and Captain Lothrop agreed to pilot them to Monomoy.

Reaching Jo Stewart's Tavern at Wreck Cove, the passengers were taken ashore and fed. The grateful survivors were billeted in the fishing village at Monomoy that following winter, after which they left Cape Cod for Ulster County, New York. The head of the surviving Scotch-Irish colony was Charles Clinton, and among his descendants are included General James Clinton of Revolutionary War fame, Vice-President George Clinton, and DeWitt Clinton, New York Governor and builder of the Erie Canal.

35

Lighthouses of Nantucket

Residents of the "faraway isle," as we like to call Nantucket, were among the first in America to have a lighthouse. Preceded in their action only by the people of Boston, the inhabitants of Nantucket erected a beacon at the entrance to their harbor in 1746. The effectiveness of the old New England town meeting was demonstrated when the sea captains of the island spoke out for the lighthouse on January 24, 1746. Before the evening was over, a favorable vote was given the project, the sum of two hundred English pounds was appropriated for the purpose of building the lighthouse, and Ebenezer Calef, Obed Hussey, and Jabez Bunker were chosen as "the men to take care to build the light house . . . on Brant Point."

By April 28 the lighthouse had been completed, for the town meeting held that day decreed that "whereas there is a light house built at the Charge of the Town on Supposition that the owners and others concerned in the shipping will maintain said light as they shall think to be the most for their conveniency During the pleasure of the Town." Thus, in no uncertain terms, the inhabitants of Nantucket made the ship owners understand that the lighthouse was their own maritime responsibility. That the ship owners did their work well is attested by the fact that Brant Point Light gleamed nightly for the next twelve years, until it was destroyed by fire.

When another town meeting was held the people of Nantucket agreed that the light should be rebuilt at once, and within a short time the tower was replaced. Incidentally, from all available records, it seems that Nantucket's Brant Point Lighthouse has been built and rebuilt more than any other tower in New England. I can find records of seven different lighthouses built at the entrance to the harbor of Nantucket.

On March 9, 1774, what might be considered a minor tornado visited the Isle of Nantucket, for at eight o'clock that morning a tremendous blast of wind ripped along the waterfront, destroying all buildings in its crooked path around Brant Point. Although the tornado took barely a minute to sweep across Nantucket Island at this point, many shops, barns, outhouses, and other small buildings were flattened completely. The worst loss, however, was the lighthouse, which was utterly destroyed.

The unhappy citizens met again two weeks later and agreed to build another tower "as High as the former one that blew down lately . . . at the Town's Expense."

Many captains from other ports were not in accord with Nantucket's system of lighthouse dues, which paid for the upkeep of Brant Point Light. To be on the safe side, the townsmen drew up a petition asking the General Court of Boston for permission to collect "Light Money" from "all the shipping using the Harbor." The General Court later passed such an order to the effect that, beginning on August 1, 1774, any vessel which was over fifteen tons was subjected to a charge of six shillings the first time each year it entered or left Nantucket Harbor. All went well for a time, with the

Nantucket inspector collecting the dues and applying the money toward the upkeep of the Brant Point Light, but another disastrous fire took place, destroying the lighthouse. A new tower was constructed and made ready for use in 1768. When the government of the United States in 1790 took over all the lighthouses, this light was among those ceded.

Because of the War of 1812, it was deemed necessary by the citizens of Nantucket to ask for the extinguishing of Nantucket Lighthouse. In a letter from the Treasury Department dated March 22, 1813, Albert Gallatin authorizes his Massachusetts representative, Henry Dearborn, to "give notice of lights being extinguished in newspapers."

In the year 1825 the lighthouse was considered no longer suitable for the purpose it had been erected, and a small tower framework was built on the top of the keeper's dwelling. When Captain Carpender reached Nantucket in 1838 on his tour of American lighthouses, he inspected this light on the roof of the keeper's dwelling. In his report he states that the tower had eight lamps arranged in a double row, six in the lower series and two lamps in the upper tier. These lamps were each backed by twelve-and-a-half-inch reflectors.

On April 8, 1831 Caleb Cushman was appointed keeper of Nantucket Light, and Aaron Folger was made the keeper of Nantucket Harbor Light. They were both cautioned by David Henshaw, local representative of the Treasury Department, about the necessity of "residing and being themselves in the houses provided for the Keepers." This admonition came because too many keepers delegated their work to other men while they went fishing for days at a time.

In 1831 the aged keeper of the Brant Point Light, David Coffin, was forced to retire, and his son, David Coffin, 2nd, was appointed to the position. At the same time Aaron Folger was retained as the keeper of the special light known as Nantucket Beacon, an auxiliary light for inner Nantucket Harbor, and not to be confused with the Brant Point Light.

Two great buoys, to be located at the discretion of John P. Norton, were placed at the harbor of Nantucket in 1835. Each cost six hundred dollars, and Stephen Pleasonton directed Norton to place them "aided by the best information you can obtain on the subject."

In 1852 William R. Easton of Nantucket, district superintendent of lighthouses, received the following letter from Stephen Pleasonton:

> Treasury Department
> Fifth Auditor's Office
> June 23, 1852

"Sir,

"Your General Report of the condition of Lights in your district without date but accompanied by your letter in relation to buoy boats, dated 19th inst., is received.

"The repairs recommended therein you are authorized hereby to have made, viz:

"In relation to changing the red glasses in the Lenses here I will write you further—Great Point (otherwise called Nantucket Light House) painting, cementing, and flagging shingling roof of dwelling and supplyng deficient glass—estimated at $279.

"Nantucket Harbor—Erecting a shed or outbuilding for the Keeper, as described, shingling the porch roof leading round the chimney, painting the Lantern and repairing or replacing oil cans—$112.

"Nantucket Cliffe—replacing the old iron lantern with a new copper one—$32. . . .

> I am, S. PLEASONTON

WM. R. EASTON, *Esq.*
Nantucket, Mass."

Various auxiliary navigation guides have been erected in Nantucket as the bar off the island changed its size and direction. When Inspector Carpender visited the island he found that two ordinary oil lamps had been placed on an old shack eleven feet high. The mariner entering the harbor would make a range of lights in the shack and the Brant Point Light to clear the bar and enter the harbor at the right location. This shack was given the glorified name of Nantucket Beacon.

Nantucket Beacon was given up on June 30, 1869, but was reestablished on the north side of the lighthouse the following November. In April 1870 it was moved back to the original location.

At the time of Carpender's inspection of Nantucket lighthouses, two supplementary range lights were being erected on the beach northwest of Nantucket Harbor. These beacons were soon called the Cliff Range Beacons, but Nantucket citizens christened them the Bug Lights. The buildings, still standing, were small light towers three hundred feet apart, the front lower light being a fixed white beacon, and the upper rear light having a fixed red characteristic.

In 1865 a brick tower was built at Brant Point to take the place of the light showing from the keeper's residence. Erected at a point approximately 135 feet to the south of the earlier lighthouses, the new beacon was built to a height of forty-two feet at its focal plane, and was visible for fifteen miles. Keeper F. B. Smith was in charge in 1882.

Much confusion existed as to the exact titles of the property adjoining the lighthouse, and in 1887 a fence was built by the government to indicate the boundary limits. Included in the area were three summer dwellings and a hotel. For many years the dispute continued, but in 1901, with the selling of six acres of land by the government, most of the difficulties were solved.

Construction of a new wooden tower began in 1900 on the beach, some distance from the 1856 beacon that still stands. Lighted for the first time on January 31, 1901, its white cylindrical tower with a bridge to shore has been seen by hundreds of thousands of people as they pass Brant Point and enter Nantucket Harbor. The flashing red gleam of 1,300 candlepower is only twenty-six feet above high water mark. There is no lower lighthouse in all New England.

There are resident personnel at the lighthouse.

GREAT POINT LIGHT

The first mention of a light at Great or Sandy Point was in 1770, when the town fathers chose a committee to ask the General Court to put up "a lighthouse on the end of Sandy Point of Nantucket." Another method was agreed upon, however, and the local Nantucket representative was told to "use his Influence in the General Court to get a Light House on our Point according to his own Discretion."

The General Court of the Commonwealth of Massachusetts on February 5, 1784, passed a resolve providing for the erection of the Great Point Light at Nantucket, and the building was soon completed. On November 11 of the same year Richard Devens, the commissary general, was granted 1,089 pounds, 15 shillings, and 5 pence in addition to 300 pounds already paid out for the erection of the lighthouse there.

In 1812 the keeper at Great Point was in charge of one of the most difficult light stations in all New England. There was no dwelling at the light for Keeper Jonathan Coffin, and it meant that he had a long walk or ride from his home to reach the tower every evening. Because of this, Albert Gallatin, Secretary of the Treasury, raised his salary to $166.67 a year and began preparations for the building of a residence.

In November 1816 Great Point Light was entirely destroyed by fire. Winslow Lewis visited the site a few weeks
later and expressed an opinion that the fire was deliberately
set. "It can hardly admit of a doubt . . . that the Lighthouse
. . . was purposely set on fire," were the words of Winslow
Lewis. S. H. Smith, Commissioner of the Revenue, asked him
for more details about this serious matter, but nothing was
ever proved one way or another.

Two years after the fire, masons completed a handsome
stone edifice, which still stands today, seventy feet above the
sea, giving its twelve-thousand-candlepower beam a fourteen-
mile visibility range.

A petition was sent to Washington in 1829 signed by many
citizens and ship owners of Nantucket, for the removal of
Captain Bunker, keeper of the Great Point Light, because of
intemperate habits. The petition suggested George Swain as
a new keeper. After Stephen Pleasonton had conducted a
thorough investigation, it was decided that the whole affair
had been instigated by some disappointed lighthouse appli-
cant anxious to take over Bunker's position.

The lighthouse report of 1838 on Great Point follows:

"On the northern extremity of the island stands the great
light of Nantucket. This light is 70 feet above the level of
the sea, in a stone tower 60 feet high. It consists of 14 lamps,
three with 15, and eleven with 16-inch reflectors, arranged
in the usual way, in two circles parallel to each other and to
the horizon. The lantern is 8½ feet high and 9 in diameter."

When the committee investigating American lighthouse
conditions reported on Great Point Light in 1851, the beacon
had fourteen lamps, arranged in two parallel circles. The
keeper had actually moved seven of the lamps from the chandelier and fixed them on a shelf against the window. Accord-

ing to the report still in the National Archives at Washington, there was a covered way that was a necessity in winter, when the "snow must drift."

Finally, in 1857 the tower was fitted with a Fresnel lens. Whale oil was used as fuel for the lamps for many years at Great Point. Colza, lard oil, and mineral oil were also employed to light the beacon.

In the old shipwreck journal kept at Great Point from 1863 to 1890 and authorized by Thornton A. Jenkins, secretary of the Lighthouse Board, we learn that in this period there were forty-three shipwrecks within the jurisdiction of the lighthouse. G. F. Coggeshall was the keeper when the journal was started. The first wreck occurred on April 20, 1863, when the Prussian bark *Elwine Frederick* hit on the rip during a moderate northeast gale. A schooner lay to nearby and removed the crew at half past twelve, taking them into Nantucket Harbor. The bark shortly afterward capsized and completely disappeared, a total loss. The following December Captain Willard Crowell, the Nantucket wreckmaster, took charge of salvaging the *Elwine Frederick,* and the schooner was afloat by high tide and later proceeded to Holmes Hole.

The number of vessels that mistook the Great Point Light for the Cross Rip Light Ship is amazing. First to be wrecked on this account was the schooner *William Jones,* whose captain was Stephen Jones of Saint George, Maine. In clear moonlight on April 17, 1864, the schooner, together with two other vessels, mistook the light for Cross Rip, and all three went ashore on Great Point Rip. The other two were able to work clear by morning. Jones jettisoned part of his cargo and got off, but came on again and was not able to sail away until April 23, when an unusually high tide freed him. Another schooner hit the bar during a heavy gale on October 12, 1865. Her captain, George Sawyer, by skillful maneuvering, was able to get his wife and three children, together with the crew, into the vessel's long boat and row to the Great Point Beach, where the keeper had a carriage waiting for him. Brought to the lighthouse, the shipwrecked sufferers watched their schooner go to pieces a short time later.

In September 1866 the schooner *Leesburg* of Portland, Maine, commanded by a Captain Smith, struck on Great Point Rip and was rescued by the island steamer and brought ashore. When the light keeper learned that it was another case of mistaking Great Point Light for the Handkerchief Lightship, he determined to interview Captain Smith.

"How came you on the Rip?" asked the keeper.

"I mistook the light for the lightship," was the reply.

"What kind of a light was there?" asked the anxious light keeper.

"As good a light as ever was anywhere," was the comforting answer, and Keeper Coggeshall ended the interview then and there, his mind at ease on learning that his own light was bright and satisfactory.

The next wreck occurred at ten p.m. on October 4, 1866, when Captain Samuel Thompson of the brig *Storm Castle* mistook Great Point Light for Handkerchief Lightship. After the lumber cargo had been thrown over, the *Storm Castle* was towed into Nantucket Harbor, November 1. The next month a sugar and molasses brig hit Great Point Rip the day before Christmas, and proved a total loss. The crew reached shore in safety. The following May another schooner was lost on the Rip, and the entire crew landed at Great Point.

On December 22, 1867, Keeper W. S. Allen noticed the schooner *Nil Desperando* aground on the Rip, and went out to her. Her captain, Benjamin Oliver, told Keeper Allen the usual story, that in the night he had mistaken the Great Point Light for Handkerchief Lightship. The schooner was later saved. It is hard to understand why no action was taken year after year as the report of these disasters reached the Lighthouse Board in Washington.

On March 19, 1869, another schooner, the *L. L. Adams,* hit the bar after Captain Robbins had made the same mistake about the light. The following April still another schooner, the *Juliet,* hit under similar circumstances.

The schooner *Chase,* under Captain A. Ingraham, bound from Rockland, Maine, to New York with a load of lime, hit the bar on September 22, 1877, but managed to get off shortly afterward. The following January the light keeper rowed out in a thick snowstorm to rescue the crew of the American schooner *Harriet Fuller.* The schooner, loaded with coal, was a total loss.

The strange experience of the British schooner *Ann Cornelia,* which hit in a driving snowstorm, is worthy of recording. Ashore on the Rip, on December 26, 1878, the *Cornelia* worked off the next day, but a northwest gale soon came up that pushed the vessel high against the bar, a position from which she was not moved until the following May 27!

The schooner *West Wind,* loaded with a cargo of ice, was sighted by the keeper on the morning of March 29, 1880, flying a distress flag. Shortly afterward she hit on the east end of Nantucket Bar, four and a half miles from the lighthouse. When the keeper reached her later, he found the boats and crew gone. The vessel soon went to pieces. Later the keeper heard that members of the crew had been picked up on April 9.

On February 1, 1881, the keeper sighted the schooner *U. B. Fisk* caught in the ice floe. The crew had abandoned ship, but were unable to make shore. Wading out in water up to his armpits, the keeper threw over a small line that the shipwrecked mariners made fast. Then he sent out a heavier line that was used to pull the men ashore. The schooner soon went down in the ice pack.

On March 12, 1887, the English two-masted schooner *James Watson,* commanded by Captain Robert Holder, hit at the Galls, a section of the beach located between Great Point and Wauwinet. A strong northerly gale was blowing, which caused them to slip their anchor to prevent foundering near Pollock Rip. The schooner struck on Great Point Rip, and the mate, completely exhausted from his exertions, was washed overboard and drowned. The rest of the crew were saved and brought to the Coskata Life Saving Station.

The Italian bark *Nostri Ginitori,* under Captain Lamone Cataloni, with a load of salt from Sicily to Gloucester, hit Great Point Rip on December 5, 1889. The crew made shore at Wauwinet, and wreckers later went aboard. The bark, towed off the bar, eventually reached Boston in a badly water-logged condition.

The last entry in the old wreck logbook is for February 14, 1890, when the *Eva B. Douglas,* a four-masted coal schooner, mistook the buoy on Great Point Rip and went aground. One side wheeler and two tugs soon came to her aid, but the wind breezed up and all went back into the harbor. The next day the steamer *Island Home* went out to free the vessel, and the *Douglas* set her sails and got off.

Theodore L. Chase, another keeper at Nantucket Light, Great Point, rendered valuable assistance to the fishing schooner *Elizabeth Foley,* which caught fire two miles from the light. Shortly after the fire started, there was a violent explosion of fuel tanks. The crew started out in a dory but were swamped and about to sink when Keeper Chase and his assistant, Otis E. Walsh, arrived. The keepers brought them ashore in the station boat, and lodged them until they could later be taken to Nantucket.

Keeper Archford Haskins came to Great Point Light with his large family in 1937 and stayed there happily for seven years before he was transferred to Sankaty Head Light. He was relieved at Great Point by Keeper Antone S. Sylvia.

While walking along the sand on February 10, 1945, some distance from Great Point Lighthouse, Keeper Sylvia discovered a strange wreck buried under a six-foot sand bank near the water's edge. More than sixty feet long, the wreck was probably thrown up on the beach in the 1890's.

We visited Coastguardsman Sylvia at Nantucket just as he was relinquishing his post at Great Point to the new keeper, Nicholas E. Norton. The Coast Guard command car took us out over the dunes through the dense fog then rolling in.

Climbing the old tower's 84 steps was quite an experience, and we soon stood at the top looking out through fog so thick we could scarcely see the keeper's residence at the foot of the lighthouse. When we descended to the ground again, we were invited to have crackers and coffee with the incoming keeper.

Keeper Norton had been a beachcomber for twelve years, and had an intense love of the sea. A Martha's Vineyard resident, he had helped Captain Levi Jackson save the crew of the *Marcus L. Uran* off Edgartown. "It was sometime before 1915, I think," said Norton, "for it was after the wreck of the *Mertie B. Crowley*. I was on Edgartown Wharf and some people told me about it. I went to Captain Levi Jackson's home and got him. We went down to the wharf and picked up a bunch of men, leaving the pier in the sloop *Priscilla*. The wind was southwest. We anchored in the lee. We found that the *Uran* was wrecked on the Wasque Shoal. Men were in the rigging and the seas were breaking over her. There were thirteen men and a woman and a cat. We took them all off in the dory." Boatswain's Mate Norton, keeper of the Great Point Light, had in his possession a medal presented him for his share in the rescue.

On our way back to Nantucket, Chief Boatswain's Mate "Tony" Sylvia told us of his help in saving the crew of the

Elizabeth Foley, wrecked early one morning. The remains of the *Foley* can still be seen near the station. Another vessel whose bones are still showing near Great Point is the *Governor Fuller,* a Gloucester fisherman wrecked during the summer more than a dozen years ago. There were thirteen men aboard. Tony helped bring them all ashore, and shortly afterward the vessel blew up and drifted ashore. A spectacular sight it became, half-buried in the sand, some distance away from the lighthouse itself. Although the tower at Great Point is still standing, there is no keeper there today. The beacon flashes white once every five seconds and also shows a red warning sector to keep mariners away from Cross Rip and Tuckernuck Shoals.

SANKATY HEAD LIGHT

When Lieutenant Charles Davis was conducting sounding operations off Nantucket in 1847 he located a newer and more dangerous reef of shoals farther out from Nantucket than any previously discovered. These dangerous shoals were soon named in his honor, the Davis South Shoals. A cliff near Siasconset was chosen for the erection of a lighthouse which would help to warn the mariner from the Davis Shoals, and the place chosen was Sankaty Head, the most southeastern headland in New England. Erected in 1849, the tower was built under the direction of Benjamin F. Isherwood at a cost of $10,333. A Fresnel lens was installed at Sankaty Head Light in 1850.

In the summer of 1850 Sankaty Head Light was superior to every other American Light, according to Lieutenant John N. Maffit, who was conducting operations off the coast. For three months that year he found Sankaty Head Light brighter than Boston Light and more than forty other beacons. "I know of no light superior to it," were Maffit's remarks.

Captain Alexander Bunker was the first keeper at Sankaty Head, lighting the temporary beacon on February 1, 1850. He and his two assistants, both of whom lived some distance from Sankaty Head, took their turns at standing a four-hour watch apiece each evening. While the tower itself was of brick laid in cement, the lower turret just below the lantern was built of granite.

In the lighthouse report book we find the following statement about the Sankaty Head Light:

Jan 30 1852

"Apparatus constructed in Paris by Henry Lepaute, under direction of Mr. Isherwood.

"Tower is placed on an elevated point on Island of Nantucket, upon the recommendation of the Supt of the Coast Survey, based (1848) upon the then recent discovery of new shoals by Lt Commanding Charles H. Davis, U S N, and his report of November 1847, strongly recommending it for both the general as well as local wants of navigation.

"The present principal light-keeper in charge is a most respectable and intelligent retired sea captain, who commanded a merchant ship for twenty-five years . . . assisted by two persons, who for want of quarters at the lighthouse, are compelled to reside at some distance from it, to the detriment of the service.

"The present keeper took charge of the light the night it was first lighted, (February 1, 1850), without previous knowledge or instruction.

"Journal of expenditure:

"370 gallons consumed for 11 months and 7 days, or about 395 gallons a year."

Samuel Adams Drake visited Sankaty Head in the year 1875. Commenting on the lighthouse, Drake says that "when built, this light was unsurpassed in brilliancy by any on the coast, and was considered equal to the magnificent beacon of the Morro. Fishermen call it the blazing star. Its flashes are very full, vivid, and striking, and its position is one of great importance, as warning the mariner to steer wide of the great Southern Shoal. Seven miles at sea the white flash takes a reddish hue."

At the present time, Sankaty Head Light gives a white 3,200,000 candlepower flash every seven and a half seconds. One hundred and sixty-six feet above the ocean, Sankaty Head Light is an easily distinguished marine mark in the daytime, its white tower identified by a single wide band of red around the middle of the lighthouse.

36

Martha's Vineyard and Cuttyhunk

There are five lighthouses on the island of Martha's Vineyard—Gay Head, Edgartown, East and West Chop, and Cape Poge. Six miles to the northwest of Gay Head Light lies Cuttyhunk Island, which has a single lighthouse, located on the southwestern point. The oldest light on either island is the Cape Poge beacon, erected in 1802.

GAY HEAD LIGHT

Across Vineyard Sound from the Elizabeth Islands lies Gay Head and its welcome lighthouse, perched high on the cliffs of Martha's Vineyard. The location of the lighthouse has long been a place of wonderment not only for the inhabitants but also for visitors who come from all over the United States. The various colors of the high cliffs that slope down to the ocean from the Gay Head promontory cannot be rivaled anywhere else in New England, with their green, yellow, black, brown, red, and white streaks of intense and vivid hues running up and down the embankment. Bartholomew Gosnold, the explorer, was the first to name this attractive headland, calling it Dover Cliffs when he sailed by the island in 1602. The name was later appropriately changed to Gay Head.

In 1799 the government decided the location was a suitable one for the erection of a beacon to guide shipping to and from Boston, and Ebenezer Skiff was appointed the first keeper. Skiff was seemingly a remarkable man. Two of his letters that have come down to us through the years show what a resourceful character he was. His annual pay had originally been two hundred dollars. As the years went by, he believed that the position was worth a substantial increase, and so composed the following letter to Albert Gallatin, Secretary of the Treasury:

Gayhead, October 25, 1805

"Sir: Clay and Oker of different colours from which this place derived its name ascend in a Sheet of wind pened by the high Clifts and catch on the light House Glass, which often requires cleaning on the outside—tedious service in cold weather, and additional to what is necessary in any other part of the Massachusetts.

"The spring of water in the edge of the Clift is not sufficient. I have carted almost the whole of the water used in my family during the last Summer and until this Month commenced, from nearly one mile distant.

"These impediments were neither known nor under Consideration at the time of fixing my Salary.

"I humbly pray you to think of me, and (if it shall be consistent with your wisdom) increase my Salary.

"And in duty bound I am your's to Command

EBENEZER SKIFF,
Keeper of Gayhead Light House

ALBERT GALLATIN *Esquire"*

An increase of fifty dollars was recommended and approved by President Thomas Jefferson. Possibly without the knowledge of the government, Skiff soon decided to expand his activities, becoming a farmer of no little ability and then branching out to solicit pupils among the native Indians for a school he conducted in a nearby house.

Again in 1815 Ebenezer Skiff decided to request a further increase in pay. Perhaps his Indian school had failed; it may be that the lighthouse keeper decided that ten years without an increase was long enough to wait. As his other letter had been so successful in accomplishing his objective. Skiff began his introductory paragraph in the same effective manner:

"To Samuel Smith Esquire
"Commissioner of the Revenue

"Sir: Clay ochre and earth of various colours from which this place derived its name ascend in a sheet of wind from the high clifts and catch on the glass of the light-house, which glass requires to be often cleaned on the outside:—Tedious service in cold weather and not so commonly necessary in any other place in the Massachusetts, nor in any of the New England States.

"The spring of water in the edge of the clifts, by means of their late caving has become useless. I cart the water used in my family more than half a mile, necessarily keep a draught horse and carriage for that purpose and frequently have to travel in a hilly common extending five miles to find the horse. Truely I catch some rain water and it is as true that many times I empty it coloured as red as blood with oker blown from the clifts.

"My firewood is brought from the Mainland and, there being neither harbor nor wharf here, is more expensive than in seaports. Keepers in some places get their wood with little cost; but here the native Indians watch the shores to take all drifts.

"The lately constructed light with a stone revolves by a clock which is to be stopped every time anything is done to the fire, which, in cold weather, must be kindled the sun an hour high or sooner, and recruited until eleven o'clock, or after, when I have to trim the lamps and wind up the weights of the clock and can go into bed at nearly midnight until which a fire is kept in the dwelling-house consuming more wood than when I tended the former light.

"It is about eight miles from here to a grist-mill and in the common way of passing are creeks not fordable at all seasons.

"The business respecting the light is, mostly, done by me in person, yet I occasionally leave home to procure wood and many other necessaries; previous to which I have to agree with and instruct some trusty white person to tend the light in my absence: If my salary would admit I would hire some person to live constantly with me lest I should be sick—I have no neighbors here but Indians or people of colour.

"Tending the former light might be deemed a simple business if compar'd with the tendence of the present complicated works and machinery, which requires much time care &c.

"Almost any man or lad under my wife's care could light the former lamp and do the business a short time: but the case is not so now.

"When I hire an Indian to work I usually give him a dollar per day when the days are long and seventy-five cents a day when the days are short and give him three meals: Now supposing the meals worth twenty-five cents each they amount to seventy-five cents which is seven cents more than the wages for my service both a day and night (while I board myself) only sixty-eight cents, computing my Salary (as it now is) at two hundred and fifty dollars a year and the year to consist of three hundred and sixty-five days.

"I have the use of two acres of land intersected with buildings, the use of a small dwelling-house and a small barn.

"I refer you to Capt. Winslow Lewis Superintendent of the Lamps &c. for the truth respecting all of the above particulars that he is acquainted with—and before I forward this Application shall lay before the Selectmen of Chilmark, which adjoins Gay Head, for their inspection; And in duty bound I humbly pray you to take this Matter into your wise consideration and afford me relief by granting an increase to my Salary.

"I am sir with all possible respect yours to command

 EBENEZER SKIFF.

Gay Head 2nd November 1815."

Skiff's writing ability again brought results, for Commissioner Smith recommended a further increase of fifty dollars in his pay. President James Madison approved the suggestion and fifty dollars more was given to Keeper Skiff each year.

In 1884 Horace N. Pease was keeper at Gay Head Light. On the afternoon of January 18, the popular coastwise steamer, *City of Columbus,* sailed from Boston to New York and the south, with many excursionists eager to reach the warmer climes of Florida. At 3:45 a.m. the next day the great steamer piled up on the terrible Devil's Bridge ledge, which runs off the shore from Gay Head, just under the lighthouse. One hundred persons drowned within twenty minutes.

Sighting the wreck soon after the accident, Keeper Horace N. Pease gathered together a crew of Indians to go out to the vessel. On their first attempt the lifeboat capsized in the raging surf, but all crew members reached shore safely. Their next attempt was successful, and they arrived at the wreck. Shouting across to the survivors huddled on the icy deck, they told the freezing victims to leap into the sea. One by one the terrified passengers jumped into the ocean, and were quickly pulled aboard the lifeboat, which, because of the swell, could not approach any nearer the steamer. Finally the overcrowded lifeboat headed for the shore, but capsized just off the beach. All were saved, however.

Another lifeboat started out from Squibnocket and brought several more survivors ashore. By this time the Revenue Cutter *Dexter* arrived at the wreck. The lifeboats rescued seventeen more survivors, but two men were still clinging to the rigging. Lieutenant Rhodes, volunteering to go to their rescue, leaped into the water. Struck by floating wreckage, he was forced to return to the *Dexter,* but later rowed a small boat across and actually boarded the *City of Columbus.* Climbing the ice-covered futtock shrouds, he reached the men but found that they had both frozen to death. Laboriously he cut them down and brought the bodies back to the *Dexter.* The wreck was then left alone in the sea, its icy rigging glistening in the sun.

Of the many keepers who have served at Gay Head Light, none has been more popular or willing to show the visitor around the lighthouse grounds than Keeper Charles Wood Vanderhoop, an Indian. Accepting the position at Gay Head Light in 1910, Keeper Vanderhoop probably took one-third of a million visitors to the top of Gay Head Light, to see the wonderful view from the 170-foot vantage point at Martha's Vineyard. His assistant for many years, Max Attaquin, was also a Gay Head Indian. Both married Gay Head Indian women, and both had two children at the time of the head keeper's retirement in 1933. Keeper Vanderhoop was succeeded at Gay Head by James E. Dolby, formerly at Sankaty Head Light, Nantucket Island.

The Gay Head Light today, perched high on the cliff near the Devil's Den at Martha's Vineyard, has a distinctive lighting combination of three white flashes and one red flash every forty seconds. The lantern room on the brown brick tower is 170 feet above the ocean, and the light can be seen nineteen miles away. It is automatic, and has a maximum candlepower of 160,000.

WEST CHOP LIGHT

In 1817 the Holmes Hole or West Chop Light was illuminated. The light shone from a stone tower twenty-five feet high and sixty feet above the sea, and there were ten lamps in the lantern room. By 1838 the sea was encroaching on the tower, and Inspector Carpender recommended that the buildings be moved three hundred yards southward. Although his recommendation was approved by the local pilots, years passed without any action. Finally, in 1891, a new tower eighty-four feet above the water was established on firmer ground and still stands to warn the mariner of the dangers of the deep. The light is now electrified. Coast Guard personnel live at the light today.

A terrific gale in 1877 threw a schooner loaded with bricks ashore near the light, and the bricks were tossed overboard to lighten the schooner. They can still be seen at low tide where they were thrown so long ago.

EAST CHOP

For many years the residents of Martha's Vineyard maintained a private lighthouse at the East Chop, and in this were helped by subscriptions from owners of several steamers that sailed in the vicinity. In 1873 the government considered the possibility of taking over the running of the light, and two years later purchased the site and property for about five thousand dollars. After an inspection of the buildings, the Lighthouse Department decided to erect a new cast-iron tower and keeper's residence, which was completed the following year. At a height of seventy-nine feet above the sea, the green flashing light is seen for fifteen miles.

EDGARTOWN

On the west side of the inner harbor at Edgartown a lighthouse was erected in the year 1828 on the roof of the keeper's dwelling house located at the end of a wooden breakwater. In 1838 there were ten lamps inside the tower, a number considered quite excessive by Carpender on his inspection tour. In 1845 the fixed light, forty feet above the sea, was visible for fourteen miles. From time to time through the years repairs were made at this lighthouse, until in 1939 the old Essex Light at Ipswich, Massachusetts, was dismantled and shipped to Martha's Vineyard, where it was set up again at the end of the old Edgartown breakwater, and there it shines at the present time far from its original location.

From a white conical tower the light flashes red every two seconds. It is an automatic station.

CAPE POGE LIGHT

On the northeastern point of Chappaquiddick Island, across from Martha's Vineyard, stands the white tower of Cape Poge Light. Its white flash every six seconds shines from the white tower to help the mariner find his way. The area around Cape Poge has been the scene of many terrible shipwrecks since the old tower was erected in 1802. The five-thousand candlepower light is a welcome aid to navigation in these dangerous waters.

In Carpender's report on New England lighthouses, he mentions that he visited Cape Poge in 1838, when workmen were moving the wooden tower back from the sea. He spoke of the five upper series of lights and the six lower series, and recommended the suppression of the upper series.

Keeper Edward Worth feared that the light would completely wash away because of the sea's sweeping in and removing the sand around the tower. The building was moved a substantial distance inland the same year, thus temporarily averting the danger. In 1922, however, a new tower was erected, which stands fifty-five feet above the ocean.

Often called one of the bleakest locations south of Cape Cod, Cape Poge is isolated by water from the rest of Martha's Vineyard. Because of its lonely situation, it has been extremely difficult at times to get keepers to remain long at Cape Poge Light.

Keeper Henry L. Thomas had a longer career at Cape Poge than any other man of the twentieth century. Early in his stay here he also doubled as keeper of the Humane Society's life-saving station, and between tending the light and rescuing shipwrecked sailors he was a very busy person.

Keeper Marcus Pieffer became the guardian of Cape Poge Light in 1930. In the summer he went ashore to Martha's Vineyard for provisions by journeying the entire length of Cape Poge and crossing to the main island in a ferry boat. During the winter Keeper Pieffer operated his motorboat when land travel became impossible.

The light is now automatic.

CUTTYHUNK

Originally spelled Poocutohhunk-konnoh, Cuttyhunk Island was the scene of the first English colonization in New England. In the year 1602 the first English spade was driven into New England soil here. Bartholomew Gosnold landed at Cuttyhunk Island from a small bark, the *Concord,* together with thirty-two other men, including Gabriel Archer, John Brereton, and Sir Humphrey Gilbert's son, Bartholomew Gilbert. Gosnold had already explored the southern New England coastline, and picked Cuttyhunk as the ideal location for settlement, with its pond of fresh water "in circuit two miles, on the one side not distant from the sea thirty yards, in the centre whereof is a rocky islet, containing near an acre of ground full of wood, on which we began our fort and place of abode."

For three crowded weeks these adventuresome explorers stayed on Cuttyhunk Island, building a sedge-thatched house. They also constructed a flat-bottomed punt, on which they ferried men and materials across the lake to the inner island. Scores of exploring expeditions to the surrounding islands and mainland were carried out from their headquarters at Cuttyhunk. They planted Martha's Vineyard with wheat, oats, and barley, while strawberries, raspberries, and gooseberries abounded in the region. "Scollops, Muscles, Cockles, Lobsters, Crabs, Oisters, and Wilks, exceeding good and very great," were eaten as food by these English pioneers. Their real discovery, however, was sassafras, which was a very expensive medical cure in England at that time. The *Concord* was loaded with sassafras and cedar wood for its return journey to England.

On May 25, 1602, Archer mentions the arrival at Cuttyhunk Island of an Indian, his wife, and daughter. Five days later the Englishmen stole a canoe from the island of Hills Hap, near the mainland. During the first week in June fifty Indians with their sachem, arrived from the mainland in nine canoes, and the first New England fish dinner was given the Indians by Gosnold. A brief description of that feast at Cuttyhunk follows:

"They misliked nothing but our mustard, whereat they made many a sowre face. . . . One of them had conveyed a target of ours into one of their canowes, which we suffered, only to trie whether they were in subjection to this leader who . . . caused it presently to be brought backe again."

* * *

This incident seemed to cause a crisis in the banquet, but after the target, or shield, was returned to the white men, who then relaxed, the Indians followed suit and went back to roasting crabs and "red herrings, which were exceedingly great."

On June 10 the Indians ambushed several of the settlers, one of whom was wounded in the side. Perhaps, as Howe hints, the incident of the stolen canoe had something to do with the affair, but at any rate the Englishmen were alarmed at the whole proceedings and a week later sailed away for England, which they reached on July 23, 1602. New England's first colony had ended.

It was many years before another settlement was attempted at Cuttyhunk Island. Gradually, however, the island assumed an important position in the navigational activities of the coast. A lighted beacon was erected in 1823 on the south-western point of the island. In those days the island was usually called Cutterhunk. In 1838 the light was in a stone tower twenty-five feet high, shining from a height of forty-eight feet above the sea. There were ten lamps, with thirteen-inch reflectors. When Carpender visited Cuttyhunk, he found that "the reflectors were cleaned in the too ordinary acceptation of the term. Instead of being burnished with whiting, as they require to be, every day, the smoke of the preceding night had merely been wiped off them. . . . This tower was originally of stone, but was so badly built as to require twice to be encased in brick."

In 1860 the lighthouse-keeper's residence was changed from a single to a double-storied building, on top of which the lantern room was built.

Captain A. G. Eisener came to Cuttyhunk Island as keeper in 1890. Having lived at Thacher's Island as keeper there since 1882, Eisener welcomed the larger island with its greater number of inhabitants. A new lighthouse tower, forty-five feet high, was erected in 1891 at the island.

On March 11, 1892, a fearful gale came out of the sea to beat against the shores of Cuttyhunk Island. At the height of the gale Eisener noticed thousands of laths coming ashore, and felt that a terrible shipwreck must have taken place. Stepping to a sheltered part of his residence, he threw open a window to "glass the offing" with his telescope. A short lull in the gale enabled him to discern the outlines of a vessel less than two cables' lengths off shore. Through the driving sleet he saw that the masts were carried away, the rigging was in a hopeless tangle of confusion on the deck and over the side, and there were four men clinging to the windlass bitts.

Keeper Eisener hurried to get into his oilskins, and then called his wife and daughter. While they prepared themselves for the coming ordeal, he hastened to the homes of two islanders, and ten minutes later all five were down at the lifeboat of the Massachusetts Humane Society, ready to launch it into the breakers off the shore. The two women and three men finally chose a moment between two smaller waves, and successfully launched the heavy lifeboat into the sea. Time and again the great combers broke over the craft, but Keeper Eisener kept her headed into the seas, and finally, after half an hour of hard rowing, they reached the wreck.

It proved to be the British ship *Rob and Harry*. A line was made fast to the bowsprit, and two of the crew crawled slowly out until they reached a point directly over the unsteady lifeboat. One of them climbed down into the chains and dropped. He landed safely in the lifeboat, and so the other, waiting his proper time, dropped from the bowsprit to land beside him a moment later. Before they could pull away, however, a gigantic wave formed just in front of them and crashed into the lifeboat, filling it with laths and water and sweeping all but two oars overboard in the confusion. The line snapped and the lifeboat began to drift helplessly away from the British vessel.

Fifteen minutes later the lifeboat hit the rocky beach at a point half a mile up the coast. Everyone aboard managed to escape alive, although the lifeboat was stove in at several different parts of the hull. Climbing out on the shore, Keeper Eisener soon had the battered lifeboat pulled up above the reach of the waves. He hurried to his workshop to obtain tools and new planking for a temporary repair job.

At this time the United States Life Saving crew arrived, under Captain Bosworth. After a quick survey of the situation, Bosworth decided that beach apparatus was worthless in the attempt to rescue the two men still aboard the vessel. All hands pitched in to finish repairs to the life boat, after which Captain Eisener and a crew from the Life Saving Station launched the boat. Reaching the *Rob and Harry*, they assisted in getting the men aboard, but one was already dead from exposure. The lifeboat reached shore and landed safely.

Two days later Captain Eisener paid some of his carefully saved money for a casket for the dead sailor, who was buried in the Cuttyhunk cemetery. The Canadian government later repaid the thoughtful captain. The Massachusetts Humane Society awarded Eisener a silver medal and twenty dollars for his heroic action in saving the survivors of the *Rob and Harry*.

On February 20, 1893, in below-zero weather, the *Douglas Dearborn* piled up on the ledges off the island, one hundred yards from shore. Every man on the island was soon down on the beach near the scene. It was a terrible day in the history of Cuttyhunk. The rescue, which took from seven o'clock in the morning until four that afternoon, was conducted in such icy weather and biting wind that casualties ran high. It is true that all aboard the *Dearborn* were saved, but many of the islanders who helped save the crew suffered the loss of fingers and toes, and several lost their hands and feet.

The following year Keeper Eisener was assigned to a new station, that at Gurnet Head off Plymouth, Massachusetts, and in 1902 he was made the keeper of the new range light station at Lovell's Island, Boston Harbor.

The hurricane of 1944 completely changed the contours of Cuttyhunk Island, which was near the center of the storm. The Coastguardsmen say that the houses were shaking terribly at the height of the gale. The men had given themselves up for lost, but the gale finally went down.

There is no regular light at Cuttyhunk today, but the Coast Guard listing tells of a flashing white light every five seconds on the southwest point of the island.

37

Lighthouses Around New Bedford

Generations of New Bedford whalers have been guided into their home port by the three lighthouses that stand at the entrance to the harbor of this thriving southern Massachusetts city. Today the fishing fleets bound for New Bedford use the same aids to navigation. Clark's Point, now Butler's Flats Light, Dumpling Rock Light, and Palmer Island Light all stand as monuments to New Bedford's maritime past as well as symbolic beacons of the future.

PALMER ISLAND LIGHT

At the entrance to beautiful New Bedford Harbor, perhaps a little nearer to the New Bedford shore than to the town of Fairhaven across the harbor, stands the lighthouse on Palmer Island. Even before the building of the lighthouse this little island of six acres had a dramatic history, beginning in the trying King Philip's War of 1675 and 1676. The reader may recall that Philip, alias Pometacom, was the grandson of Massasoit, and stirred up all New Englanders by his savage attacks on the white settlers.

Early in the war the famous Indian fighter, Captain Ben-jamin Church, engaged in a conference with Awashonks, a woman sachem, at Little Compton, Rhode Island. During the parley another Indian named Little Eyes, hiding nearby to ambush the settlers, tried to kill Captain Church. The cap-tain's scouts soon captured Little Eyes and took this intended murderer to the Acushnet River, where plans were made for his detention. Palmer Island, because of its relative isolation, was chosen as the location for the imprisonment, and a friendly Indian named Lightfoot was placed in charge of the detention camp there.

A few months later Captain Church, again on the trail of King Philip's warriors, captured Philip's wife and son, whom he took with 124 other Indians across to Palmer Island, where the lighthouse stands today. In August 1676 Philip was slain at Mount Hope, and the Indian War came to an end.

From earliest times until about 1800 Palmer Island was heavily wooded with cedar trees. One by one the trees were removed from the island. In 1936, Arthur Small cut down the last cedar tree, a withered, gnarled, and weather-beaten survivor.

In 1849, because of agitation by the many sea captains and whaling ship owners, the government purchased an acre of land on the northern extremity of Palmer Island for the pur-pose of building a lighthouse. The tower was completed the same year, and on August 30, 1849, William Sherman be-came the first keeper.

A seawall six rods long was built on the eastern side of Palmer Island in 1852. During the same year Samuel Rod-man conducted experiments at Palmer Island with a special type of whale oil. He used seventy-nine and a half gallons of whale oil, and then terminated his experiment, sending a bill for the oil used. Stephen Pleasonton was surprised that Rod-man charged the government for what Pleasonton called an "experiment," but after consideration, Pleasonton approved the bill as presented. Actually, Rodman had agreed to charge the government exactly the same amount as the average cost for lighting the Clark's Point Light, during a similar period, $105.80. The government, although it paid Rodman's bill, did not adopt his system of lighting.

Shortly after the Civil War ended, a hotel, dance hall, and wharf were erected on the southern side of the island with steamer service from New Bedford. It was not long before the sedate citizens of New Bedford heard rumors that the returning whalers were enjoying themselves too much on Palmer Island, and the hotel acquired a reputation of unsavory nature. By 1890 the hotel failed and went out of business, and then the five acres on the southern end of the island were acquired for an amusement park. The difficulty of getting on and off the island was an insurmountable obstacle, and after several seasons of doubtful prosperity, the enterprise collapsed.

Abbott P. Smith purchased the area shortly after the hotel failed, and used it for many years as a summer home, but in 1904 sold his interests to a cotton mill group that planned to store coal there. The plan proved impractical and was given up.

Throughout the long period of New Bedford's prosperity in the whaling business, the keepers of Palmer Island Light constantly maintained their vigil day and night. When the last whaling square rigger, the *Wanderer,* left New Bedford Harbor, it was Keeper Arthur Small who stood high in the tower and waved farewell as the whaler sailed out to sea on August 25, 1924. A short time later the *Wanderer* was a helpless wreck on Cuttyhunk Island, a terrific summer gale having pushed her ashore there.

Arthur Small, mentioned elsewhere in this saga of the New England lighthouses, had a remarkable career. He came to

Palmer Island Light from Bug Light in 1922 with his wife, Mabel.

A singularly gifted artist, Keeper Arthur Small was probably the greatest painter who was ever in the lighthouse service. Palmer Island was the scene of many of his canvases, and he is known throughout New England as the artist-lighthouse keeper.

Arthur Small tells us that the average person does not realize the great weight of responsibility on the shoulders of the lighthouse keepers day and night all year long. "It is a popular idea that there is very little to do except for striking a match once a day to light the lamp," Keeper Small told me. "Few of these landlubbers realize that if a fog comes in during the middle of the night the keeper must be ready to turn on the fog signal at once, for if the fog bell is silent for a moment, even then a great vessel may be feeling her way up into the harbor, depending on the ringing of the fog signal bell for her safety."

"The channel in New Bedford Harbor is so narrow," Keeper Small said, "that if a large vessel went down, all shipping in or out of the harbor would be at a standstill. The coal for the electric light company could not reach the pier, and the cotton steamers likewise would find it impossible to dock. In a short time all the city would be seriously crippled. That is what makes me angry when I hear of the easy job of a lighthouse keeper, as described by some fair weather sailor or inland resident."

Small and his wife, Mabel, were content and happy to remain at their island home, keeping the fog signal sounding and making sure that a steady light gleamed from the tower. Their happiness was not to last, however.

In the great New England hurricane of 1938 Keeper Arthur Small was washed off the island by a gigantic wave and struck time and again by all kinds of debris. His wife ran to the boathouse to try to launch the dory to go after him while the wind raged 110 miles an hour. Mrs. Small probably never knew about the giant wave that crashed into the boat-house with such fury that the house, the dory, and everything else was swept into the sea. She was drowned. In some un-known way he was saved, waking up two weeks later in the Chelsea Marine Hospital.

Today the ruined tower still stands, a memorial to those lost in the 1938 hurricane.

DUMPLING ROCK LIGHT

Nine miles closer to shore than Cuttyhunk Light, on the opposite side of Buzzard's Bay, stands Dumpling Rock Light, guarding ships entering New Bedford Harbor from the ledges off Round Hill Point. The lighthouse was built in 1829. Inspector Carpender, after his visit in 1838, said Dumpling Rock was a

"Useful light in guiding vessels into Dartmouth Harbor, and in enabling them to avoid the dangers of this immediate navigation but, like most of the lights in this district, it is much larger than is necessary. . . . I recommend, strenuously, the suppression of the upper lamps, and a compact arrange-ment of the remaining six. They are now seven inches apart.

"I visited this light in the afternoon, and found the keeper absent on the main, without having paid the least attention to the lights since he extinguished them in the morning. The reflectors appeared not to have been burnished for some time, and the lantern covered with smoke. This keeper and his family were in danger of being drowned out, until Govern-ment built a wall round the dwelling; since which, they have lived in safety. Located as this light is, on a small barren rock, with fewer advantages to the keeper than, perhaps, any other light in the district, it would seem proper that I should notice the fact of the salary being smaller by $50 than that of many others."

During the early years of the nineteenth century the keeper of the Dumpling Rock Light would signal into New Bedford to his friends whenever a homeward bound vessel was sighted approaching the harbor. He had fixed an arm on a post near the lighthouse tower and would raise it or lower it in code to give advance notice so that merchants of New Bedford could send their representatives out to the ships to sell their goods.

The great New England Hurricane of 1938 damaged Dumpling Rock considerably, and two years later it was entirely rebuilt. The skeleton tower has a flashing green light shining from a height of fifty-two feet above the water and is situated on a rock off Round Point Hill. There is no keeper attached to the light now.

CLARK'S POINT LIGHT AND BUTLER'S FLATS

In the year 1804 it was deemed necessary by the sea captains and mariners sailing in and out of New Bedford to establish a beacon or lighthouse at Clark's Point, and so a lighthouse was erected in that year on the south end of Clark's Neck.

The "raising" of the lighthouse at Clark's Point, as was often the case in those days, was the occasion for a celebration with a hundred gallon "try pot" of chowder for the participants after the lighthouse frame had been hoisted into place. The first lighthouse caught fire several years later during a violent thunderstorm, although it was never ascertained whether the tower had been struck by lightning or not.

Edward Carpender, on his inspection tour in 1838, noted that the stone tower at Clark's Point was fifty-two feet high.

"I visited this light in the forenoon, and have good reason to think that fewer lamps differently attended, would afford equal light; one of the lamps was without a fountain, and appeared not to have been used the previous night. Two of the chimneys, or tube-glasses, were broken, and some of the others so much smoked as to show that they had been carelessly trimmed."

Seven years later, in 1845, Robert Mills speaks of the light as *stationary*. Mills continued as follows:

"It may be considered as the key of the sound. Steer N.E. by N. about three quarters of a mile till in 5½ to 6 fathoms, sucky bottom, when Clark's point light will bear N. W. by N. half N., then steer N. by W. and run into the river. After passing Clark's point light, you will see a small island, (the outer Egg island) just above water, which you will leave on your starboard hand giving it some birth, as their are rocks which lie southwesterly from it, say one-third of a mile distant, but still keeping nearer to it than to the mainland, to avoid Butler's flat, which makes off from the west shore. To steer clear of the flat, keep the lighthouse open a ship's length to the westward of the Round hills; as soon as you see the north line of the woods with the cleared land about a mile north of the light-house, you are to the northward of the flat, and may steer either for the hollow or the high part of Palmer's island, hauling a little to the eastward as you approach it."

During the 1850's the coasting vessel that brought supplies to the lighthouses of New England had aboard surreptitiously a negro slave woman and her two children, a boy and a girl. Brought in from the lighthouse during the night, the family were given refuge in New Bedford itself. The boy grew to manhood in the city, driving a hack for many years. Known as Charlie, he was a well-known figure around the New Bedford of the 1890's.

As the harbor grew more active, the merchants of New Bedford started agitation for a beacon on Butler's Flats, and the famous artist-writer-architect, F. Hopkinton Smith, was chosen to build the tower. As the flats were unusually soft, lighthouse builder Smith was forced to construct a large iron cylinder thirty-five feet in diameter at Crow Island and then take it down the harbor to Butler's Flats, where five feet of soft mud had been dredged away, leaving the hard pan foundation. When it was in position, the cylinder was filled with stone and concrete, and the rooms of the lighthouse tower were built on the foundation. In general appearance the tower resembles Deer Island Light in Boston Harbor and Duxbury Pier in Plymouth. There is a wide balcony on the first floor for exercise with a door opening into the circular kitchen. Upstairs are the keeper's quarters, while on the upper level the light itself shines out from a height of fifty-three feet above the waters of New Bedford Harbor.

F. Hopkinton Smith completed the Butler's Flats Light on April 30, 1898, at which time the Clark's Point Light was extinguished as no longer necessary. Three generations of one family have been active at these two lighthouses. When Captain Baker retired from the sea in 1872 he became the keeper of the Clark's Point Light, and continued there for seven years. His son, also Captain Baker, took over the duties as keeper and was at Clark's Point for twenty-three years, transferring from Clark's Point to Butler's Flats when the new tower was erected. With him at the time went his son Charles A. Baker, who was then the assistant. In 1912 Charles A.

Baker assumed full duties as keeper on the retirement of his father. Thus we have the unusual situation of three generations of lighthouse keepers in one family serving more than seventy years in outer New Bedford Harbor.

Butler Flats Light, a white conical tower on a black cylindrical pier, stands in thirteen feet of water on the west side of the channel leading to New Bedford Harbor. There is a flashing white light that shines from a height of fifty-three feet above the water.

38

Other Massachusetts Lights

Point Gammon and Bishop and Clerks

Hyannis Harbor for many years had a beacon at Point Gammon, situated at the entrance to the harbor. Erected in the year 1816, the light was placed in charge of Keeper Peak. Peak's son John lived with his father at the light from 1816 until Keeper Peak's death in 1824, when John Peak took over the duties. His salary in 1842 was $350 a year.

When Edward Carpender visited Point Gammon Light in 1838, he found the lighthouse situated seventy feet above the sea, at a point twelve miles northwest of Monomoy Light. At that time the light had ten lamps with thirteen and a half inch reflectors, six in the lower tier and four in the upper, with about four or five inches between the reflectors. The dwelling was connected with the tower by the kitchen, "enabling the keeper to attend to the light without exposure to the weather."

Seven years later Inspector I. W. P. Lewis had Keeper Peak sign a prepared statement after Lewis had interviewed the keeper. Peak said in part that his "dwelling-house is extremely leaky, particularly on the east side, where the rain leaks in, so that we always have to move our beds during an easterly rain, and also to mop up bucketfuls of water; the roof leaks, and the shingles are rotten and nail-sick. . . . I am allowed a boat, but there is no boat house. The curb of the well is so rotten that we have difficulty in obtaining water."

The nearby Bishop and Clerks Rock was still a menace to navigation in spite of Point Gammon Light, so in 1855 a lightship was placed near the rocks. Proving impractical, the lightship was superseded by a lighthouse on the ledge at Bishop and Clerks Rock, and on October 1, 1858, it flashed out for the first time.

With Bishop and Clerks Light in operation, Point Gammon Light was eventually given up. In 1872 the unused buildings at Point Gammon were sold along with the site itself, but the lighthouse tower was not taken down.

Finally, the Coast Guard considered it unsafe. Bishop and Clerks Lighthouse was blown up in 1952, leaving only a mass of rubble where once stood a proud beacon that guided shipping past the perilous ledges in the area.

TARPAULIN COVE LIGHT

Tarpaulin Cove Light was established in 1817, at which time John Hayden was made keeper. It is located at the west side of the cove, which, according to Inspector Lewis, is a "small indent in the shores of Nashawn Island, where coasters freqently anchor when met by head winds." Nashawn is one of the Elizabeth Islands in Buzzard's Bay, now known as Naushon Island.

John Hayden was still keeper at Tarpaulin Cove Light in 1842, when Inspector Lewis made his visit. At the time, Hayden said that the "tower is leaky from top to bottom, so that I have to cut the ice off the staircase in winter. . . . I have a well, thirty-six feet deep, without a drop of water in it."

The keeper at Tarpaulin Cove Light, Richard Norton, obtained his position because the Confederate raider *Alabama* sank the square-rigger of which he was captain and part owner. Losing all his possessions, Captain Norton was assigned to be keeper at the lighthouse on Naushon Island, Massachusetts, in partial recompense.

Today Tarpaulin Cove Light is a white tower with a small house attached to the west side of the building on Naushon Island. An automatic flashing white light shines from a height of seventy-eight feet.

BIRD ISLAND LIGHT

Bird Island Light in Buzzard's Bay was built in 1818 at the east side of the entrance to Sippican Harbor. Because of the commerce in Marion Harbor the lighthouse was soon given a similar rating with the important Gay Head Light on Martha's Vineyard, with a revolving light system. The light was erected thirty feet above the sea, in a stone tower twenty-five feet high. The dwelling was also of stone. When Carpender visited at Bird Island in 1838, he expressed surprise that Bird Island had been fitted with a revolving apparatus. "I see no reason," said Carpender, "why this should be a revolving light. . . . I now recommend that it be converted from a revolving white to a fixed red light, to consist of 6 instead of 10 lamps; the lamps to be arranged in a circular form. . . . The keeper of this light informs me that the head of the bay is always frozen over for long periods during the winter, and that no instructions have ever been given to extinguish the light during such periods."

In 1842 John Clark, keeper of Bird Island Light, made a statement, on the request of Inspector Lewis, in which he told of his appointment in 1834 at a salary of four hundred dollars. "The dwelling-house is tolerably comfortable," said Keeper Clark, "but requires new shingling; the chimneys smoke; the east and south side of the island are washing away fast. Last winter the stone wall on three sides was knocked away by the sea. I have been at work this summer rebuilding the wall on a more substantial scale. The superintendent allowed me forty dollars for the work. . . . My oil is good. There is a well here, but no water. I am therefore obliged to boat my water from the mainland, over two miles distant, and carry all our clothing ashore to be washed."

Bird Island Light was abandoned, but for some years was visited by adventuresome sailors and landlubbers.

Nobska Light

Nobska Light at Wood's Hole Harbor was originally built in 1828 at the top of the keeper's dwelling, and shone from a height of eighty feet above the sea. When Carpender visited there in 1838, he found the keeper unable to maintain a boat, because of a new government ruling forbidding keepers on the mainland to have boats. Carpender recommended that regulations be waived in favor of the Nobska Light keeper.

In 1876 the government rebuilt Nobska Light of steel, and it now illuminates the area with a fixed white light that has a red sector to prevent vessels from being wrecked on the Hedge Fence or L'Hommedieu Shoals.

At Nobska Point Station there is a memorial plaque for pilot Alfred Aucoin, who was murdered in his airplane when his heavily insured passenger decided to commit suicide near the light. The plane crashed in the vicinity.

An important radio beacon is located at Nobska Point fifty yards from the tower. Storm warnings are displayed nearby both day and night, and the tower is floodlighted from sunset to sunrise. Coastguardsmen at the station are active with the many duties they are called upon to perform.

On November 3, 1972, the last government lighthouse keeper, Joseph Hindley, retired after forty-four years of service. His first government employment came in 1921 when he enlisted at Wood's Hole for duty aboard the revenue cutter *Acushnet*.

He enlisted in the Lighthouse Service on August 3, 1928, and was sent to Whale Rock Light in Rhode Island. Other stations where he served include State Pier, Rhode Island; New Bedford, Massachusetts; Manhattan Beach, New York; Greenland; Gay Head Light, Massachusetts; Sakonnet Light; and Nobska Point, which was his final tour of duty.

NED'S POINT LIGHT

At the northeast side of the entrance to Mattapoisett Harbor, the beacon known as Ned's Point Light has for many years warned mariners of the dangers in the vicinity. Erected in 1837, the lantern was forty-one feet above the sea and gave a fixed white light. Rebuilt in 1888, the tower still stands today, showing a white flash every six seconds to vessels which are within the area 299½°–119½° from the tower.

Charles S. Mendell, Jr., tells of an interesting anecdote connected with the building of Ned's Point Light. Uncle Leonard Hammond, as the contractor of the light was called, had been unable to finish building the tower in the specified time. When the inspector arrived, Uncle Leonard steered him into the local tavern, which was the Plymouth County House, operated by Hammond himself. Meanwhile Uncle Leonard's employees ran down to the lighthouse tower to get things in readiness for the inspector's visit. Where the completed floor should have been, the men placed planking on barrels, which at least gave the appearance of flooring. The inspector arrived, but unfortunately he stepped on the end of a plank and disappeared with a crash into the foundation of the tower. He recovered, with only his dignity seriously injured.

During a period of governmental economy Ned's Point Light was offered for sale. By mistake, it was advertised in the local papers as being for sale to the "lowest bidder." Captain James Stowell of Mattapoisett promptly posted his offer of one cent. The government, in embarrassment, sent him eight pages of information as to why his bid was not accepted.

The light is run automatically at present.

MAYO'S BEACH LIGHT

A year after Ned's Point Light was first built, a light on the other side of Cape Cod was erected at Mayo's Beach, Wellfleet. Situated at the head of Wellfleet Bay, six miles northeast by north of Billingsgate Island, the lighthouse was in the process of construction during the visit of Inspector Carpender to Cape Cod in 1838. "I was surprised to find a lighthouse building on Mayo's Beach," said the inspector, who wrote to Washington asking that the construction be stopped. In this he was not successful, but in 1843 Fifth Auditor Stephen Pleasonton also suggested that the light was not needed. Pleasonton claimed the beacon was useful "to a few fishermen only, who could very well enter the port without it, and that it was considered a useless expense." Pleasonton therefore directed that the number of lights in the tower be reduced to three.

By 1878 the waves had undermined the keeper's home at Mayo's Beach to such an extent that in 1880 repairs were necessary. After moving the residence to a more suitable location, the government once more was forced to protect the building from the sea by putting up a heavy bulkhead.

A screen was erected at Mayo's Beach around the light so that the birds, which were attracted by the glare and had been killing themselves by the score, would not damage the lantern room itself. Many panes of plate glass had been broken by the terrific impact with which the birds crashed into the light, several of them even penetrating to the interior of the lantern room itself.

As the years went by, however, Mayo's Beach Light became more and more unnecessary in the opinion of the government, and finally was extinguished for good.

WING'S NECK LIGHT

On December 15, 1848, Stephen Pleasonton asked that a lighthouse be erected at Wing's Neck, Buzzard's Bay, Cape Cod. The lighthouse was approved, planned, and built by December of the following year for $3,251. It was found necessary to rebuild the light in 1889. Believed by some to be one of the most important lighthouses on the Atlantic coast because of its proximity to the Cape Cod Canal, the Wing's Neck Light formerly gave a white flash every six seconds, with a beam of 37,000 candlepower.

The keepers who have been at Wing's Neck Light through the years have left fine records of daring and outstanding achievements, but the rescues of Keeper George Addison Howard and his brother, Assistant Keeper William Howard, attracted nationwide attention in 1932 because of their many rescues during the first eight months of the year. Singly or together, the two keepers saved eight lives between January 1 and August 30, while William Howard saved, during his career, at least thirty-seven lives.

According to the official Coast Guard *Light List* of 1972, Wings Neck Light is no longer in existence, but it still can be considered a daytime sentinel.

Stage Harbor Light

It was not until 1880 that Stage Harbor Light was erected, and so its entire history has been of relatively recent nature. Located at Harding's Beach on the northeast side of Chatham Roads, the Stage Harbor Light shines from a height of forty-eight feet above the high water mark, its 400-candlepower gleam giving a flashing white light visible for twelve miles. The lighthouse was changed to a white skeleton tower in the year 1933, and now has a white flash every six seconds.

Cleveland Ledge Light

Cleveland Ledge Light is the last major beacon to be erected in Massachusetts. Marking the east side of the southern approach to Cape Cod Canal, the light is built in twenty-one feet of water on a ledge two miles from shore. The caisson that forms the foundation for the light was built in New London, Connecticut, and on October 7, 1940, was towed out to the ledge where it was sunk into its permanent position. A year later the lighthouse was turned over to the government in a partially completed condition because of the international situation, with a temporary light installed. Only recently has the full permanent installation of lighting, fog signal, and radio equipment been made.

The caisson is fifty-two feet in height and also fifty-two feet in diameter. The interior of the caisson is filled with rock. The top of the caisson forms the main deck of the structure, and above this rises the two-story reinforced concrete building, on top of which stands the lighthouse tower, fifty feet high, also of concrete. An antenna tower and platform of structural steel also rise from the main deck.

Lieutenant Olie P. Swenson of Bourne was commanding officer aboard the Cleveland Ledge Light when the terrific

September hurricane of 1944 hit the beacon from the southeast on September 14. Four hours later the wind changed to southwest, and within half an hour a glass block skylight on the southwest side of the tower gave away, allowing tons of water to pour into the lighthouse. The entire personnel of nine men rushed to the engine room, where they bailed the water from the floor. As they worked, other waves came crashing down upon them, and only the presence of a porcelain laundry tub into which they emptied their pails saved the day. The tub drained quickly every pail of water thrown into it. Some of the Coastguardsmen tried to stop up the break in the skylight, but were thrown back by the force of the waves which swept in.

The men were only able to stop the water rising in the battery room when it had reached a point less than two inches from the top of the batteries. One by one various pieces of electrical equipment flared out a warning as they were short circuited. Finally Seaman LaMar Steed and Chief Boatswain's Mate Thomas E. Norris managed to reach the broken glass block and erect a barrier of oil drums, planking, and mattresses against the sea. The men saved the lighthouse from being extinguished at a time when both the telephone and the radio were out of order.

During the gale, the launch secured to the davits thirty feet above high water mark was badly damaged by the force of the waves. The little wire-haired terrier, the only other occupant of the tower besides the nine men, showed great fright during the ordeal. But the nine men of Cleveland Ledge Light had successfully "ridden out" the first real test of the lighthouse.

The cylindrical tower and dwelling, as well as the caisson, are now white. Every ten seconds there is a white flashing light of 200,000 candlepower. A radio beacon utilizing the antenna at the light tower is used as a distance finding station for the area.

Coastguardsmen live at the light to ensure the safety of those entering the Cape Cod Canal.

PART **IV**

SOUTHERN NEW ENGLAND

39

Rhode Island Beacons

Smallest in size of all states in the Union, Rhode Island is one of the most important in lighthouse history. Many of the old beacons have been vital to the development of Newport and Providence.

BEAVERTAIL LIGHTHOUSE

Conanicut Island, where Jamestown, Rhode Island, is situated, is also the location of the third oldest American lighthouse. Beavertail Point Light was built in 1749. The island is also famous for its association with that great privateer William Kidd, who is called a pirate by many otherwise well-informed people. Captain Kidd went ashore on Conanicut Island on his return from his ill-fated voyage, which began at New York in 1696. His good friend Thomas Payne awaited him on Conanicut Island and advised him against going to Boston, where he would be captured, but Kidd trusted Governor Bellomont, one of his royal partners, who was then in Boston. Bellomont deceived Kidd by pretending all was well. For his trust in Lord Bellomont, Kidd was later hanged.

321

There are many who claim that Kidd's treasure is still buried at Conanicut Island, but without question little of his relatively small treasure was ever buried in the ground. Kidd, it is true, did leave money with Thomas Payne, but it was later used for his wife, Sarah Kidd, and their children.

Thirty-seven years after Kidd was hanged in England, the General Assembly of the English Colony of Rhode Island and the Providence Plantation passed an act for the erection of a lighthouse at Beavertail Point. No action was taken, however, until the year 1748, when the same Provincial Government passed an act, part of which we quote below:

"Whereas the General Assembly of this Colony, at their session in Newport, on the Twenty-second Day of August, in the Year . . . 1738, . . . Enacted, That there should be a Light-House . . . at Beaver Tail. . . . But a War breaking out with Spain, before the said year's interest was paid into the Treasury it was thought proper to postpone the building said Light-House till the War was over."

Levies had been made as early as 1730 for the building of a lighthouse at Conanicut Island. In May 1744 a tonnage duty of 6 _d_ per ton was ordered. Immediately after the treaty of Aix-la-Chapelle and the resumption of normal trade, the above act was passed.

Within a short time of the passage of the act, construction of Beavertail Light was begun. By the following year the light, built of rubblestone, was finished. The keeper lighted the beacon the same year. Incidentally, tonnage duties fell far below the cost of keeping up the lighthouse. From May 1763 to May 1765 receipts amounted to £5,292, while lighthouse expenses were £6,355.

Little is known of the early history of the beacon. When the British sailed into Newport Harbor in the summer of

1775, they burned Beavertail Light. Repairs approved by President Washington in 1790 were soon completed and Beavertail Light again warned the shipping entering Newport Harbor.

In the great September hurricane of 1815 the keeper's dwelling house at Beavertail was destroyed by the sea. In 1816 a new five-room stone building was contructed for his use.

Inspector Edward Carpender's report of November 1, 1838, calls Beavertail Light a "useful light on the southern extremity of Conanicut Island, 98 feet above the level of the sea." At that time the light was in a stone tower, sixty-four feet high, and consisted of fifteen lamps, with nine-inch reflectors. When Carpender visited the lighthouse one morning he found that the keeper had left home without having cleaned or shined the reflectors or lamps. In fact, said Carpender, "the reflectors had the appearance of not having been cleaned for some days." The premises were in "sufficient order."

Lieutenant George M. Bache also inspected the lighthouse the same year. He found that the dwelling house walls were badly laid, and mentions that in "1829 a bellhouse was built near the base of the tower, and a bell placed in it; these were removed in 1833. A portion only of the wall of the house is now standing." Bache's description of the Beavertail tower of 1838 is worthy of being recorded.

"The tower, from which the light is shown, is sixty-four feet in height; the masonry is of rubblestone, of small size, roughcast on the exterior; it is ascended by an interior spiral stairway of wood, having landings at convenient distances. The oil is stored under the lower landing."

Fog signals have played an important part in the history of Beavertail Light. Keeper Sylvester R. Hazard, who for many

324 SOUTHERN NEW ENGLAND

years was at Beavertail, admitted that the fog bell placed there in 1829 was a failure, for shortly afterward the steamer *Providence* ran ashore in a bad fog and the lives of several hundred passengers were endangered. Luckily, the *Providence* was got off without loss of life. Some years later, when Celadon L. Daboll, of New London, invented his fog whistle, former Keeper Hazard wrote to the Secretary of the Treasury that the Daboll trumpet was a great improvement over anything he had ever heard, for he had listened to it from a distance of six to eight miles. Twenty-four other men signed Hazard's letter in concurrence.

Many others testified to the strength of the Daboll signal. Port Collector Edward W. Lawton of Newport testified that he was awakened from his bed at his house in the middle of Newport by the trumpet! Captain S. L. Fremont, at Fort Adams, thought that the Daboll trumpet was so loud that he mistook it for the mail steamer's whistle passing the fort! At this time Newport or Beavertail Light was under the care of Mrs. Dermaris H. Weeden, widow of former Keeper Weeden. On October 8, 1855, Mrs. Weeden had been keeper under her own name for almost eight years.

Celadon Daboll seems to have been an interesting character. When his foghorn did not please a prospective purchaser, he would sell a fog whistle. If there were those who objected to working the hand pump that furnished the pressure for the whistle blast, Daboll would arrange a treadmill or horse windlass. In 1852 a horsepowered fog signal was in operation at Beavertail Light. In spite of the favorable reception, Beavertail Light's fog signal was discontinued a few years later.

In 1857 a steam whistle was installed at the light, and was used at Beavertail for eleven years. When it wore out in 1868, a new invention of Daboll's, a fog signal with a hot air engine, was substituted. The hot air engine had been planned by

John Ericsson, who designed the iron-clad *Monitor*. The new signal seemed to please everyone concerned, and remained at the station until 1881, when an improved steam engine was installed to replace the hot-air engine.

1888 saw the adoption of the Crosby automatic fog signal controller, which allowed the characteristic of the lighthouse fog signal to sound accurately, while in 1900 Beavertail was fitted out with a new compressed air-operated siren. At present diaphragm horns produce the fog signal.

Ice, which in 1875 caused so much damage around Cape Cod, did not spare Beavertail Light. When the ice in the Providence River began to break up early in March, the pier and the keeper's dwelling were swept into the sea, while some of the protecting stone at the base of the light was dislodged. The keeper and his son narrowly escaped death at the time.

In 1856 a square granite lighthouse was erected at Beavertail, and the light now shines from a height of sixty-four feet above the sea, its green flash of 45,000 candlepower visible eight times every thirty seconds. The tower, the upper half of which is painted white, is attached to the keeper's dwelling.

In the great September hurricane of 1938 the keeper's dwelling and other buildings were damaged at Beavertail. When the storm went down it was found that the water had exposed the foundation of the ancient 1749 tower nearby. It had not been realized until after the storm that any part of the historic structure actually existed.

NEWPORT HARBOR LIGHT

Since 1823 a white stone tower has stood at the entrance to Newport Harbor. Rebuilt in 1922, the edifice is at the northern end of the breakwater. The 2,500 candlepower beacon has a fixed green light, while the fog bell sounds every ten seconds.

PRUDENCE ISLAND

In 1852 a lighthouse was built at Sandy Point, Prudence Island. The white octagonal tower gives a flashing green light. The fog bell sounds every fifteen seconds during fog or stormy weather.

The worst disaster in the entire history of Prudence Island was during the terrible September hurricane of 1938, when five persons, including the wife of the lighthouse keeper, were carried out to sea and drowned when the dwelling house on the lighthouse reservation was swept away by the savage fury of the tropical gale. The keeper was also thrown into the sea, but another wave swept him back ashore.

DUTCH ISLAND LIGHT

On the southern point of Dutch Island a lighthouse was erected in 1827. Rebuilt in 1857, Dutch Island Light is a white square tower that has a five-second red flash followed by a five-second eclipse. The 500-candlepower light is fifty-six feet above the sea.

WARWICK LIGHT

Warwick Light, which stands on the northern side of the entrance to Greenwich Bay, has a flashing green light in a white conical tower, fifty-one feet above the sea. Built in 1827, it was remodeled in 1932. The diaphragm horn gives one two-second blast every fifteen seconds.

PLUM BEACH LIGHT

A comparatively recent station, Plum Beach Light was built in 1897 in sixteen feet of water on the northeastern edge of the shoal in Western Passage, Narragansett Bay. It has a single white flash every five seconds. One of the memories of the 1938 hurricane at this light was a streamlined yacht that swept along at the height of the gale right by the lighthouse at more than a mile a minute to pile high on Anthony's Beach, North Kingston. After the storm it was found fully one thousand feet inland.

The lighthouse has been replaced by a black buoy.

WHALE ROCK LIGHT

On Whale Rock, in the western side of the Western Passage, a lighthouse was built in 1882. It was a white conical tower on a red, cylindrical pier, the light giving its steady green beam from sunset to sunrise. The fog bell sounded a double stroke every twenty seconds.

This strongly built edifice was a victim of the great New England hurricane. The keeper probably prepared as best he could when the first signs of that almost unbelievable cyclone swept out of the south, but all was in vain. We will never know when the tower went over, or if the brave keeper tried to reach land. The solid cast-iron tower, built on a rocky ledge with a concrete and reinforced steel base, fell over into the sea, carrying the keeper to his death.

In 1940 a new skeleton tower was erected at Whale Rock, and at that time the characteristic was made a green flashing beacon that gave out its light every four seconds. It is now a black gong buoy that gives a green flash every four seconds.

BULLOCK'S POINT

On the east side of the Providence River Channel the Bullock's Point Light was erected in 1872, a square tower attached to the keeper's dwelling on a granite pier. The light was a fixed red beam, and the fog signal in bad weather sounded a double stroke every fifteen seconds.

When the 1938 hurricane hit Bullock's Point Light, the keeper climbed into the tower and stayed there during the remainder of the storm, keeping his beacon going all that terrible night. When dawn came, he found that the wall of the building facing the gale had been ripped off, and the stairs had washed out as well, but Keeper Andrew Zuius descended to the first floor over the ruins of the staircase.

Bullock's Point is now a red skeleton tower that gives a red flash every six seconds.

BLOCK ISLAND NORTH LIGHT

Block Island North Light was erected in 1829 on Sandy Point. Rebuilt in 1867, the present tower is fifty-eight feet above the sea, and can be seen a distance of thirteen miles. It is a brown tower on a granite dwelling. It is now unattended and the 2,000-candlepower light flashes white every five seconds.

In 1967, at the one-hundredth anniversary of the building of the new tower, members of the Massachusetts Marine Historical League conducted services at the abandoned tower.

BLOCK ISLAND SOUTHEAST LIGHT

High on the cliffs of Block Island stands the attractive building and tower of Block Island Southeast Light. The 160,000-candlepower light flashes green every 3.7 seconds from a height of 201 feet above the water on Mohegan Bluffs. It is the strongest Rhode Island beacon and the only primary seacoast light in New England with a green flash.

WATCH HILL LIGHT

In spite of its isolated location, there is something about Watch Hill Point that has always attracted me. It is located on the northern side of the eastern entrance to Fisher's Island Sound. Perhaps the attraction is partly in the name, suggestive of countless visits to this hill to watch one's dear relative sailing away for a voyage of several years, or it may be the long ride overland down to the point itself.

Whenever a wreck has been sighted off this dangerous location, word spreads rapidly, and soon the entire section is crowded with people from the surrounding towns and cities, peering off at the tragedy that may possibly unfold before their eyes.

It was in 1807 that Watch Hill Light was built. Across the bay from Montauk Point, it is approximately fourteen miles away from the Long Island beacon. When first erected, its elevation was seventy-three feet above the water, although it now shines from a point sixty-one feet high.

Watch Hill Light flashes white and then gives a double red flash every fifteen seconds. It is an attended beacon with resident Coast Guard personnel.

POINT JUDITH LIGHT

Point Judith Light was established in 1810 on the western side of the entrance to Narragansett Bay. Built of rough stone, the lighthouse was only thirty-five feet high, although the light flashed from a height seventy-four feet above the sea. There were ten lamps, each having an eight-and-a-half-inch reflector. The lamps were arranged in two clusters. When Lieutenant George M. Bache visited the station in 1838, he paid special attention to the revolving table that turned the apparatus to make the light flash. Bache observed that the mechanism took 144 seconds to complete its 360-

degree turn. A 288-pound weight provided power that turned the table.

Gilbert Pendleton was the keeper of Point Judith Light in the year 1843. Appointed July 11 of that year, Pendleton received $350 annually.

In Mill's *American Light-House Guide* of 1850, Point Judith Light is called "a *revolving* light, erected on a stone tower 40 feet high, on the S. E. point of the Narragansett shore, and 74 feet above the bay; time of each revolution of the light 2¼ min., and visible 17 miles. Latitude 41° 21' 35" N., longitude 71° 29' 35" W. This light is distinguished from Newport light, which is stationary, and bears from it N. E. half N., distant 3 leagues; and may be distinguished from Watch Hill light by its not wholly disappearing when within 3 leagues of it."

Rebuilt in 1857, the Point Judith tower is now an octagonal, pyramidal edifice, the lower half painted white and the upper section brown, and it is connected with a dwelling. It has a 20,000-candlepower light, which flashes three times every fifteen seconds. Every fifteen seconds the fog siren gives a two-second blast.

Point Judith, or Point "Jude" as it is sometimes called, has been the scene of many shipwrecks. The *American Eagle* foundered there in 1870, and the same year the steamer *Acusionet* was wrecked nearby. In 1885 the *Almon Bacon* went down, followed the next year by the *Allen Green*. The *Amanda E.* sank off Point Judith in 1902. The *Agnes* foundered there in 1898.

A partial list of other vessels lost at Point Judith follows: *Blue Jay*, 1896; *C. B. Hamilton*, 1866; *Catherine W. May*, 1876; *Cuckoo*, 1882; *Anita*, 1888; *Edward M. Laughlin*, 1898; *Henry W. Scavey*, 1875; *Harry A. Barry*, 1887; *Normandy*, 1864; *Venus*, 1877; *Mars*, 1892; and *Swallow*, 1900.

40

Ida Lewis and Lime Rock Light

February 25, 1842, was the birthday of Rhode Island's most famous heroine, Ida Lewis. It was on that date that she was born at the home of Captain Hosea Lewis in Newport, Rhode Island. Although the lantern that she tended so faithfully has become an exhibition piece, and the lighthouse on the Lime Rocks is now the Ida Lewis Yacht Club, the unselfish and truly remarkable deeds that Ida Lewis accomplished have made her life's record one that will shine through the years in unending glory.

Captain Hosea Lewis was appointed keeper of the Lime Rock Light in 1854. At that time there was no residence for the keeper's family at the rock. Ida was then only twelve years old, and her father's appointment offered countless outlets for her remarkable energy and unusual maritime interest. Already known as the most outstanding girl of her group, she could row a boat to beat any boy her own age, while by the time she was fourteen Ida was easily the best swimmer in all Newport.

One day Ida discovered that a load of lumber was being taken ashore at the lighthouse, and she joyfully realized that her father was going to have a house built there so that his family could live with him on the rocks. On June 29, 1858, Captain Lewis moved his family into the newly completed home on the island.

Captain Lewis had been a pilot aboard a Revenue Cutter for twelve years, and transferred to the lighthouse service because of failing health. His first wife died, and he later married the daughter of Dr. A. C. Wiley of Block Island. His second wife's name, Idawalley Zorada, was bestowed on her daughter at birth, but as the child grew older her friends shortened the name to Ida.

The family was very happy in the new keeper's home at Lime Rock Light, but their joy was changed to sorrow when Captain Hosea suffered a shock the following October. Although he recovered enough to sit up and later to walk with a cane, Lewis became but a shell of his former self, constantly needing the help of his loved ones.

This emergency gave Ida an opportunity to show her true abilities. While her mother trimmed the light and fed its fountain with oil, Ida brought out supplies from the mainland and rowed her little sisters and brother to school every day. The bitterness of an April wind, the hot sun of July, the gales of September, and the icy blasts of January were all accepted and overcome by this daring girl. Some idea of her remarkable courage can be gained by her father's comments at this time.

Captain Hosea Lewis said that again and again he had seen the children returning from school in some heavy blow. "Old sailor that I am, I felt I would not give a penny for their lives, so furious was the storm," said Keeper Lewis. "I have watched them until I could bear it no longer, expecting every moment to see them swamped and the crew at the mercy of the waves, and then I have turned away and said to my wife, 'Let me know if they get safe in,' for I could not endure to see them perish and realize that we were powerless to save them. You cannot tell the relief when she cried out, 'They have got safe to the rock, Father.' I have seen Ida in the bitter winter weather obliged to cut off her frozen stockings at the knees," concluded the lighthouse keeper.

In the fall of 1858 four young men were sailing between Fort Adams and Lime Rock Light, when one of them, a boy named King, climbed up to the top of the mast and amused himself by rocking the sailboat back and forth. Young Ida, watching the strange antics from her lighthouse door, gave a shrill cry as the craft suddenly turned bottom up, and she saw four heads bobbing in the water. The sixteen year old girl ran for the boat house, slid the lifeboat down to the water, and rowed rapidly for the scene of the accident.

Reaching the boat Ida cleverly avoided the frantic clutches of the drowning boys until she had maneuvered her craft to a safe position. Then, one by one, she pulled the four lads over the stern of her boat to safety. All the while her father, who had hobbled slowly to the window where the telescope was in position, had been watching the spectacular deed, and collapsed into his chair the moment Ida had pulled the last boy aboard. Ida rowed swiftly toward the Lime Rock Light, and a short time later landed the young men safely. The other boys besides King were identified as Powell and Smith of Philadelphia, and a young Mr. DeJongh of Newport. The boys acted as many others have since, returning home without letting their parents know of their narrow escape from death. It was eleven years before the accident became known, and only then because of Ida's later rescues. King, who had been responsible, later gave his life in the Civil War.

Eight years after this rescue, Ida's second exciting adventure took place, in February 1866. The Civil War had ended less than a year before, and a party of three soldiers from nearby Fort Adams, with the recklessness that every war necessarily creates, and aided by certain stimulating beverages from town, were returning to their garrison by the old fort road. Upon reaching Jones' Bridge, six hundred yards from the Lime Rocks, they noticed the skiff belonging to Ida's brother on the beach. It was but a minute before they had decided to use his skiff for a shortcut across the bay to the fort, and they were soon in deep water, two of them pulling an oar apiece.

Without warning, the soldier in the stern suddenly started to bang his foot down on a plank in the bottom of the skiff, and soon the plank was kicked out and the skiff began to sink. The men at the oars, now swimming, struck out for shore, while the culprit who had kicked out the plank clung desperately to the skiff, barely able to keep his head out of water. Ida Lewis had already noticed the accident, and was even then rowing to the scene. Reaching the drunken soldier just before he was about to give up hope, Ida found to her dismay that he was not only extremely heavy, but so drunk that he was wholly unable to aid himself in any way.

In her efforts to get him into the boat she suffered a severe strain, from which she did not recover for more than a year. Despite all her desperate struggles, the man could not be pulled into the boat. Finally, she bent a line around his body under his armpits, and made it fast. Exhausted by her struggles, Ida rowed slowly toward the shore, where she shouted to two men for help. The combined efforts of the three succeeded in bringing the soldier back to life. Warm and dry clothing loaned the soldier by Ida's brother, whose boat the soldier had damaged and sunk, was readily donned by the now-sober Civil War veteran, and he soon left for the fort.

His two companions were never heard from again. Whether they perished in the harbor or seized the opportunity of the accident to leave for parts unknown is an unsolved mystery. Their bodies did not come to the surface if they drowned, so their fate will never be known. The soldier who stove the boat and borrowed the suit of clothes never returned with the garments.

Shortly after nine o'clock on a cold January morning in 1867 three laborers employed by August Belmont were driving a valuable sheep along the streets of Newport. Without warning the sheep suddenly ran out on the Old Mill Wharf and plunged into the water. The three workmen ran down to the shore, where the new skiff belonging to Ida's brother was pulled up on the beach near Jones' Bridge.

A heavy southeast gale was then blowing. Pushing off into the storm, they were soon a short distance from their prized sheep, but they found themselves in great personal danger as the waves buffeted and turned the tiny craft. Ida Lewis, at the time, was sewing by the window of the kitchen, her father and mother close by. The alert girl noticed the three men in her brother's skiff, and was attentively watching when they were hit by a wave higher than the rest and capsized. In less than a minute Ida was out of the door and down with her lifeboat, which she pushed off and rowed swiftly toward the scene of the capsizing.

Despite the danger, Ida could not help laughing as she drew up with the three men, who, regardless of their dangerous predicament in the water, were still shouting after the lost sheep. Pulling them into her craft one by one, Ida rowed the three men ashore, where they thanked her profusely, although they were still thinking of the lonely sheep, now almost out of sight as the wind and tide swept him out to sea. But good-hearted Ida again launched her boat, and an hour later brought the animal ashore for the grateful men, whose happiness then knew no bounds. Whether the great August Belmont ever heard about the adventure of his lost sheep or not, Ida told the story for many years as one of her most unusual incidents.

Two weeks later Ida's mother, who by nature was an early riser, looked out and saw a sailor stranded on Little Lime Rock, near the lighthouse. Calling to Ida to go to his help, the mother waved signals of encouragement to the desperate mariner, who had been clinging to the rocky ledge all night. The waves had risen higher and higher as drawn broke, until only his head was above the water. Dressing quickly, Ida ran to the boathouse and launched her craft in the direction of the shipwrecked mariner. Soon he was pulled aboard her faithful boat and taken back to the lighthouse, where he declined further benefits from the Lewis family and asked to be landed at the nearest wharf. The reason for his strange attitude was later apparent when Ida returned the wrecked sailboat to the owner, whose boat had been stolen from him. The owner declared that if the man who had taken his sailboat without pay or permission had been left to drown he would have gladly given Ida fifty dollars.

On March 29, 1869, while a heavy gale was raging outside, Ida was sitting in her favorite chair beside the kitchen fire when she heard her mother cry from upstairs.

"Ida, O my God, Ida! Run quick, a boat capsized and men are drowning, run quick, Ida!"

Without stopping to don her shoes, the girl rushed to the boat and launched it into the heavy seas. Before she reached the shipwrecked sailors, one of them had already gone to his death beneath the waters of Newport Harbor, but two soldiers were still floundering near the craft. Ida pulled them aboard the boat and headed back to the lighthouse, where she got the men safely into the kitchen. After drying themselves and resting, the soldiers left for the fort. It was one occasion that was suitably rewarded, for Colonel Henry J. Hunt, stationed at Fort Adams, sent Ida Lewis a letter of appreciation containing $218 that had been contributed by the officers and men at the fort.

Gradually Ida Lewis became better known in Rhode Island, and then in the whole nation. The Life Saving Benevolent Society of New York, having heard that up to May 1869 she had saved eleven persons, sent her a silver medal and one hundred dollars. Other organizations in Rhode Island and Massachusetts also acknowledged her unusual abilities. Ida really became famous when *Harper's* and *Leslie's*, the *Life* and *Look* magazines of that generation, engraved pictures of her in their respective publications. Then the whole nation realized the daring and ability of the Newport heroine. Because of the national publicity, her mail became enormous and the usual marriage proposals and other freak letters arrived from all parts of the Union.

The residents of Newport honored Miss Lewis on July 4, 1869, by presenting her with a new lifeboat at an occasion on Long Wharf in the presence of a large, enthusiastic gathering. The modest girl accepted the gifts with humility and appreciation. Ida Lewis then stepped aboard the new lifeboat and rowed it away from the wharf, with thousands of people gathered on the pier and along the shore cheering her as she rowed out to the Lime Rock Light.

When her father died, Ida's mother for a time was officially the keeper of the light, but in 1879 General Sherman, after a special act of Congress, appointed Ida Lewis keeper of the Lime Rock Light.

Because of the nationwide interest in Ida Lewis, she received a visit from President Ulysses S. Grant and Vice-President Colfax in 1869. As they landed on the shore, President Grant stepped in the water and got his feet wet.

"I have come to see Ida Lewis," said President Grant, "and to see her I'd get wet up to my armpits if necessary." The President and Ida Lewis had a long chat, during which Grant asked the twenty-eight-year-old woman to tell him of her life at the wave-swept rock. She took him around the house, showing President Grant the light that she had tended for so many long nights. Returning to the mainland, Grant later said that his visit to Ida Lewis was one of the most interesting events in his life.

Ida Lewis performed her last act of bravery when she was sixty-four. A close friend was rowing out to the lighthouse, when she stood up, lost her balance, and fell overboard. Ida, with all the vigor of her past youth, ran to the boathouse and launched the lifeboat. Soon reaching her friend's side, Ida Lewis hauled the woman aboard and rowed back to the lighthouse. This woman was the twenty-third person whom Ida had saved from drowning!

Many notables made the journey to see this woman lighthouse keeper. Around the year 1907 she told of some of the visits, which included "every Mrs. Astor and every Mrs. Vanderbilt and every Mrs. Belmont you ever heard of." When these ladies visited, they "called on me with whole boatloads of men and women that all talked at once and treated me as if I were a kind of real queen," said Ida.

On July 1, 1907, Keeper Ida Lewis had been on duty at Lime Rock Light for half a century, or over 18,250 nights! Such a record any man would envy, and yet it was made by a woman! Keeper Ida Lewis was then sixty-six, and spoke of plans for the summer.

"I've got to paint the whole house inside, this year. That's Government work, so I do it myself. . . . My brother—I let him do the outside work, because I'm getting old, I guess, and I really can't handle a boat like I used to.

"Sometimes the spray dashes against these windows so thick I can't see out, and for days at a time the waves are so high that no boat would dare come near the rock, not even if we were starving. But I am happy. There's a peace on this rock that you don't get on shore. There are hundreds of boats going in and out of this harbor in summer, and it's part of my happiness to know they are depending on me to guide them safely.

"For many seasons the Newport papers told of excursions to this light. My helpless father's chief occupation was to sit and count the number of visitors. Once he actually counted over six hundred in one day! In those times I shook hands with more people during a summer than did the President at Washington. I couldn't get my housework done. Hundreds from each state in the Union have been here, including men and women of highest distinction. For example, there was Admiral Dewey. When he was Secretary of the Lighthouse Board he came here one day and said: 'Miss Lewis, I want to smoke on your half-acre rock for half an hour.'

"General William Tecumseh Sherman sat out on the rock for nearly an hour, asking me questions about my life, and saying he was glad to get to such a peaceful place. Yes, there's hardly a great admiral or noted general that hasn't been here to see me. There was one cabinet minister the Secretary of the Treasury under Grant. He said he came purposely to thank me personally for saving the life of a soldier from Fort Adams, because the light was in his department and he was proud to have a woman in his department who was not finicky about getting her hair wet."

There were many trials and tribulations in Ida's last years at Lime Rock Light. New regulations and restrictions of the Lighthouse Department worried her to no small degree, but two staunch friends stood by her till the end, Robert Grosvenor and Amelia Shaw Kerr.

On the afternoon of October 24, 1911, the commanding officer at nearby Fort Adams received a request that the coast artillery practice, then in full swing, be temporarily suspended, as Ida Lewis was very ill. The guns were silenced at once. A few hours later the brave heroine passed away. When the steamer *Priscilla* sailed by Lime Rock Light that night, the bells of all the craft then anchored in Newport Harbor were tolling, in memory of Ida Lewis, the lighthouse keeper. Her remarkable career had ended.

The storms and gales of almost a century have swept up and down Newport Harbor since Ida Lewis first tended Lime Rock Light. Her impressive tombstone in the Newport cemetery is mute testimony to the love and respect the people of that city felt for her. Although we live in an age of women champions in various sports and activities, and women have taken their place alongside of the so-called stronger sex, it will probably be many, many years, before the remarkable feats of this Newport heroine are equaled.

Index